THE
SECRET
ALLIANCE

THE
SECRET
ALLIANCE

*The Extraordinary Story of the
Rescue of the Jews Since World War II*

TAD SZULC

Farrar, Straus & Giroux · New York

Copyright © 1991 by Tad Szulc
ALL RIGHTS RESERVED
PRINTED IN THE UNITED STATES OF AMERICA
Published simultaneously in Canada by HarperCollinsCanadaLtd
Designed by Tere LoPrete
First edition, 1991
Library of Congress Cataloging in Publication Data
Szulc, Tad.
The secret alliance : the extraordinary story of the rescue of the
Jews since World War II / by Tad Szulc.
p. cm.
Includes bibliographical references and index.
1. Refugees, Jewish. 2. Holocaust survivors. 3. Jews—
Migrations. 4. Palestine—Emigration and immigration. 5. Beriḥah
(Organization) I. Title.
HV640.5.J4S98 1991   325.5694—dc20   91-25542   CIP

Contents

Contents

Preface

The Secret Alliance is the story of the vital but secret role played by American Jewry in the rescue of approximately two million Jews in Eastern Europe, North Africa and the Middle East from the mid-1940s to the present day. It is also a history of illegal immigration into Palestine, and later into Israel.

Illegal immigration was the framework in which private American Jewish organizations operated in absolute secrecy, contributing personnel and funds, in support of the clandestine operations run by the Palestinians in the first phase and by the government of Israel and the Mossad, its intelligence service, in the second phase. One of the most remarkable aspects of these enterprises was the intimate cooperation between American Jews and Palestinian and Israeli figures in meeting the challenge to "bring forth the children of Israel" (Exodus 3:10) from the "countries of distress."

My own attraction to this theme, once I became aware of the scope of the illegal immigration history, was based principally on my realization that, contrary to much conventional (and guilt-ridden) wisdom then and now, American Jews had *not* failed to do their share in attempting to save and help their brethren during the war years and subsequently, when Jewish populations were in peril in the Moslem world.

In fact, I think there is considerable evidence pointing to the conclusion that without the participation of private

American Jewish organizations—and their leaders and their men and women in the field—a million or more Jews of Europe, North Africa and the Middle East would not have been rescued. I would even venture a more daring historical conclusion: that the birth of the State of Israel in 1948 was rendered possible by the immense pressures created by the migrations set in motion in postwar Europe by the underground Palestinian operatives and their American partners. Finally, hundreds of thousands of Jews were saved from starvation in the immediate aftermath of World War II by the American Jewish organizations that were simultaneously engaged in illegal immigration to Palestine. One should add in passing that the private American financial contribution to these projects was in the hundreds of millions of dollars, although the individual donors had no idea at the time how the money from the fund-raising campaigns was being used; they can learn it now.

I must state at this point that I had known for many years a number of key personalities engaged in the American Jewish Joint Distribution Committee (the Joint) and the Hebrew Immigrant Aid Society (HIAS) operations, some of them since as far back as 1955. I also played a very limited personal role in at least two HIAS operations. In 1956, I was able to introduce the HIAS director for Latin America, Gaynor I. Jacobson, to Brazil's President Juscelino Kubitschek, whom I knew fairly well in my capacity as a *New York Times* correspondent. This introduction led to the agreement between the Brazilian government and HIAS for permission for Moroccan and Egyptian Jews to emigrate to Brazil, and it was the first time Brazil had agreed to such Jewish emigration. In 1967, when I was the *New York Times* correspondent in Madrid, I also introduced Jacobson, the HIAS European director at the time, to a senior official in the

Spanish Foreign Ministry. I was told, consequently, that HIAS and Spanish government officials would permit Spain to grant passports and visas to Jews in the Middle East who were endangered by the Arab-Israeli Six-Day War, and that it would be possible in this fashion to save Jewish lives and keep Jews out of prison. This was the only time in my newspaper career that I took the decision *not* to write a story that I knew to be topical and with which I was thoroughly familiar; I made the judgment that Spain might be prevented from carrying out its commitment to help the Jews if an article on this subject was published—because of the intimate Spanish-Arab relationships—and that saving lives came before an exclusive story.

In the most literal sense, this book could not have been planned and written without the inspiration, advice and phenomenal personal recollections of my old friend Gaynor Jacobson, the only person who was directly and decisively involved in *all* the phases of this story. As head of the operations in Greece, Czechoslovakia and Hungary for the Joint and then as a top executive of HIAS, Jacobson has lived through the experience of postwar Eastern Europe and through the astonishing adventures of the North African and Middle East operations. Jacobson retired as HIAS's executive vice president in 1981 (he is now honorary executive vice president), but he remains very much in touch with Jewish migratory processes—most recently the exodus of Soviet Jews to Israel.

Gaynor Jacobson and his wife, Florence, a social worker who worked with him during their assignments in Prague and Budapest, magically brought to life for my benefit the people, the situations and the mood of the time more than forty years ago. I have taped uncounted hours of conversations with Gaynor Jacobson, and the thousands of pages of transcript became the historical road map and the preliminary draft of my book.

Moreover, Gaynor Jacobson opened for me all the doors in the United States and Israel, introducing me to men and women of whom, in most instances, I had never heard before, but who turned out to be the heroes and heroines of my tale. This was especially true in Israel, where the Jacobsons accompanied me in the autumn of 1989 for a stay that was a marathon of interviews. It was an easy task because the Jacobsons are so beloved in Israel that a single telephone call from Gaynor was sufficient to produce at a moment's notice *everybody* who had anything to do at any time with the sagas of Jewish illegal immigration.

Through Gaynor Jacobson, I gained the invaluable co-operation of Yehuda Dominitz, probably Israel's greatest authority on immigration, who has since become a personal friend as well. Dominitz served as director general of the Jewish Agency's Aliyah (Immigration) and Absorption Department and now heads the Israel office of United Jewish Appeal–Federation of New York. Dominitz taught me much of the history of contemporary Jewish migrations and steered me toward other sources of inquiry.

Yehuda Bauer, professor of Holocaust studies at the Hebrew University in Jerusalem and the leading authority on the European phase of illegal immigration to Palestine, gave of his time to guide me through the political subtleties of that period. His own books were most helpful in my research, as was the work of Dina Porat, a historian at Tel Aviv University.

One of the great heroes of Palestinian illegal immigration was Shaul Avigur, the head of the clandestine organization in charge of it. Avigur was an obsessively private individual. He was also the co-founder of the secret intelligence service a decade before Israeli independence. Scores of Americans and Israelis dealt with him, but Avigur was a man who did not wish to be publicly known—and he almost succeeded. His daughter, Mrs. Ruth Hillel, was of crucial assistance in sharing with me her recollections of him and in providing me with his published but virtually unknown writings, available only in Hebrew.

Avigur's American counterpart, Dr. Joseph Joshua Schwartz, is the other hero of my story, but Schwartz also died before I embarked on my work. I was fortunately able to find marvelous material about him from his many friends, and I hope I have done justice to his memory.

In Israel, I was able to interview in depth most of the surviving people who were active in both phases of illegal immigration.

Concerning the European phase, some of the most important information was obtained in two long conversations with Asher Ben-Natan, who headed the secret Palestinian network in Austria at the end of World War II; he later served as a leading intelligence service officer and as Israel's first ambassador to West Germany and then to France. Daring and inventiveness were the specialties of Yesheyahu (Shaike) Dan, who parachuted into Romania during the war to become the principal Palestinian illegal immigration operator in the Balkans. At the age of eighty-one, his trademark cigar butt clenched in his teeth, he remains as active as ever in areas that are still secret, and he is a fine storyteller.

Significant contributions were also made by Mordecai Surkiss, who was the first European commander of the Brichah underground Palestinian and European organization for illegal immigration; Levi Argov, who, as Brichah commander in Slovakia, played a major role in organizing the flow of Jewish refugees from Eastern Europe; Elhanan

Gafni, the first clandestine emissary from Palestine to reach Prague and later Israel's ambassador to the Cameroons; Yehiel Kadishai, a Jewish Brigade soldier who worked with the Brichah at the end of the war and served in the 1970s as secretary to Prime Minister Menachem Begin; Chaim Herzog, President of Israel, whose father, the Chief Rabbi of Palestine, brought a transport of Jewish children out of Poland; Jossi Harel, the commander of the ships *Exodus* and *Pan*, whose dramatic voyages with illegal immigrants are famous in Palestinian history; Aharon and Lea Assa, who worked in Czechoslovakia with the Brichah and the Joint in helping with the flight of Jewish refugees from Eastern Europe; Bubu Landa, a Slovak partisan who joined the Brichah and had a major part in organizing the passage of Jews fleeing from Poland to Czechoslovakia and on to Austria; Frieda Koren, a New Yorker (she was born Freda Cohen) who was on Gaynor Jacobson's staff in Prague and spent long months on the Polish-Czechoslovak border during the Jewish exodus there; and Zev Hadari, a Palestinian illegal immigration emissary in Istanbul and Bulgaria during the war and now a scholar of post-Holocaust history.

Concerning the African and Asian phase, the bulk of the most fascinating material came from interviews with Isser Harel, who, as director of the Mossad, supervised the Moroccan operation; Shmuel Toledano, then a deputy director of the Mossad, who helped to coordinate the Moroccan operation from headquarters in Israel; Shlomo Havillio, a former senior Mossad officer, who was the first field commander of the Moroccan project, based in Paris, and Efraim Ronel, who succeeded him; Shlomo-Zalman Shragai, a high official of the Jewish Agency, who coordinated the political aspects of the Moroccan operation with the chiefs of the Mossad; General Uzi Narkiss, who served as military attaché in Paris during the Moroccan enterprise, later commanded Israeli forces that captured East Jerusalem in the 1967 war, and then headed the Jewish Agency's immigration department; Nat Bar-Giori, who was a key covert operator for the Mossad in Morocco; Carmit Gattmon, the widow of Alexander Gattmon, who was the Mossad's station chief in Morocco, and herself a Mossad operative; Haim Halachmi, a Mossad officer in Paris and Morocco, who is now HIAS director in Israel; Shlomo Hillel, who was the field commander of the Mossad operation in Iraq, then Minister of Police and Speaker of the Knesset (Parliament); Lova Eliav, a Mossad officer who worked with the Kurds in Iran and attempted to bring Egyptian Jews out of Port Said during the 1956 Sinai war, and later a Knesset member; Hanan Bar-On, the first Mossad officer under diplomatic cover to initiate secret negotiations in Addis Ababa for the emigration of Ethiopian Jews; and Nehmiah Levanon, who was involved in wartime illegal immigration activities in Europe, then was engaged in clandestine work with Soviet Jewry in Moscow.

In New York, I learned much about all of these operations from Ralph I. Goldman, a Bostonian, who quietly helped the Brichah in Europe while he served in the U.S. Army, later becoming the American adviser to Prime Minister David Ben-Gurion and the Joint's executive vice president and honorary executive vice president. Goldman and Jacobson reviewed this manuscript, saving me from potential errors. I also extend my gratitude to Melvin Goldstein, who was Joe Schwartz's right-hand man during the Joint's wartime operations in Lisbon and Paris; the Joint's Herbert Katzki, who worked with Schwartz in Lisbon, Marseilles and Istanbul; Laura Margolis Jarblum, a senior Joint officer in Shanghai and Paris; Irving Haber, who held key positions with the Joint in Europe and with HIAS in Casablanca during the

Mossad's great Moroccan operation; and Edward M. M. Warburg, former chairman of the board of the Joint. In Paris, Paula Borenstein recalled for me the immediate postwar period of the Joint's operations there. From California, Nathan Schwartz spoke to me about his late father, Joseph Joshua Schwartz. Also in California, Zoltán Toman, who was Czechoslovakia's Deputy Interior Minister and head of the secret police between 1945 and 1948, enraptured me with his poignant recollections when I spent a weekend at his home in 1989.

In terms of archival research, I received full access to all of the materials at the headquarters of the Joint and HIAS in New York. At the Joint, I was greatly helped by Ralph Goldman, Herbert Katzki and Miriam Feldman, who translated for me the Hebrew sections of David Ben-Gurion's diaries, and Denise Bernard Gluck, the archivist.

At HIAS, my gratitude goes to executive vice president Karl D. Zukerman, Lorraine Stein, who assembled all of the research material for me, and Roberta Elliott, who came up with fine leads for me to follow.

In Washington, I received sound advice from my friend Alvin Rosenfeld at the U.S. Holocaust Museum. Moshe Shualy of the museum staff performed brilliantly in translating Shaul Avigur's writings from the Hebrew. Gila Flam translated the account of Rabbi Herzog's rescue of Jewish children from Poland. Abraham Edelheit, also of the museum staff, helped greatly with the bibliography.

My very special appreciation goes to William Nylen of Miami for the extraordinary feat of transcribing with superb accuracy all of my interviews, running into thousands of pages, and overcoming every conceivable foreign accent in English as well as coping with Hebrew and Yiddish expressions and obscure geographical names. Without Bill Nylen's highly intelligent transcript technique, I would not have been able to take full advantage of my interview material.

My literary agents in New York, Mort Janklow and Anne Sibbald, encouraged me mightily to go on with this book when I developed doubts about my capacity to handle it. My friend Steve Wasserman, then at Farrar, Straus & Giroux, encouraged me just as powerfully by signing it up. John Glusman, my editor there, carried the project to its conclusion. My gratitude to all of them.

At home in Washington, my wife, Marianne, once more offered all of the vital psychological and editorial support that makes the difference between a book being finished or not, and she deserves much credit for this one.

Finally, this book would not have been possible without the belief, on the part of individuals associated with the Joint and HIAS in the United States and the Mossad and the Jewish Agency in Israel, that the time had come to tell an extraordinary story that has been kept largely under cover for decades.

The First Rescues

I

Silent Partners

On a rainy April afternoon in 1946, nearly a year after Nazi Germany surrendered, two Russian-born Jews blessed with extraordinary vision, imagination and courage—one an American and the other a Palestinian—met in a nondescript office at 19, Rue de Téhéran in midtown Paris. There they planned and set in motion a clandestine course of action to rescue hundreds of thousands of their fellow Jews from war-ravaged Eastern Europe. Their goal was to transport them, by any means possible, to British-governed Palestine. It was the beginning of an immensely ambitious joint enterprise spanning forty years that led to the escape of close to two million Jews from three continents. The American was Dr. Joseph Joshua Schwartz, chairman of the European Executive Council of the American Jewish Joint Distribution Committee, and the Palestinian was Shaul Avigur, a mystery figure in clandestine

POST-WAR EUROPE

	Miles	
0		400
0		600 km

Zionist activities. Their relationship marked the start of a private intelligence and covert operations alliance between American and Palestinian Jews that remains in effect to this day.

Jewish immigration to Palestine has traditionally been referred to as Aliyah, meaning literally "ascent." The movement of Russian Jews to the Holy Land in 1882, prompted by anti-Semitic persecutions and the gleam of nascent Zionist ideas, was known as the "First Aliyah." Prior to Israeli independence in 1948, legal immigration was referred to as the Aliyah A. The Aliyah Bet was secret, organized by the Haganah, the Jewish underground army, and the Histadrut, the General Federation of Jewish Labor, after the British government issued its White Paper on May 17, 1939. Although providing for an independent Palestinian state in the future, the White Paper confined Jewish immigration to 75,000 people over the next five years. It thus set limits on Jewish entry to Palestine, guaranteeing, in effect, that the two-to-one Arab majority in the population would not be reversed and that there would not be a sovereign *Jewish* nation. To the Palestinian Jews, therefore, illegal immigration was the principal weapon available in the struggle for an Israeli homeland. The British became the immediate adversary, even if they had been allied against Hitler in the war.

The Aliyah Bet, run by Shaul Avigur, and the Haganah's intelligence service, the Sherut Yediot (Shai, for short), were the direct forerunners of Israel's present-day secret intelligence service, the Mossad. But in the pre-independence days "Mossad" (meaning "institute" in Hebrew) stood among the initiated for the illegal immigration operations organization, and "Aliyah Bet" and "Mossad" were used interchangeably. Naturally, the Aliyah Bet was no longer required after Israeli independence and it was dissolved in 1951. The new Mossad absorbed Aliyah Bet's secret illegal immigration functions and concentrated on bringing the Jews of the Middle East and North Africa to Israel. Private American Jewish organizations would cooperate with the new Mossad as they did with the old Mossad, often providing a cover for and financing the Israeli intelligence agencies' immigration work.

In the immediate aftermath of the war, these illegal immigrations to Israel, in addition to the clandestine transfers of vast Jewish populations from Eastern Europe to displaced persons (DP) camps in Germany, Austria and Italy, were crucial in creating the political pressures that forced the United Nations to vote in 1947 for the partition of Palestine and led to the birth of the Israeli state the following year. There is no question, however, that the illegal immigrations would have been impossible without the support of private American Jewish organizations working hand in hand with Palestinian Jews and Jewish survivors in Europe.

Indeed, American Jews, acting independently of the U.S. government through private American Jewish organizations, played a much greater role—both during and after the war—in rescuing Jews in Europe, the Middle East and North Africa than is generally acknowledged. Now that the shroud of secrecy has been lifted from these operations, the historical record should revise the public misapprehension that virtually nothing was done by Americans to help save Jews. Clearly, much more should have been accomplished by America—certainly by its government—to prevent, slow down or halt the Holocaust, but this is part of the broader history of World War II and its origins.

Official British and American policy toward Jewish refugees in wartime and postwar Europe—and toward *potential* Jewish refugees while the fighting still went on—gradually pushed private American Jewish citizens to amazing efforts to save their fellow Jews. These Americans were filling the vacuum left by London and Washington regarding Jewish rescues.

British policy was simple and straightforward. In the spirit of the 1939 White Paper, Britain firmly and consistently opposed for nine years—until Israeli independence—*all* Jewish immigration to Palestine over the meager annual quota set by the government of Prime Minister Neville Chamberlain and maintained by his successor, Winston Churchill. Invoking the supposedly overriding political need to avoid antagonizing the Arabs in Palestine and throughout the Middle East, the British often diverted the Royal Navy and the Royal Air Force from combat in the Mediterranean theater to capture, often with the infliction of bloodshed, the defenseless freighters smuggling Jewish refugees from Europe. No senior British official or leading politician ever rose against this inhumane and inflexible policy, even after 1942 when word began to filter out about the massive extermination of Jews in Nazi death camps and Jewish leaders repeatedly implored the government to help.

When it came to the Palestinian question, President Franklin D. Roosevelt chose to accept the State Department's advice not to try to influence the British to change their rigorous policy; wartime unity among the Allies was paramount. There were joint Anglo-American military operations in North Africa and the Middle East, and the fate of Jewish refugees was clearly secondary to the larger requirements of achieving victory over Hitler. At the same time, throughout the war the Roosevelt administration maintained strict quotas on the entry into the United States of Jewish refugees from Europe, even though the President and especially Eleanor Roosevelt were personally sympathetic to the Jews' fate. And although a White House conference on refugees was held in October 1940, nothing meaningful resulted.

Curiously, one man in Washington stood out as the principal advocate of keeping Jewish refugees out of the United States. He doubted the veracity of Holocaust reports, and he succeeded for years in having his way. Breckinridge Long, a Missouri lawyer who had befriended Franklin Roosevelt when they both worked for the government during World War I and later served as FDR's ambassador to Italy, was named in 1940 as Assistant Secretary of State for European Affairs and head of the Special War Problems Division. In this new post, Long exercised complete power over the granting of U.S. visas, and one of his first steps in office was to enact even more stringent procedures. Long was never seriously challenged, and he was thus able to block all initiatives toward finding an American solution to the Jewish refugee dilemma. Between 1941 and 1943, his chief ally was Loy Henderson, a career diplomat who ran the department's Eastern European section under Long.

To this day it is not clear what really motivated Long. He claimed to fear that Nazi and Communist "fifth column" agents would slip into the United States under the guise of being Jewish refugees, thereby justifying the visa restrictions he imposed. It is hard to understand the political power Long was able to command, but his absurd policy was never directly challenged.

Many top government officials, including Interior Secretary Harold L. Ickes, Treasury Secretary Henry Morgenthau, Jr., himself a Jew, and Attorney General Francis Biddle, favored help for the Jewish refugees in the only remaining haven—the United States. Ickes proposed letting the Jews come to the American Virgin Islands, and FDR suggested settling Jewish refugees in Alaska. Roosevelt also demonstrated his support for the Jewish cause by receiving Dr. Chaim Weizmann, a top leader of the Jewish independence movement, at the White House during the war. Two immensely influential American Jews, Governor Herbert Lehman of New York and Judge Samuel Rosenman, a personal adviser to the President, actively pushed the Jewish refugee issue, supporting both immigration to Palestine and an increase in the number of American visas granted. Secretary of State Cordell Hull appeared to be essentially neutral in this controversy—he seemed totally uninterested in the Jewish question—while Under Secretary of State Sumner Welles, who had direct access to Roosevelt, tended to favor terms of compromise. But none of this support for the Jews could sway Long, who negated all efforts to help the refugees.

When the first telegrams reached the State Department in August 1942 revealing that the Nazis had plans to exterminate as many as four million Jews in Europe—following the Wannsee conference in Berlin in January of that year, which called for the "definitive solution" of the Jewish problem— the initial reaction in the State Department was to describe the reports as being of a "fantastic nature." And although Sumner Welles in time helped persuade the State Department of their veracity, U.S. policy remained unchanged. Not until 1944 did Roosevelt adopt a more liberal policy, creating the War Refugees Board (and allowing one thousand Jewish refugees to enter the United States on a one-time basis) and speaking out publicly in favor of settling Jews in Palestine.

Roosevelt's belated efforts, however, had no impact on British policy. In practical terms, the British tactics of keeping Jewish refugees out of Palestine and the Americans' acquiescence left no alternative but illegal immigration. American Jews who moved to support and finance rescues thus operated in a political environment immensely ambivalent concerning the whole question of Jewish refugees.

It was against this background that Joe Schwartz's American Jewish Joint Distribution Committee (widely known as the Joint or JDC) moved quietly to assist in the illegal immigration of Jewish refugees to Palestine. The Joint was formed in 1914 after Henry Morgenthau, Sr., then American ambassador in Turkey (and father of the future Treasury Secretary), appealed to his Jewish friends for relief for Palestinian Jews caught up in the fighting in World War I. Palestine was then a part of the Ottoman Empire. A nonpolitical organization, the Joint was active during the ensuing years in providing relief to Jews in over seventy countries, including programs to settle Russian Jews on farms in the Ukraine and the Crimea during the 1920s.

It was during World War II, however, that the Joint began to discreetly fund illegal immigration operations. Although its support of illegal immigration was kept secret from the public (and at the outset from the British), the Joint meticulously informed the United States government of all of its activities. In return, the Joint enjoyed the tacit approval of Washington, where its friends, from Secretary Morgenthau to Mrs. Roosevelt, managed to keep Breckinridge Long in the dark about an emerging alliance with Aliyah Bet.

During the war years and after V-E Day, the Joint would "buy out" Jews from Europe, feed and house them and finance illegal transport ships to bring refugees to Palestine through the British blockade. These operations were underwritten almost entirely by American Jewry. During and immediately after the war, individual donors in hundreds of Jewish communities in the United States contributed hundreds of millions of dollars for the relief of European Jews, although they had little idea that much of their money supported secret immigration operations. Since 1939, when the war erupted in Europe, funds for the Joint came principally from annual campaigns by the United Jewish Appeal on the national and local levels. Some Jews contributed millions of dollars; others single dollar bills.

Prior to Israeli independence, these operations were run in Europe and the Middle East by Shaul Avigur's handpicked "emissaries"—Palestinian Jews, young Eastern European and Russian Zionists, American representatives working in foreign posts for the Joint and soldiers of the British Army's Jewish Brigade. The movement in Eastern Europe and later in the displaced persons camps in the West became known as the Brichah, the Hebrew word for "flight" or "escape." The Palestinians and the soldiers helped to build it up. Nobody seems to remember how or when this name emerged, but the Brichah was fashioned spontaneously by young Jews, some of whom were veterans of partisan bands that had fought the Germans in the forests and mountains of Poland, Slovakia, Lithuania and the Ukraine; others were returning from Nazi concentration camps or Soviet wartime exile. The Brichah quickly multiplied into a number of loosely structured organizations that cooperated increasingly with one another to protect Jewish refugees and to open roads to Palestine. Thus, there was a Polish Brichah, a Czechoslovak Brichah, an Austrian Brichah and so on. The "emissaries" from Palestine were dispatched clandestinely by Avigur to reinforce and coordinate the Brichah groups. Soon they took over most of the national Brichah organizations as well as the overall European Brichah command. Schwartz's Joint network provided the money for the operations and often a "front" for the Brichah "boys and girls," who formed the backbone of the movement for mass illegal Jewish immigration to the "Promised Land."

II

The Mystery Man

No two men could have been more unlike in background and personality than Joe Schwartz and Shaul Avigur. Yet both men shared the same ideals, respected one another and together formed a formidable team. Their common goal: to lead Jews to an independent Palestinian homeland.

Israeli history books hardly reflect the fact, but Avigur,* along with his brother-in-law Eliyahu Golomb and several other single-minded young Palestinian Jews, founded the Haganah armed forces in the 1920s.

Golomb, who was older than Shaul and had served in the Jewish Legion in World War I, became quite famous as the

* Avigur (which in Hebrew means "Father of Gur") changed his name from Shaul Meyerov in memory of his son Gur, an Israeli Army commando trooper killed at the age of seventeen in the 1948 war of independence against the attacking Arab states.

man "at the heart of everything" during the pre-independence struggle, as Israeli Prime Minister Golda Meir put it. After he died in 1945 a Haganah refugee ship was named after him, but nothing is named after Avigur.

Avigur was born in the small town of Dvinskoy, east of St. Petersburg, on November 18, 1899. Four years later, his family moved to Mogilev in the Ukraine before emigrating to Palestine. Shaul was twelve when he arrived, and spent his adolescence in Tel Aviv—then barely more than a large village—and later on a kibbutz with his father. Shaul's father, a dentist who practiced sporadically, was a Jewish Micawber, a man who lived in the clouds. His mother, Sara Meyerov, was of German Jewish parentage and a strict moralist who exercised great influence on Shaul and his sister Zippora, who would marry Moshe Shertok, Israel's first Foreign Minister and then Prime Minister, under the name of Sharett. The brothers-in-law were Israel's Founding Fathers. In the early days in Tel Aviv, Shaul's mother suspected his involvement in the anti-British underground when he installed a secret radio transmitter in the attic.

Avigur grew up to be an invisible man, austere and a loner. Because of his military—and, later, intelligence—work, he never had time to complete a university education. Apart from his deep knowledge of classical Hebrew texts, which he studied as a child, he was largely self-taught. He "certainly wasn't an intellectual," his daughter Ruth Hillel admitted. But Avigur was an intensely practical man who was knowledgeable about weapons, undercover work and the character of men and women. And he was one of the few Jewish leaders of importance who was not an active politician. Avigur had no time for politics and no use for self-promotion, though he belonged to the exclusive Jewish elite that built the State of Israel in Palestine. His great-

great-grandfather Rabbi Meir Shalom Ha Cohen Karlitzer, from Minsk, Russia, was one of the first European Jews to travel to Palestine. He arrived in 1837 and died there two years later. No other Meyerovs tried their luck until Shaul's immediate family came in 1911.

During the winter of 1920, before his twenty-first birthday, Shaul fought the Arabs in the defense of the remote Jewish settlement of Tel Hai in northern Palestine. It was a legendary engagement in modern Israeli history; for Shaul, a young farmer from a kibbutz, it was his first major battle. He had rushed to Tel Hai, where 90 Jewish men and women, armed with ancient rifles, held off 500 attacking Arabs in the snowy hills. And he saw Joseph Trumpeldor and Aaron Sher, the two Jewish commanders, killed in the fighting. Shaul survived the battle, in which the Jews were forced to abandon the settlement, and returned to his kibbutz. It was "Tel Hai that pushed me to the Haganah," he later wrote. Never again would he lead a peaceful civilian existence. Until his death Avigur would be a military commander, conspirator and spymaster.

As a young Haganah fighter, Avigur had a hard and lean look. He was dour, secretive, and his conversation was normally confined to a few brief sentences which he hoarsely whispered in Hebrew or heavily accented English. His blue eyes were usually half closed when he spoke, though they could be stiletto sharp when he was displeased. Avigur was an ascetic: he never smoked, touched alcohol or womanized. His favorite beverage was hot tea with honey or dates. He made people uncomfortable, his daughter Ruth maintained, "because he had so few vices." Avigur detested small talk and social life, and he never set foot in a cabaret. He dressed informally, and even when he was a man of great power in Israel, he owned no more than two pairs of trousers (he was partial to khaki) and a few shirts. He had no hobbies, primarily because he had no time for them, but he was very good with his hands. On those rare occasions when he visited his kibbutz in adulthood, he liked to do blacksmith work, repairing tools and implements. Avigur was most handy with weapons: it was his task to arm the men of the kibbutzim, and then to acquire weapons for the Haganah during the 1948 war. He seemed wholly devoid of a sense of humor, though there are some amusing passages in his memoirs on life in the Haganah—mainly his characterizations of his companions.

Reminiscing about their family life many years later, Avigur's wife, Sara, recalled that even when she first met him at Kibbutz Kinneret on the Sea of Galilee in 1923, he was "a mystery man." He was only twenty-four years old at the time, but he was already a top Haganah commander. As Sara wrote in her memoir, "He appears and disappears . . . doesn't sleep at night and sleeps all day . . . late in the night he goes out on a wagon somewhere . . . Where is he going, this man covered with mystery and secrets?" The answer was to work for the Haganah and arrange weapons transfers. But with his family Avigur was able to let himself go emotionally. His writings, in rich and poetic Hebrew, reveal a deep—almost romantic—passion for his land, along with a profound sense of history. His daughter remembers him as "a warm and loving father."

From its creation in 1939, Avigur headed the ha-Mossad le-Aliyah Bet, the special undercover agency for illegal Jewish immigration to the Holy Land. Aliyah Bet had just begun to function full-time under Avigur's stewardship. As Mossad "chief," Avigur often traveled abroad. Even before it was born, he went to Poland in 1929 to contact the Jewish community there, and during the 1930s he made extended visits to London, where he used the offices of the Jewish Agency at 77 Great Russell Street. The Jewish Agency had been organized in 1930 by Jewish Palestinian labor movements and was the ruling political body of the Zionist movement before independence. Whenever Avigur heard about a young Zionist activist from the Continent, he insisted on interviewing him at immense length about the situation of Jewish communities in his native country.

Ehud Avriel (born Ueberall), who years later became Avigur's deputy, first met him in London when he was visiting some friends in 1936. His initial encounter with Avigur left a lasting impression, and he described it in his memoir: "Shaul interrogated me closely about every aspect of Jewish life under [Chancellor] Dollfuss's Christian Socialist Fascism, the civil unrest, the reliability of the Zionist movement and the urgency of emigration from Vienna in view of the growing anti-Semitism. . . . I was astonished by the degree of intimate knowledge that the commanders of the Haganah had about our life in remote Vienna."

Avigur's London operations ranged from illegal immigration to Palestine to the purchase of weapons for the Haganah and general intelligence gathering. When Avigur turned up in Warsaw a few months before the Nazis attacked on September 1, 1939, the acquisition of weapons for the Jewish underground army was one of his top priorities. Although the Poles were not selling armaments to foreigners on the eve of the war, Avigur was able to obtain a large amount of arms and he succeeded in dispatching them to Palestine through circuitous secret Zionist networks. Jossi Harel, who became commander of the big postwar illegal immigration ships, including the famous *Exodus*, met Avigur for the first time in 1937. Avigur was "a man you could swear by," he recalled, "and for him to get armaments for the kibbutzim and for defense was as important as bringing in immigrants." The Jewish anxiety about arms was heightened by the fact that the Haj Amin al-Husseini, the Moslem mufti of Jerusalem, was ardently pro-Nazi and had moved to Berlin, from where he was helping to arm Arabs against both the Jews and the British.

Among Avigur's many assets was his quiet friendship with Colonel Orde Wingate, a British officer stationed in Palestine in the 1930s, who privately supported the Jewish cause. One of the great guerrilla warfare experts of his time, Wingate discreetly advised his friends in the Haganah on clandestine operations. Shaul Avigur was among the principal beneficiaries of his efforts. Wingate subsequently became famous for his guerrilla exploits in Burma, where he was killed fighting the Japanese in World War II.

During the war, Avigur's operations were centered in Tel Aviv, but they extended throughout the Middle East, Eastern Europe and Western Europe. He also set up headquarters in Istanbul, a major center for organizing illegal emigration from the Balkans to Palestine through Turkey, Teheran and Beirut. After the war, Yugoslavia became the principal transit channel for Jews escaping from Eastern Europe to Palestine. But of all postwar nations, France proved to be the most hospitable operations base for organizing the transport of Jews. And it was in Paris, of course, that Avigur and Schwartz began to conspire full-time.

III

The Miracle Worker

In contrast to Avigur, Joe Schwartz was an explosively dynamic individual, a man with a steamroller approach who never deviated from his goal and often ignored established authority. Unlike Avigur, he was a bon vivant on an impressive scale. Schwartz seemed to know everybody who mattered.

He was born on March 23, 1899, in Novaya Odessa in the Ukraine, eight months before Avigur. When Joe was eight his parents brought him to the United States, and the family settled in Baltimore. Schwartz was naturalized in 1912, and he became American to the core. His most intimate friends called him "Packy," a nickname he had chosen for himself as a young boy after a Baltimore prizefighter named Packy MacFarland. Later in his life he still signed some letters and telegrams—most frequently to his wife, Dora—with his childhood moniker. The son of the chief Orthodox rabbi of

Baltimore, Schwartz was himself an ordained rabbi and an eminent scholar. He graduated from Yeshiva University in New York (when it was known as the Rabbi Isaac Elchanan Seminary), served as rabbi for three years and later earned a doctorate in Oriental studies from Yale University. Schwartz was an authority on Semitic languages and literature; he had lectured at the American University in Cairo and at Long Island University, and he was the associate editor of *Scripta Mathematica*.

Elegant, handsome, with sparkling brown eyes and a shock of brown hair, Schwartz—just over six feet tall—was almost Lincolnesque in appearance. Worldly and suave, he was a natural leader who could be as fun-loving as he was work-consumed. He relished pitched political and academic debates, which he punctuated with outbursts of profanity, and he often spent hours drinking his favorite Scotch whisky—twelve-year-old Ballantine—and chain-smoking. Schwartz also loved nightclubs, among other pleasurable pastimes. He was stunningly popular with women of all ages, and flirted effortlessly and delightfully, according to women who knew him well. A romantic figure, Schwartz led an intriguing semi-secret life during the war. One Polish-born woman who worked with him in 1945, when she was barely in her twenties, grew misty-eyed when his name came up forty-five years later; the memory of "our Joe" had never left her. But Schwartz's charm embraced men as well, and this translated into fierce loyalty; he could do no wrong as far as his associates were concerned. As authoritarian as he could be, Schwartz never issued strict orders; his subordinates took his suggestions as law.

Despite his warm and outgoing personality, Schwartz was an intensely private man. He spent much of his time alone and kept his personal problems to himself. Most outsiders were unaware that he had a Ph.D. from Yale. Nor did friends ever know why he left the rabbinate. If he had lost his faith, he never gave any explanations. And Schwartz seldom spoke of his less than happy family life, which was complicated by the fact that his work often kept him away from his West Seventy-sixth Street home in New York. His favorite form of solitary relaxation was to work on the most difficult crossword and acronym puzzles he could lay his hands on. As his son Nathan recalled, Joe was enamored of linguistics from his Yale days.

Schwartz abruptly abandoned his academic career and religious calling to devote his life to the cause of Jewish refugees worldwide. He signed on with the Joint in 1940 as its director of European operations. Schwartz set up his headquarters in Paris and promptly became the Joint's beloved miracle worker. Working out of war-torn Europe for more than a decade, Schwartz was not to be questioned. He had no patience for administrative details, especially when they concerned his far-flung lifestyle and personal activities. In spite of eyebrows raised at the Joint's Paris office, nobody at New York headquarters thought about confronting Schwartz when it came to the issue of his personal accountability.

Schwartz was as dedicated and tireless as Avigur, and he crisscrossed Europe in his efforts to help Jewish refugees. After the Nazis invaded Belgium, the Netherlands and France in May 1940, he dashed to Budapest with Morris Troper, then the Joint's European Council chairman, to help organize relief mechanisms for the Jews in Hungary and Romania in case the war cut off that part of Eastern Europe. They returned to Paris in early June, just two days ahead of the Nazis. The chief concierge of the Prince de Galles Hotel—one of France's most distinguished hotels and

Schwartz's Parisian home—met them at the door and told them he had kept the empty establishment open because he was certain that Monsieur Schwartz would stop by on his way back from the East. Schwartz then fled to Bordeaux, where the French government sat briefly before its ultimate collapse, and went on to Lisbon, which became the Joint's operational center throughout the war. The Portuguese capital had reasonably good communications with the United States as well as with much of Europe and the Middle East. And Lisbon was the center for numerous clandestine operations for the Allies and the Nazis alike.

Schwartz and Avigur's initial encounter probably took place in August 1943 somewhere in Palestine. It was Schwartz's first wartime visit to the Holy Land. His fat green U.S. passport bore the stamp "SECURITY CONTROL—R.A.F. STATION—LYDDA—2.8.1943." Schwartz had flown to Palestine on U.S. military aircraft via Lisbon and Algiers. His priority access to military transportation was part of the discreet support the Joint's operations received from highly placed friends in Washington.

The purpose of Schwartz's trip was to clarify numerous misunderstandings that had arisen between the Joint and the Jewish Agency over the nature of their cooperation. A key issue stemmed from internal differences within both the Joint and the Jewish establishment in Palestine over what policies were to be pursued regarding the immediate fate of Jewry in hostile environments. This was invariably linked to the question of Palestine's ultimate destiny. Indeed, Jews everywhere were still deeply split over the desirability of a sovereign Jewish state.

David Ben-Gurion, who headed the Jewish Agency and

became the first Israeli Prime Minister, had advocated a federated Jewish-Arab state in Palestine back in the mid-1930s. The Yishuv—the Jewish community in Palestine with roots in turn-of-the-century migrations—generally supported his position, and used the war and the impact of the Holocaust as a means of garnering support for an Israeli state. But the American Jewish community then was considerably less interested in the Israeli cause. In fact, Schwartz was one of the few militant Zionists among top Joint officials. Even Judah-Leib Magnes, the American-born rabbi who was the first president of the Hebrew University in Jerusalem and chairman of the Joint's Middle East Advisory Council, was in favor of a binational state and, therefore, against illegal immigration endeavors.

When Schwartz arrived in Palestine in August 1943, he discovered that Magnes had turned down on his own a request from the Jewish Agency for funds to support the rescue of Jews in Europe. The Joint, Magnes incorrectly explained, did not engage in "illegal" work. Schwartz therefore came under concerted attack by the Jewish Agency and Histadrut over what was seen as the Joint's refusal to contribute to rescue and illegal immigration operations. This, of course, was not the case. It is quite possible that the Palestinian leadership simply did not know that the Joint had secretly helped finance the Warsaw Ghetto uprising earlier that year through its Swiss banking network. Magnes too may have ignored this fact. One Jewish hand often did not know what the other was doing. Indeed, there was intense turf rivalry among Jewish political and relief groups.

Schwartz was further embroiled in the Yishuv's running controversy over whether rescue operations in Europe should take precedence over illegal immigration, an argument that remains unresolved in Israel to this day. Schwartz realized that some Yishuv politicians were trying to undercut Avigur's Mossad. But as far as he was concerned, both goals were equally important. His conversations in Palestine—conceivably without Magnes's knowledge—laid the groundwork for agreements between the Jewish Agency and Avigur's Mossad to enable the Joint to become increasingly involved in rescues as well as illegal immigration.

After their initial meeting in Palestine to coordinate Mossad and Joint activities, Schwartz and Avigur met again a few weeks later in Istanbul. The Mossad and the Jewish Agency had been operating in Istanbul since 1939, and the Joint had recently established its own American-staffed office there. Istanbul was rapidly becoming the principal center for rescue and immigration enterprises in Eastern Europe and the Balkans. Like Lisbon, it was a neutral city where communications were quite good and emissaries of many governments and groups could come and go freely. Istanbul was ideal for intelligence and diplomatic manipulations by the belligerent powers—and special interests such as those of the Joint and the Palestinians. Turkish officials proved to be most helpful when money was involved.

Schwartz and Avigur also met periodically in Teheran. The Joint kept vast reserves of food and clothing in warehouses for Jewish contingencies in the Soviet Union and the Nazi-occupied countries. From Teheran, Avigur supervised relief for tens of thousands of Jewish refugees streaming from Russia through Persia. His sister Zippora, whose husband, Moshe Sharett, was the Jewish Agency policymaker and would later become Israel's Foreign Minister and Prime Minister, was stationed in Teheran as a social worker looking after the refugees.

But it was in Paris that Schwartz and Avigur began to work together in earnest. In the autumn of 1944, just after the capital's liberation, Schwartz reopened the Joint's office at 19, Rue de Téhéran, near Place St.-Augustin. He couldn't wait to get back. By mid-1945 Avigur had moved his personal headquarters to Paris, where he ran the Mossad and the Brichah and shopped for weapons all over Europe.

They widened their contacts later in the year when both organizations became convinced of the urgency of producing a comprehensive plan for moving Jewish refugees out of Eastern Europe through Germany, Austria, Italy and France en route to Palestine. After visiting Nazi death camps and camps for displaced persons in Germany that October, Ben-Gurion noted in his diary that "70 percent of the survivors do in fact want to go to Palestine," and he proclaimed a firm policy on illegal immigration. "In the struggle ahead we have on our side three major forces: the Yishuv and its strength, America, [and] the DP camps in Germany. The function of Zionism is not to help the remnant to survive in Europe, but rather to rescue them for the sake of the Jewish people and the Yishuv; the Jews of America and the DPs of Europe are allotted a special role in this rescue."

In late 1945, in a speech to the survivors of Auschwitz, Ben-Gurion affirmed that only an independent Israel could guarantee that a Holocaust would never happen again.

Avigur and Schwartz now had a firm mandate.

IV

Money for Blood

Though it was not until 1939 that the Mossad was formally constituted to conduct illegal immigration, Avigur had been busy for years devising ways of bringing Jews to Palestine from Europe, especially from Nazi-occupied countries. As early as 1937 he had begun dispatching Haganah emissaries to Eastern Europe to enlist local Zionist youth organizations in helping Jews—with or without British entry permits—to emigrate to Palestine. Avigur encouraged them to set up clandestine camps in their own countries to learn how to farm and to use weapons while they awaited departure.

Palestine's total population in the late 1930s was 1.5 million, of whom 450,000 were Jews, the rest being Arabs. The British were intent on keeping legal Jewish immigration to a minimum. A record 60,000 permits were granted in 1935, but the annual quota fell to 30,000 in 1936, and then to only 15,000 under the provisions of the White Paper in 1939. By

1945, acting on British instructions, Palestinian Arabs were to determine the annual entry quotas for Jews. Inevitably, European Jews were forced to the alternative of illegal immigration. Palestinian Jews, primarily through the Mossad, orchestrated this task to accommodate the largest possible numbers.

Mossad emissaries were already active in Paris, Warsaw, Belgrade, Bucharest, Athens and Istanbul. A key figure in the Mossad's European operations was Moshe Agami. A Latvian-born kibbutznik and Haganah officer who had lived in Palestine since 1926, Agami was among the first to be tapped by Avigur for delicate foreign missions. Agami was the emissary sent to Vienna to coordinate the rescue of Austrian Jews. He arrived in Vienna a few weeks after the Anschluss on March 11, 1938, when the Germans annexed Austria. Among the first young Zionists he contacted was Ehud Avriel, a twenty-year-old member of the Hehalutz (Pioneer) Zionist youth movement. Their meeting in Vienna was the start of a lifetime association concentrating on organizing illegal Jewish emigration to Palestine from a half dozen European countries. At the war's end the post in Bucharest was held by Ruth Aliav-Klieger, a close personal friend of David Ben-Gurion and one of the most daring and successful Palestinian operatives. The emissaries in each European capital, including Agami in Vienna, Yehuda Arazi in Rome and Dani Shind in Istanbul, immediately set up a telephone communications network—not an easy undertaking considering the appalling quality of prewar telephone services in Eastern Europe and the Balkans—and they kept in touch by speaking in a secret code prepared by Mossad experts.

In attempting to launch illegal immigration to Palestine

before the war, the Mossad leaders—as well as the Jews in much of Europe—confronted an extraordinary paradox and a situation that conceivably could have prevented untold Jewish deaths during the Holocaust if it had been properly handled at the time. It is one of those horrifying historical misperceptions that are so difficult to comprehend even today. This was the Nazis' willingness—indeed, an overwhelming anxiety—to have Jews leave the territory of Greater Germany (which then included Austria) and adjacent nations such as Czechoslovakia and Poland.

By early 1939, Hitler and his principal associates had not yet decided on the "Final Solution" of the Jewish problem in Europe—this would come in 1942. The policy followed by Nazi authorities in Vienna—including Adolf Eichmann, the SS officer in charge of Jewish Affairs—was to get rid of the Jews through orderly emigration to Palestine or wherever they wished to go. Eichmann, in fact, stood ready to expedite the emigration from Austria and, as Avriel has written, established a smoothly working relationship between his office and the Mossad commanders in Vienna. This relationship was the precedent for Eichmann's unsuccessful attempts toward the end of the war to trade Jewish lives for dollars and vehicles in Eastern Europe. The Nazis, however, never communicated this policy forcefully enough, and neither the Jews nor the Western governments had the imagination to grasp what was being proposed. It was a unique opportunity. Naturally, nobody could foresee the Holocaust, but as Avriel wrote in his memoirs, "Jewish refugees were an especially unwelcome commodity: the Germans wanted to get rid of them at all cost, and the British refused them admission to territory under their control."

Avriel, who worked with Agami and other emissaries in Europe organizing the first illegal immigration departure for Palestine (the *Attrato I* left Bari, Italy, on March 9, 1939, with 385 young Polish Jews), soon found himself dealing directly with Eichmann. Avriel had gone to Palestine on a quick visit late in 1938, and Avigur, who instantly learned of his presence, instructed him to try to increase the new flow of refugees through Yugoslavia—which made transit visas readily available—and then across the Mediterranean to the Holy Land. The Mossad, Avigur promised, would provide ships and escorts from the Palyam, which was the naval branch of the Palmach, the Haganah commando force. Vienna would be the center of all illegal immigration operations, it was decided, in part because of Eichmann's willingness to cooperate.

The Mossad was able to operate throughout Europe, even after Germany occupied Czechoslovakia in March 1939 and war was imminent. Eichmann established in his headquarters at Vienna's Rothschild Palace a "Center for Jewish Emigration," and ordered that all illegal convoys for Palestine be controlled by one of his deputies. He urged the Mossad men to channel the Jewish refugees out of Austria through the Slovak "Republic," the puppet state set up by the Nazis after they had dismembered Czechoslovakia. When Avriel traveled to Bratislava, the capital of Slovakia, he was ·driven there from Vienna in a luxurious black limousine with a uniformed SS driver. It was a state of affairs verging on the surreal, but Eichmann and the Mossad plodded ahead in this bizarre partnership. In August 1939, Mossad emissaries from all over Europe met at a discreet conference in Geneva to coordinate their activities. Two weeks later, on September 1, the outbreak of World War II was marked by the German attack on Poland, but it seemed to make no difference in the Vienna operations.

Eichmann soon issued 1,000 passports for Jewish refugees

in Austria, who were to go down the Danube to Bratislava
and then on to Yugoslavia, where the Mossad supposedly
had a ship waiting for the voyage to Palestine. Avriel was
summoned to the Gestapo headquarters, where Eichmann
reprimanded him:

> "Progress is too slow!" he barked at me. We did not
> work quickly enough. Why did we get so few people
> down the Danube to the Black Sea and through Yu-
> goslavia to the Adriatic and from there to Palestine?
> And why did we not push more people into England
> and America? Were we not aware that he had had
> enough of us? It was time to make the place *judenrein*
> —and soon!

While Agami and Avriel had gathered the 1,000 refugees
in Vienna, the Mossad was unable to procure a ship. The
Mossad tried to buy one in the Romanian port of Constantsa
with funds provided by the Joint—the first time the Joint,
at Schwartz's behest, actually financed illegal immigration—
but no one was willing to sell ships to Jews. In fact, the
Mossad had briefly owned a ship, the *Darien*, intended for
this operation, but on the Haganah's orders it was sold to
the British for intelligence missions.

At this point, Haganah military intelligence thought it
prudent—with a view toward future relationships—to be
involved in British covert operations. Regardless, the exodus
continued as the refugees were transported from Bratislava
to the port of Kladovo on the Yugoslav Danube. But the
river froze for the winter and the emigrants could go no
farther. After nine months in Kladovo there was still no ship
available, so the refugees were transferred to a camp in the
small river town of Šabac. Then in the spring of 1941, the

Nazis invaded Yugoslavia, and on April 7, 1,100 Jews at the camp were executed by the SS. These were the very same Jews Eichmann had encouraged to escape German territories two years earlier.*

The Eichmann affair and its consequences raise, even a half century later, the fundamental question of why the Western powers—regardless of whether they could have visualized the Nazi "Final Solution"—failed to act with wisdom, to say nothing of generosity, when it was still possible to save Jews. Savage Nazi anti-Semitism was already in full evidence. Tragically, Britain remained steadfast in its refusal to allow the number of Jews emigrating to Palestine to exceed the meager annual quota set by the White Paper—even though the Nazis were not yet holding Jews back.

A charitable explanation is that the generalized Western tendency was to minimize all these signals. Another reason is that Western political leaders did not care enough; in the maelstrom of prewar politics, Jews were nobody's priority. And for that matter, the United States was also closed to mass Jewish immigration from Europe. Annual quotas for entry visas to the United States were absurdly low, set at 27,370 refugees from Germany and Austria during all of 1938.

Yet there were still a number of times during the war when Nazi commanders, including Eichmann, offered to

---

* In June 1938, 386 young Jews left Austria for Greece and then boarded an illegal ship for Palestine after Eichmann had granted permission for their departure. This was negotiated in a series of extremely unpleasant meetings between Eichmann and Willy Israel Perl, a thirty-two-year-old Viennese lawyer, who represented the faction of Zionist Revisionists. Perl's refugee organization in Vienna—a minor ideological rival of the Mossad—was called the Action, and it ran parallel to Avigur's Mossad. The Revisionists were able to arrange several relatively small shipments in 1938 and 1939, each time with Eichmann's assent for the departure from Austria. Perl later became a colonel in U.S. Army intelligence, settling in the United States.

barter Jews for money—agreeing either not to deport them from Eastern Europe to the death camps or to release large groups of them altogether. Eichmann seemed to be involved from the outset in all of the deals concerning Jews—as well as killing them when the Nazis took that course.

In 1943, a proposal known as the Europa Plan, elaborated by the Slovakian Jewish leadership in contact with local Nazi SS commanders, reached Joint, Mossad and Jewish Agency representatives in Istanbul, among them Schwartz, Avigur, and Avigur's brother-in-law, Moshe Sharett. The plan suggested a halt to deportations of Jews from Slovakia, and the idea soon emerged that in exchange for vast sums, deportations elsewhere in occupied Europe might cease too. No longer certain of the Reich's victory, SS officers were beginning to think about money for themselves, and the word from individual Nazi commanders in Hungary and Slovakia was that for two or three million dollars most of the European Jews could be saved. Although it is impossible to say whether the Europa Plan was truly feasible, it is known that after $400,000 was sent to Slovakia and deposited for the Nazis in Swiss bank accounts, some deportations were stopped or delayed. Negotiations were then broken, for reasons that remain unclear. Perhaps enough money could not be raised in time, or perhaps the whole exercise was a Nazi fraud. In any event, the Europa Plan provided another opportunity for the Joint to become involved in Jewish rescue efforts. It was largely on Schwartz's recommendation that the Joint provided over $120,000 in cash for the plan (over $1 million at 1991 values); its secret Swiss banking network handled funds channeled through the Jewish Agency. Deep as the doubts may be about the ultimate prospects of the Europa

Plan, the nagging question persists: could tens of thousands of Jewish lives have been saved if the Allied governments had participated in it?

The standard reaction to "money for blood" plans presented by the Foreign Office in London, and halfheartedly by the Roosevelt administration, was that the war effort would be damaged if payments in cash or in equipment were awarded to the enemy. This was the case as well in May 1944 when Eichmann sent Joel Brand, a leader of the Jewish community in Budapest, to Istanbul with the famous offer to exchange one million Jews for 10,000 trucks and other commodities—or for $400 million. Eichmann's idea was that the Joint would finance this immense operation, but the veto by the British Cabinet put an effective end to Brand's mission. British intelligence agents first abducted him from the Mossad en route from Istanbul to Palestine, and then imprisoned him in Cairo for four months.

Would Eichmann have lived up to the deal? There is no way of knowing. But the fact remains that 400,000 Hungarian Jews were murdered after Eichmann's August deadline for the Brand deal had expired. The final British position was summarized by Lord Walter Moyne, the Minister for Middle Eastern Affairs, who was quoted as asking Brand: "What will I do with a million Jews? Where will I put them?" Moyne was later assassinated in Cairo by members of a Jewish underground organization.

There is at least one instance of Jews being "bought out"— and saved—in a complex cloak-and-dagger operation. Not surprisingly, the Joint was a central player. After two months of secret negotiations between Saly Mayer, the former president of the Federation of Swiss Jewish Communities—who quietly served as the Joint chief financial representative in Switzerland for over a decade—and middlemen representing top Gestapo and SS commanders, 1,673 Hungarian Jews held at the Bergen-Belsen concentration camp were permitted to leave for Swiss exile in June 1944. The ransom in dollars, gold, platinum, diamonds and jewels was valued between eight and twelve million Swiss francs ($50 million today). It also appears to have prevented the execution of an estimated 100,000 Jews in the Budapest ghetto. A 1946 affidavit presented to the U.S. occupation authorities in Austria by Rudolf Kaestner, the representative of the underground Jewish Agency's Rescue Committee in Budapest, affirms that these executions were halted. Kaestner had been allowed to travel to Switzerland to negotiate with Mayer as a middleman on behalf of General Kurt Becher, the SS Standartenführer in Budapest, who originated the proposal.

Kaestner believed that the deal had been authorized by Heinrich Himmler and Adolf Eichmann of the SS. This agreement coincided with Eichmann's approach to the Palestinians in Istanbul through Joel Brand. The Brand fiasco may have cost 400,000 Jewish lives in Hungary, but there were no further executions in Budapest after the deal concluded by Saly Mayer. A total of 180,000 Jews in Hungary survived the Nazi occupation. Mayer deposited another $5 million of the Joint's money in an escrow account in a Swiss bank to entice the Nazis to "sell" more Jews, but there was no response.

According to Kaestner's affidavit, gold and valuables were collected from Jewish families in Budapest, and Kaestner personally delivered them to General Becher. But the dollars came from the Joint via Saly Mayer. Mayer thought of the 1,673 Hungarian Jews brought to Switzerland by way of Bergen-Belsen as the first contingent, a Nazi "down payment"

on additional Jewish groups. Kaestner was led to believe that
the Germans were prepared to "sell" Jews if the Joint stood
ready to pay for them. He was convinced that the Nazis
could be bought, and in a twelve-point proposal he sent to
General Becher in July 1944 he demanded that "all" Jewish
executions be stopped. It is not known why the Mayer-
Becher channel went dry after the Bergen-Belsen rescue,
though it is possible that the collapse of the Brand mission
led the Nazi commanders to suspend all transactions of this
type.

The postscript to this affair is that on May 11, 1945, three
days after the German surrender, General Becher returned
the entire ransom he had received in Budapest a year earlier
to a Yugoslav Zionist leader named Moshe Schweiger, who
had been interned in the Mauthausen concentration camp
in Austria. For reasons that remain unclear, Schweiger had
become General Becher's protégé. In fact, Becher released
him from Mauthausen shortly before V-E Day and then
handed him the ransom treasure. Schweiger, who had just
been named the representative of the Joint and the Jewish
Agency, soon turned it over to a U.S. Army military intelligence unit, the CIC Unit 215. General Becher was then
arrested and the ransom was entered in the property register
of the U.S. Military Government in Austria. In July 1946,
the Joint's secretary, Moses A. Leavitt, wrote Secretary of
State James F. Byrnes that the money and the valuables
should be returned to the Joint and the Jewish Agency "for
the purpose of relief and resettlement of Jewish victims of
Nazi persecution." As far as can be determined, the Joint
never collected more than $25,000 from the U.S. government
on this claim.

Mayer's operation proved that some Jews, at least, could
be wrested away from the Nazis in exchange for payments

if every opportunity was used to the fullest. And the Joint's records show that both the American and British governments were kept informed throughout the entire Budapest operation, without posing any objection.

The most famous single instance of a U.S. government-approved rescue during the war, of course, was the Wallenberg case. Raoul Wallenberg was the young Swedish diplomat sent to Budapest to set up a mechanism to protect and save Hungarian Jews, and in June 1944 the U.S. government authorized the Joint to transfer $100,000 to him as the first installment in financing this undertaking. The Wallenberg mission, one of the most remarkable and successful of its kind, was funded in its entirety by the Joint. Wallenberg paid Hungarian and Nazi officials for exit passports—he may have saved as many as 50,000 Jews—and he presided over a vast organization of hospitals and soup kitchens, employing 400 local Jews. Saly Mayer was again the financial wizard who secretly replenished Wallenberg's funds until the Swede was imprisoned in January 1945 by the conquering Soviet troops and vanished forever. The question arises why there could not have been more Mayer-Becher exchanges and Wallenberg operations.

By the same token, one must ask why the Mossad and the European Jewish communities failed to receive assistance in seeking to procure ships to transport refugees to Palestine —as in the case of the 1,100 Jews murdered by the Germans in Yugoslavia. One reason is that there weren't adequate resources for rescues until 1943, when the Joint, chiefly through Joe Schwartz's good offices, became seriously engaged in funding illegal immigration. But could the Yishuv, the established Jewish community in Palestine, have provided more in funds—over and above what the Jewish Agency collected for itself and the Mossad?

In spite of this shortage of funds, the Mossad launched 45 sailings and landed 26,000 illegal immigrants between 1937 and 1940, the bulk after 1939. The first Mossad refugee ship to set sail from Europe was the *Attrato I*, and between 1943 and Israeli independence in 1948, 64 "Haganah ships," as they were called by Avigur's people, rescued 102,000 illegal immigrants from Europe, including women and children. The Haganah's Palmach commandos and civilians helped refugees disembark at night, sometimes silently wading with them on their backs through shallow waters to the shore. These operations were carried out in the face of frequently brutal and bloody interdiction by the British armed forces on the sea, in the air and on land. Captured ships were routed to the island of Cyprus, where the Jews were interned in camps. At the same time, British diplomats in European capitals, even in newly liberated Yugoslavia and Greece, pressed local governments to prevent Jews from leaving their coasts for Palestine. It was not Britain's finest hour.

V

Official Resistance;
Tacit Approval

The American government's official position on the entry of Jewish refugees into the United States and illegal immigration to Palestine didn't really change until the last year of the war. Unofficially, however, the Roosevelt administration tolerated, and in some cases even encouraged, covert operations by American Jewish organizations in their support of clandestine movements of Jews from Europe to the Holy Land. While this was crucial to both the Joint and the Mossad, historically it does not excuse the U.S. government's failure to openly support the rescue of Jews during a war fought in the name of freedom and democracy.

In retrospect, two principal and overlapping agendas were responsible for the official American response: a domestic and an international one.

Because of the pressures applied by the State Department,

and chiefly by Breckinridge Long, only 22,000 Jewish refugees were allowed to enter the United States between 1942 and 1945. In the famous case of the German liner *St. Louis*, which in May 1939 was prevented by the Cuban government from landing its 930 Jewish passengers in Havana even though they held valid Cuban visas (purchased for cash from Cuban consulates in Europe), Roosevelt did not let them enter the United States either, and the ship had to return to Europe. In this instance, it was again the Joint that acted when the Roosevelt administration refused: first, it offered to post a $500,000 bond to guarantee that the refugees would not be public charges while in Cuba (some of them had visas to other Western Hemisphere countries); then it mobilized European Jewish organizations to persuade local governments to let the *St. Louis* disembark her passengers in non-German ports. Belgium, the Netherlands, France and even Britain agreed, and at least a percentage of these Jews were saved on the eve of the war.

Not until eight months after the end of the war in Europe did the United States further open its doors to Jewish refugees. On December 22, 1945, President Truman authorized by executive order the entry of 39,000 displaced persons at a rate of 3,000 per month beginning in May 1946. Most of these arrivals, naturally, were Jewish. Two years later, on June 18, 1948, Congress passed the Displaced Persons Act, which allowed for the entry of 205,000 refugees over a two-year period. But as its provisions discriminated against Jews (Truman, signing the act with "very great reluctance," described it as excluding "Jewish Displaced Persons rather than accepting a fair proportion of them along with other faiths"), a subsequent amendment added 136,000 visas to make the legislation more equitable. By then, Israel was already independent and open to all Jews.

American national opposition to the admission of foreign Jews was clearly due to much more than the vagaries of the anti-Semitic Breckinridge Long in the early 1940s: his attitude symbolized the fact that dislike of the Jews ran deep in American society—often translated into job, educational and social discrimination—and Roosevelt and the Congress were aware of it.

Internationally, the U.S. stance on endangered Jews was certainly less than forceful. While Roosevelt wrote Secretary of State Cordell Hull that he regarded the 1939 British White Paper on immigration into Palestine with "a good deal of dismay" and commented that "this is something that we cannot give approval to by the United States" (he even had Ambassador Joseph P. Kennedy transmit this reaction to the Foreign Office), the administration did nothing in the ensuing years to affect British policies. Jewish refugees were simply not a wartime priority, and there is nothing to suggest that Roosevelt ever raised the Palestine immigration problem with Churchill. From the Prime Minister down to the Imperial Staff, the British had a monolithic position on this issue and it remained unchanged and virtually unchallenged by British public opinion until Britain abandoned Palestine in 1948.* American public opinion—except for Jewish voices

---

* Though Churchill did nothing to force changes in the British policy on Palestine, surprisingly he took a pro-Jewish stance after receiving a paper from the Imperial Chiefs of Staff in opposition to plans to partition the Holy Land. But he did it in a private communication on January 25, 1944, to Major General Sir Hastings Ismay, chief of staff at the Defense Ministry:

> The Chiefs of Staff seem to assume that partition will arouse Jewish resentment. It is, on the contrary, the White Paper policy that arouses the Jewish resentment. The opposition to partition will come from the Arabs, and any violence by the Arabs will be countered by the Jews. It must be

(and not nearly all of them)—hardly cared about Palestine at all. As to the Palestinian Jews, their wartime dilemma vis-à-vis the British was summed up by the Jewish Agency's David Ben-Gurion: "We shall fight with Great Britain in this war as if there was no White Paper, and we shall fight the White Paper as if there was no war."

Under these penumbral conditions, rescues of European Jewry were complicated by the State Department's European and Near East divisions, which fought tooth and nail against relaxing controls on U.S. currency transfers to occupied Europe, even after President Roosevelt and Treasury Secretary Morgenthau had approved this policy in early 1944. The official reason for this action was fear that these funds would aid the enemy—an absurd notion considering how little the $10 million aid package mattered in terms of global war. It has never been determined, however, if the State Department's resistance to assisting European Jewry, and, as alleged by many historians, its hiding the truth about the ongoing extermination of Jews by the Nazis from the American public, resulted from pro-British sympathies or from latent anti-Semitic sentiments. Treasury Secretary Morgenthau advised Roosevelt in a "Personal Report" of January 17, 1944, on what he called the "utter failure of certain

---

remembered that Lord Wavell [the Allied commander in the Middle East] has stated that, left to themselves, the Jews would beat the Arabs. There cannot therefore be any great danger in our joining with the Jews to enforce the kind of proposals about partition which are set forth in . . . the paper. I therefore cannot accept in any way the requirements for internal security set out in the table, which proceeds upon the assumption that both the Jews and the Arabs would join together to fight us. Obviously we shall not proceed with any plan of partition which the Jews do not support.

Sadly, Churchill did not pursue this theme, prescient as he was in his judgment, and, of course, he was no longer in power after mid-1945. His views on Palestine became public only when the *Closing the Ring* volume of his wartime memoirs was published in 1951.

officials in the State Department" to prevent the Jewish exterminations. He clearly had Breckinridge Long in mind, and he proposed the creation of a U.S. government agency to deal with the refugees.

Outside the State Department, the Roosevelt administration demonstrated a growing, if discreet, leaning toward the Jewish Palestinian cause, even at the price of irritating Britain. Roosevelt himself took the lead in that direction when he created, in January 1944, the War Refugee Board, a Cabinet-level group charged with taking "all measures within [its] power to rescue the victims of enemy oppression who are in imminent danger of death and otherwise to afford such victims all possible relief and assistance consistent with the successful prosecution of the war." Although the formation of the board did not actually raise U.S. immigration quotas, it was nonetheless a turning point in the official American posture toward the rescue of European Jewry. Through the efforts of those Americans chosen to direct its activities, the War Refugee Board produced remarkable results in a short period of time. The board's chairman was John W. Pehle, a Treasury Department official (not a Jew) who helped Morgenthau draft his scathing memorandum to the President.

Then, Breckinridge Long was, in effect, forced to resign when Roosevelt chose not to promote him to Under Secretary of State to replace Sumner Welles. In his gently manipulative manner, FDR wanted Long out of the way and picked the most effective strategy to achieve his purpose. Visa policies were no longer in the hands of the man who so stubbornly opposed Jewish immigration to the United States, but much time would elapse before America's gates were thrown open to foreign Jews. While the creation of the War Refugee Board was a major milestone, the Jewish cause still had formidable foes in Washington; for example, General George C. Marshall, the Chief of Staff of the Army and a powerful figure in the capital, was able to kill a proposed Senate resolution in 1944 favoring free emigration to Palestine in order to promote "a free and democratic Jewish common-wealth" when he cited military problems it would cause in the Middle East. Later, Marshall would oppose the creation of a Jewish state altogether.

Two months after the creation of the War Refugee Board, Roosevelt told the American Zionist leaders he had received at the White House that they could publicly quote his position; namely, that the U.S. government had never given its approval to the White Paper of 1939. "The President is happy that the doors of Palestine are today open to Jewish refugees," Jewish leaders quoted Roosevelt as saying, "and when future decisions are reached, full justice will be done to those who seek a Jewish national home, for which our government and the American people have always had the deepest sympathy, today more than ever in view of the tragic plight of hundreds of thousands of homeless Jewish refugees." Unlike Truman, however, Roosevelt never issued an executive order to let Jewish refugees enter the United States in large numbers.

Obviously, ways had to be found by American Jewish organizations to transfer some funds for rescue and relief operations (with the tacit support of the Treasury Department) before the Treasury act forbidding "trading with the enemy" was lifted and the Joint could engage in the large-scale enterprises envisaged by Schwartz and the Mossad. By September 1944, Schwartz was able to announce that out of $47,530,900 expended worldwide on refugees during 1940–45, the Joint had spent $6 million in the occupied countries, channeling the money through Switzerland. This included sending from Teheran 10,000 packages of food and clothing to 300,000 Polish refugees in Asiatic Russia. Some $8.3 million of this staggering $47.5 million was for immigration—mostly illegal.

Schwartz claimed that in occupied France between 1940 and 1945 the Joint helped save 6,500 Jewish children through a system he had set up just before the war with local relief committees in several European countries. Known as "Après" ("Money Afterward"), this system allowed local committees to borrow money at home with the Joint's assurance of repayment in dollars after the war. In France, local committees had borrowed $2 million in French francs in this fashion, which kept Jews from starvation. Schwartz said that "an appreciable part of this money was used in supporting Jewish children who were hidden in monasteries, in nunneries, in Christian homes and farms, often with names altered and parentage concealed." These funds, he explained, "kept children alive; they made possible boarding them among peasants or farmers or sending them into Catholic and Protestant institutions."

And help came from many quarters. In addition to material aid, Jewish children were furnished with identity cards and other papers to facilitate their escape. "That was done in a great many cases with the full knowledge of the French police," Schwartz said in a report to the Joint board, "who, when they stopped a man in the street and asked to see his documents, when they found they didn't seem to be genuine, asked him, 'Are you a Jew?' If he said 'yes,' they asked, 'Why didn't you say so in the first place?' and sent him off to safety." The Joint's work in France continued throughout the war years, "always in close contact with the general French underground movement."

But as in so many wartime situations in occupied Europe, the behavior of local authorities was unpredictable, if not contradictory. Whereas the police of the Vichy regime in France and then the Germans and the Nazi-run French police turned over to the Gestapo 75,000 Jews (two-thirds were Jewish refugees from elsewhere in Europe) and thousands of foreign non-Jews for deportation and often death as a matter of official policy, there are endless examples recorded in the files of American Jewish and other agencies of individual French police officers who helped save Jews.

Certainly more could have been accomplished for Jews in occupied Europe if the Joint (and therefore Palestinian Jewish organizations which relied on the Joint) had not been so hamstrung by the U.S. State Department's small-mindedness. But even before the establishment of the War Refugee Board, Schwartz and his associates tended to receive special treatment from American military and diplomatic authorities.

Though he remained a civilian, Schwartz was awarded an "assimilated" rank of colonel in the U.S. Army. This allowed him to wear a military uniform with a "U.S." shoulder patch and "U.S." lapel insignia, and he enjoyed top priority for travel aboard U.S. military aircraft and access to all other forms of military transportation and facilities. Schwartz's military orders specified that he was "attending to important refugee work." Other senior Joint representatives in Europe were accorded the same courtesies, which made it possible for them to function with extraordinary ease in wartime and in postwar Europe as part of the official U.S. establishment. In fact, they were assigned to the Inter-Governmental Refugee Committee, and as such were considered members of the Allied Military Government in Europe.

The Joint likewise was allowed to own and operate trucks and jeeps in Europe. American officials obviously looked the other way when these U.S. vehicles were used more or less surreptitiously by Brichah and Mossad operatives running

(45)

their illegal immigration schemes across the Continent. Sometimes these operatives also sported military uniforms with Joint insignias, which were usually—and most helpfully—mistaken for U.S. Army uniforms by the local police and frontier and customs guards. American embassies, legations and consulates in Europe and the Middle East served as communications channels for the Joint and for Joe Schwartz in particular. His cables from the field to the Joint's New York headquarters or to his Lisbon and Paris offices were handled as part of the U.S. diplomatic traffic, as were all the headquarters messages to him.

Schwartz and his Joint colleagues enjoyed such privileges because from 1943 on, top government officials—and quite possibly the White House itself—had quietly ordered military commanders and diplomatic officers to assist them. The most important of the Joint's secret allies in Washington was, of course, Treasury Secretary Morgenthau, who wielded immense influence and helped shape, if not official, then unofficial attitudes toward the Joint's operations.

In truth, Schwartz could not have operated as successfully as he did without the tacit support of many figures in the U.S. government—just as the Brichah and the Mossad could not have achieved as much without Schwartz and the Joint.*

---

* Only in 1983 did the State Department declassify a secret, thirty-five-page report drafted by unnamed department officials, titled "Illegal Emigrants' Movements in and through Italy." Dated May 14, 1947, and called by the Department "La Vista Report," the document told of a "close watch" by State Department officials on both Joint and HIAS activities. It drew no particular conclusions from it—the report was mainly descriptive—and the "watch" had no consequences. Joint and HIAS officials were unaware of it until the declassification thirty-six years later; they assume now that it was a "free-lance" operation by the State Department, not conducted on the orders of the Truman administration. In fact, the administration ignored an official British note in October 1947 protesting against private American organizations transporting Jewish immigrants to Palestine from the Balkans with the use of U.S. military vehicles with U.S. Army insignia and operatives wearing American uniforms.

VI

The Road from the Balkans

The efforts of individuals in the field were instrumental in the great Jewish rescues. One of the most active refugee workers during the war years was Ira A. Hirschmann, a forty-one-year-old New York City department store executive, educator, pianist, musicologist and fierce protector of Jewish victims of Nazism.

Hirschmann was appointed as the War Refugee Board's field representative in Turkey. He was the perfect American version of the Renaissance man. He had moved as a top executive from Lord & Taylor to Saks Fifth Avenue and Bloomingdale's, pioneering in the 1930s the stores' modern advertising and promotion. He had also served as a member of the Board of Higher Education of New York City. Hirschmann was an outspoken advocate of academic freedom and had presided over New York's University in Exile for refugee scholars. After the Anschluss, Hirschmann rushed to Vienna, where he accepted financial responsibility for over two hundred prospective Jewish immigrants to the United States. His personal friendship with Roosevelt and his U.S. diplomatic passport helped him carry out his one-man refugee-saving performance in Vienna.

When the War Refugee Board was born, Hirschmann volunteered immediately for an overseas assignment, taking an indefinite leave of absence from his job as executive vice president of Bloomingdale's. White House connections expedited his appointment, and Hirschmann's mission took him to the board's regional office in Turkey, located at the American embassy in Ankara. Though the State Department was shocked by Hirschmann's emergence as a refugee program official, Ambassador Laurence A. Steinhardt greeted him warmly as an ally. Until then, Steinhardt, a Jew, had been the lone American in Turkey trying to help Jews trapped in Eastern Europe. Hirschmann decided that he could operate better in Istanbul than in Ankara—all the intrigue was on the Bosporus—but the two men were constantly in touch.

Hirschmann quickly made friends with the Apostolic Delegate to Turkey, Monsignor Angelo Roncalli, who was later elected Pope John XXIII; with Jewish Agency and Mossad representatives in Istanbul, Chaim Barlass, Teddy Kollek and Ehud Avriel; with the principal secret intelligence officer at the British consulate general, Colonel Harold Gibson; and with Turkish officials who dealt with visas and transit permits. Naturally, Schwartz was a frequent visitor to Istanbul.

Hirschmann became one of the conduits for Joint-supplied funds allocated for the purchase and charter of ships to transport Jews from Romanian and Bulgarian Black Sea ports to Istanbul en route to Palestine. A U.S. government official, Hirschmann served as the linchpin of the Joint's operations in Istanbul, paying for Eastern European and Turkish transit visas for Jewish refugees and negotiating with the British embassy for entry permits to Palestine. Before long, Hirschmann had put together a team of American diplomats, papal envoys, British intelligence agents, Palestinian emissaries and Joint field representatives from New York. As Ehud Avriel, the Mossad's top man in Istanbul, put it: Hirschmann "practically joined the underground."

In mid-1944, in concert with the Jewish Agency and the Mossad, Hirschmann and Schwartz arranged for the illegal transport of 8,000 Jewish refugees from Constantsa to Istanbul in a flotilla of small, leaky boats. Schwartz authorized $3 million (over $20 million in 1991 dollars) to finance this expedition, the largest sum yet spent by the Joint on a single operation. The Joint's contribution represented 90 percent of the total cost of moving the refugees to Istanbul and then on to Palestine. Without it, Schwartz wrote, "there would have been no rescue program from the Balkans." The rescue of these 8,000 refugees was the largest single operation of the war.

That British intelligence officers in Turkey chose to work intimately with the Mossad, the Joint and Hirschmann is one of those inexplicable wartime mysteries. From the outset, Colonel Gibson and Major Arthur Whittal, overseers of the British secret intelligence service in Istanbul, maintained close social and professional ties with the Mossad's Ehud Avriel and Dani Shind, as well as with Hirschmann. Whenever Schwartz happened to be in Istanbul he too joined the discreet cocktail parties hosted by the British to plot refugee movements. Perhaps British intelligence judged it useful to have friendly Jewish contacts for the future. As for Turkish transit visas, a combination of pressures from Ambassador Steinhardt, Monsignor Roncalli and the British intelligence officers took care of the problem. Occasionally Mossad and Joint operatives in Istanbul contributed to the welfare of the families of local visa officials.

Though official British policy was to keep Jewish entry into Palestine at a standstill, Gibson and Whittal went to astonishing lengths to assist many clandestine undertakings, and, when necessary, to warn Jewish operatives of impending dangers. It was probably due to their efforts that in 1943 the British Foreign Office made the unexpected decision—never publicly explained—that any Jewish refugees who were able to reach Turkey "under their own power" immediately receive permission to continue overland to Palestine. (In fact, only 184 refugees made it to Turkey between early 1942 and mid-1943.) It was simple then to move them by train to their final destination. "Under their own power," a definition the British also chose to keep imprecise, was taken by the Mossad, the Joint and Hirschmann as license to organize as best they could Jewish shipments of refugees from the Black Sea. From late 1943 on, the number of refugees rose, culminating with the rescue of those 8,000 Jews in mid-1944.

The British interned a total of 49,814 illegal immigrants on the island of Cyprus prior to Israeli independence, allowing only 750 people per month to enter Palestine during the nineteen months prior to Israeli statehood. An additional 7,500 children were transported to Palestine between August 1947 and May 1948, but during the Arab-Israeli conflict of 1948, the British—following a United Nations Security Council order—refused to release men of military age. It was not until as late as January and February of 1949 that the last 10,276 illegal immigrants left Cyprus for Israel.

———

A special patron of the Jews in Turkey was Monsignor Angelo Roncalli, who was ready to help in every emergency. His contribution to the rescue of Jews during the war is little known, and it stands in stark contrast to the attitude of Pope Pius XII, who maintained an inexcusable silence on the fate of the Jews during the Holocaust. But Monsignor Roncalli was not the only one to honor his church through humanitarianism toward Jews: Monsignor Angelo Rotta, the Papal Nuncio in Budapest, worked closely with Roncalli to save Hungarian Jews, and Hungary's József Cardinal Mindszenty acted as a channel for the transfer of secret funds from the Joint to the Brichah in Budapest. Coincidentally, Monsignor Roncalli's principal partner in these matters was Ambassador Steinhardt, who often exceeded his official instructions in aiding Jewish rescues.

Almost from the moment he set foot in Turkey, the sixty-two-year-old Apostolic Delegate—a native of Sotto il Monte, near Bergamo in Italy—opened his doors to pleaders of Jewish causes. On innumerable occasions he intervened with German, Bulgarian, Hungarian, Romanian and Slovak ambassadors in Ankara and other diplomatic corps colleagues to grant safe-conduct passes and transit and exit permits for groups of prospective Jewish refugees from Eastern Europe and the Balkans. Chaim Barlass, the Jewish Agency representative in Istanbul, and Hirschmann frequently called on him with specific requests.

Roncalli's first major involvement in the rescue of Jews came in the spring of 1943 when the Jewish Agency and the Mossad sought to launch the Europa Plan to stop deportations from Slovakia. Because Slovakia was a predominantly Roman Catholic country and its Nazi-nominated puppet President, Monsignor Josef Tiso, was a priest, Barlass appealed directly to the Apostolic Delegate to urge the Slovaks to stop the deportation of Jews to Nazi concentration camps. Roncalli, who had tried earlier to help persuade governments and shipowners to make vessels available for the transport of Jewish refugees from the Balkans to Turkey, sent messages to key figures in the Slovak church and the Tiso regime. It is impossible to say how successful he was in this endeavor, but deportations from Slovakia were halted for at least a time during that period in late 1943 and early 1944. Even German diplomats in Bratislava acknowledged that Roncalli's interventions had some impact. His efforts coincided with fund raising for the Europa Plan by the Joint's Saly Mayer, which presumably added to the pressure on Slovakia.

As the war progressed and, increasingly, word began to reach the West about the systematic destruction of Jewish communities, the fate of the Jews in the eyes of many governments, and even fellow Jews who themselves were not at risk, tended to become a political rather than a human phenomenon. Too often, the Jewish problem was treated as an abstraction, perhaps because it was so difficult to imagine or visualize what was really happening. To Roncalli, who thought in terms of individual men, women and children, the question was human and anguishing.

Early in 1943, Roncalli had tried to arrange for the departure of some, if not all, of the 70,000 Romanian Jews in the German-occupied Trans-Dniestria province in the eastern part of the country. For a variety of reasons the scheme collapsed, but the Mossad was able to extricate 1,200 refugees from Trans-Dniestria and bring them to Palestine aboard two "illegal" ships early in 1944. Roncalli quietly tried to help secure the shipping, though in the end it was the Americans who obtained the vessels.

Roncalli played major roles in attempts to rescue Bulgarian and Hungarian Jews as well. In mid-1943, the Palestinian emissaries in Istanbul learned that 25,000 Jews were about to be deported from Sofia, the Bulgarian capital, to death camps in Poland. Barlass rushed over to see Monsignor Roncalli, remembering that the Apostolic Delegate had served earlier in Sofia and was a friend of King Boris and his wife. Barlass also knew that King Boris and many influential Bulgarians had gone to extraordinary lengths in the past to protect the Jews of their country. As Barlass later wrote in an essay, "Pope John XXIII and His Attitude to the Jews," Roncalli was horrified to learn about the impending deportation. "I realized that I stood before a man of lofty spiritual stature, who was truly interested in the sufferings that had befallen our people and who was prepared heart and soul to assist in whatever way he could. Whenever during my interviews he would hear of the news from Poland, Hungary and Slovakia, he would clasp his hands in prayer, tears flowing from his eyes."

In Barlass's presence, Roncalli drafted a message to King Boris, demanding that Jewish deportations be halted. As it happened, the Bulgarian government dispersed all the Sofia Jews to the countryside, where they were safe, and it is entirely possible that this was the result of the Apostolic Delegate's intervention. Shortly thereafter, King Boris mysteriously died, and many Bulgarians thought this was the consequence of his defense of the Jews. In *While Six Million Died*, Arthur D. Morse cites the account by Luigi Bresciani, an assistant to Monsignor Roncalli, of the Apostolic Delegate's reaction to the news about the treatment of Bulgarian Jews: "I had never before seen Monsignor Roncalli so disturbed . . . Even though calm and gentle as a Saint Francis de Sales come to life, he did not spare himself from saying openly that King Boris should on no account agree to that dishonorable action . . . threatening him among other things with the punishment of God."

Roncalli's aid was enlisted again in March 1944, when

Hungary was occupied by Germany and tens of thousands of Hungarian Jews were about to be deported from Budapest to Nazi concentration camps in Poland. This was part of Eichmann's lethal operation, after most of his "money for blood" schemes had failed. Roncalli was informed of the situation by two visitors: Chief Rabbi Yitzhak Isaac Halevi Herzog of Palestine and Ira Hirschmann, both of whom appealed for his help. Between May 15 and late June 1944, 437,000 Hungarian Jews were shipped to Auschwitz; 250,000 to 300,000 of them were exterminated by midsummer. On April 26, the War Refugee Board had urged Pope Pius XII to threaten the Nazi leaders with excommunication if they did not halt the extermination, but the Pontiff did not communicate with Hungary's ruler, the regent Miklós von Horthy, until June 25, by which time most of the deported Jews were already dead. And the papal message chose not to threaten excommunication.

On August 1, 1944, Hirschmann once more asked Roncalli for help. Roncalli had failed to persuade the Pope to receive Chief Rabbi Herzog, but the Apostolic Delegate had devised a solution of his own to save as many as possible of the 200,000 Jews remaining in Hungary in the absence of a political decision by the Vatican. Roncalli told Hirschmann that if Jews in Hungary were willing to be baptized as Roman Catholics "as an emergency measure," he stood ready to make the arrangements. Hirschmann replied that he felt certain that the Jews there would be happy to be saved, and Roncalli immediately sent thousands of baptismal certificates to Papal Nuncio Rotta in Budapest, along with British immigration papers for Palestine.

As Arthur Morse describes it, "within months of Hirsch-mann's visit to the Apostolic Delegate, thousands of Jews were baptized in the air-raid shelters of Budapest and thereby snatched from death. . . . Others escaped to Palestine thanks to the immigration certificates forwarded by Monsignor Roncalli, and still others survived because of 'safe-conduct' passes issued by the Papal Nuncio in Budapest." The Nuncio issued at least 15,000 such safe-conducts, and, in Morse's words, "encouraged a record-breaking number of baptisms as suggested by his old friend, the Apostolic Delegate to Turkey." Papal Nuncio Rotta delivered a note to the Hungarian government on behalf of the neutral nations represented in Budapest, stating that they knew that "the deportation of Jews is about to be accomplished . . . [They] all know what this means, even though it be described as 'labor service' . . . [They] herewith request the Hungarian government to forbid these cruelties, which ought never to have been started."

Meanwhile, in Turkey, Roncalli was busy issuing baptismal certificates to Jews there as well. As he wrote to Hirschmann: "I am always ready to help you in your charitable work as far as in my power and as far as circumstances permit." It seemed almost foreordained that Angelo Roncalli would become the great ecumenical pontiff John XXIII.

VII

The End of Overt Operations

T he rescue of European Jewry was conducted not just from Istanbul; it was coordinated among several cities on the periphery of the Nazi "empire." In the immediate aftermath of the collapse of France in June 1940, the Joint moved its European headquarters to Lisbon. The neutral capital was an ideal conduit for secret emissaries, who also set up an outpost in Marseilles. Again, the Joint and Joe Schwartz played a pivotal role in protecting Jews in France's unoccupied zone, governed from Vichy by the pro-Nazi regime of Marshal Henri Philippe Pétain and the collaborationist premier, Pierre Laval.

By July 1940, the Joint was in business in Marseilles under the direction of Herbert Katzki, a young Schwartz aide who had come to Europe the previous year. Because the United States was still a neutral power, Americans could move freely in France; indeed, there was an American embassy in Vichy.

Masses of Jewish refugees were in unoccupied France at the time, and as Katzki recalled, "though we didn't deal with the Vichy government, the Marseilles police checked into us pretty carefully." Katzki, the only American in the Marseilles office, found that "as in any other police state . . . you had to be careful. . . . You didn't know who was sitting at the table next to you when you were in a café, so you had to be discreet in what you said. You never said anything over the telephone." Sometimes Joint operatives could trust French policemen, sometimes not.

Katzki and his nine French employees were responsible for organizing both official and clandestine departures of Jews from unoccupied France—mostly to French North Africa—and for looking after the welfare of Jewish families stranded there. It was Katzki's job to gather all possible information about Jews in occupied France and elsewhere in Europe and send it to Lisbon so Schwartz could plan rescue and relief operations. For the Joint, Katzki said, Marseilles was the "last outpost" in Europe north of the Pyrenees. There was a tremendous fear of deportations to Germany, but no Jews were deported until the end of 1941. The Joint closed down the Marseilles office after the Germans marched into unoccupied France on November 11, 1942, marking the end of its operations in France.

Schwartz happened to be in France on December 7, 1941, and as a U.S. citizen he immediately became an enemy of the Vichy regime. The only commercial aircraft flying out of France were German, according to Katzki, "so Joe took a chance and got on a Lufthansa plane and landed all right in Lisbon . . . he was a courageous guy. Not foolhardy, but venturesome enough to take risks when he had to take them."

As deportations from unoccupied France began late in

1942, thousands of Jewish refugees from all over Europe were kept in camps set up by the Vichy authorities in their zone, including German and Austrian Jews who had volunteered for the French Foreign Legion in 1939 (foreigners who technically were "enemy aliens" could not join the regular French Army) and had been discharged after the armistice. Schwartz, who visited Marseilles and other areas in the unoccupied zone on several occasions, felt that the Joint should know what was happening inside the camps, even though French authorities refused access to the Americans and their French co-workers. Schwartz's idea that European rescue and relief work should be conducted by local committees with Joint assistance wherever possible paid off handsomely. "We arranged for French Jewish chaplains to enter the camps, and they were able to keep an eye on the people for us," Katzki said. Ingenuity was also required to provide sufficient food for the camps in France because of regulations forbidding the transport of foodstuffs from one French *département* (analogous to a county) to another. But Katzki succeeded in doing just that; he also managed to get food to Jews in the labor battalions which had been established by the Vichy regime.

Another American Jewish organization was also active in occupied France in the early 1940s and that was the Hebrew Sheltering and Immigrant Aid Society. Known as HIAS, it was the oldest Jewish American institution dealing with refugees, originally established in 1890. Vichy recognized HIAS as a legal refugee agency and allowed it to operate in Marseilles after Katzki and the Joint pulled out. The Joint had not yet become a full-fledged immigration organization; it still concentrated on Jewish relief and welfare, although

Schwartz was already pushing it in the direction of immigration. At that point, HIAS had a formal agreement with Vichy, and the Joint advanced funds to HIAS to pay for legal travel by Jewish refugees. HIAS had access to the French concentration camps and it was able to organize shipments of refugees to French Morocco en route to the Western Hemisphere—mainly Latin American countries willing to receive Jewish groups.

The greatest human asset to HIAS was a portly French Jew with extensive political connections in France and North Africa: Raphael Spanien. Spanien had worked for HIAS in Paris since the late 1930s. He held a law degree, served in the French Army and was wounded during the Nazi blitzkrieg in the spring of 1940. He was then evacuated through Dunkirk and made his way to Lisbon and Marseilles, where he resumed working for HIAS. Spanien was head of the HIAS office in Casablanca in mid-1941 when about a thousand Jewish refugees from France, bound for Martinique, were stranded in the Moroccan port city and placed in a concentration camp by the local authorities. It took Spanien little more than a few telephone calls to have the refugees released and sent on their way.

Spanien was less successful in saving Jews the following year, but not for lack of trying or lack of access. During the summer of 1942, the Nazis ordered the Vichy regime to deport Jewish refugees from unoccupied France to labor camps in Poland. Naturally, the Pétain government complied. Spanien, who by then was back in Marseilles, went to Vichy, where he secured a private interview with Premier Laval. His friend Gilbert de Chambrun was the brother of Laval's son-in-law, Count René de Chambrun. Laval told Spanien that he had to agree to the deportation of foreign Jews to protect the French Jews; nothing could be done to change the situation. In September, Spanien flew to Lisbon and informed the HIAS man there, James Bernstein, that between 10,000 and 20,000 foreign Jews who had lived in France since 1933 had already been deported. Bernstein cabled New York headquarters and urged some form of action by the United States to save the Jews. "We doubt if we can continue to save them," he said.

After Germany invaded unoccupied France early in 1943, HIAS was forced to close down its Marseilles office. In time, most of its French employees were deported to the East. Spanien moved to Lisbon, where he remained until he could return to Paris in 1945. This marked the end of overt American activities to try to protect and save Jews in German-occupied Europe. For the next two years or so, these European activities would be carried out underground.

VIII

Going Underground

From 1943 to 1945 the clandestine operations of the Palestinian Jews and the Americans concentrated on efforts to prevent or halt the massive slaughter of Jewish populations in Nazi-occupied Europe and to assure relief for those fortunate Jews who had survived. These were the goals of the Mossad's Avigur and his brothers-in-law, Moshe Sharett and Eliyahu Golomb, and they were orchestrated from Tel Aviv. But operations were still conducted primarily out of Istanbul with the close cooperation of the Joint and the War Refugee Board.

Schwartz used Lisbon as the Joint's European headquarters during these two years, but he was continuously in and out of Istanbul. It was there in July 1944 that Schwartz signed the agreement with the Jewish Agency and the Mossad which financed virtually all of the illegal Jewish immigration from the Balkans to Turkey and thence to Palestine. The agreement did not specify how much money would be provided by the Joint, nor did it say how long money would be available. It was simply understood that there would be sufficient funds for what was needed. All Joint-Mossad agreements were drafted with deliberate ambiguity, and their texts have mysteriously vanished. What counted was the good faith of the principals—and the authority vested de facto in Schwartz.

The negotiations with the Nazis for "purchases" of Jews —the Eichmann proposals forwarded to the Palestinians in Istanbul, and Saly Mayer's successful "buyout" through Switzerland—were part of that same effort, as were the Joint's attempts to dispatch food and clothing to surviving Jews in Europe and the Soviet Union. Through clandestine financial arrangements, provisions procured in Stockholm were to be sent in trucks under neutral flags to Warsaw and Prague, as well as to Soviet Asia.

In terms of the actual numbers of refugees, illegal immigration to Palestine was still limited due to the extreme difficulty of extricating Jews from occupied Europe and because of the stubborn British blockade. But Avigur, his colleagues in Palestine and Schwartz on the American side attached immense political and symbolic value to their effort. It was not merely a matter of saving lives; it was an assurance to Jewish communities under the occupation that they were not forgotten. Avigur insisted on sending Mossad emissaries to Europe from the very outset—as much to save from death those who could be rescued as to organize Jews there for the future.

Indeed, probably more than most of his colleagues in Palestine, Avigur thought in terms of marshaling, after an Allied victory in Europe, a body of Jewry that would lead to the establishment of a Jewish state. For Avigur, the Mossad's efforts to mount illegal immigration in the mid-1940s were as essential to the cause of Jewish nation building as was the search for weapons for the Haganah. His friend Berl Katznelson, a top leader of the Mapai (Labor) Party, summed up this view: "Save Jews . . . all the rest, later. If there are no Jews left, Palestine and the Zionist enterprise will also be annihilated." Schwartz saw it the same way, and his vision of an independent Jewish state lay behind his long-term approach to the financing of illegal immigration, even though his associates in New York were still far from embracing the idea.

As the end of the war approached in 1944, Avigur began preparing new emissaries for European missions. The Allies had invaded Italy and the south of the country was already liberated. This opened up new routes both for Mossad operatives into Europe and for organizing illegal immigration transports to Palestine. Units of the Jewish Brigade of the British Eighth Army who were fighting in Italy constituted a superb network to back up the Mossad's penetration of the Continent. The Nazis, meanwhile, were withdrawing west from the Soviet Union, and soon Romania and Hungary would be liberated. Over half a million Polish Jews had been deported to the Soviet Union in 1940, and survivors would be returning. In Yugoslavia, Tito's partisans were virtually in control of the nation. The invasion of Western Europe was imminent.

Avigur concluded that before long hundreds of thousands of Jewish refugees—the survivors—would be let loose across Europe. Urgent measures had to be readied to look after them, organize them and bring as many as possible to Palestine. Through his intelligence channels in Eastern Europe, Avigur was also aware that the Brichah partisans' activities were increasing and that they needed support and leadership as well. The Brichah would play a crucial role in the postwar wave of illegal immigration. Avigur himself was determined to be the guide for this movement, which would be unprecedented in Jewish history.

Operationally, one of the notions advocated by Avigur was to parachute Mossad emissaries into the Balkans so they could establish links with surviving Jewish communities and start preparing them for emigration to the Holy Land. But the Palestinian Jews were at the mercy of the British, who had to provide the aircraft for the drops, and Avigur soon discovered how reluctant they were to do so. Although 240 Palestinian Jews had volunteered in 1943 to be dropped over the Balkans, the British sent only three of them that year, presumably aware that the Mossad envoys would not be particularly concerned with their interests. In 1944, however, 32 Palestinian parachutists were dropped over Europe in a collaborative British-Mossad operation. Twelve were captured by the Nazis, including twenty-three-year-old Hungarian-born Hannah Senesh, a poet, who was tortured and executed, and the Italian-born philosopher Enzo Sereni, who was executed in Dachau.

Among the parachutists who eluded the Germans was Romanian-born Yesheyahu Trachtenberg, known to his friends and associates as Shaike Dan. Shaike Dan subsequently became one of the most celebrated—yet secretive— Mossad operatives, penetrating Romania, Bulgaria, Yugoslavia and Hungary after his jump over Romanian territory in June 1944. He was a friend of Communist rulers and Communist secret police chiefs (many of whom were of Jewish origin), and in the postwar years the tall, rail-thin Shaike Dan was instrumental in arranging the emigration of over 400,000 Romanian Jews to Israel in exchange for secret payments of nearly $100 million (much of it provided by American Jewish organizations) to the Ceaușescu regime. Shaike Dan claims he brought out from Bulgaria 40,000 Jews in little over one year; the payment was $1 million, or $25 per head, and the deal was negotiated with the chief of the secret police he had befriended.

He had immigrated to Palestine in 1936 and embarked on his intelligence career in 1942 while serving as a volunteer in an antiaircraft unit of the British Army in Tripoli, Lebanon. "Very confidentially" he had heard of a secret center for illegal immigration in Tel Aviv, run by a man named Avigur. "They were looking for people to go to the Balkan countries to save Jews, to try to help them, to bring them to Palestine," Shaike Dan recalled. Upon meeting Avigur he told him, "If it is true, I am prepared to go."

He was subsequently trained in Cairo by the British Army's Intelligence Service Liaison Department, which operated jointly with the U.S. Office of Strategic Services (OSS). He also attended the joint British–U.S. operatives' paratrooper school in Haifa. But the British agreed to drop him only after a recommendation from Brigadier Wingate, the friend of Jewish guerrillas, who argued that Shaike Dan was a perfect candidate for his mission since he spoke Romanian as well as Yiddish, Hebrew and English. Wingate, in contrast to most of his senior British colleagues, was in favor of Avigur's Mossad operations.

In the end, Shaike Dan made a "blind drop," jumping over a country where neither the British nor the Mossad had any connections. It was just after midnight, and there was only a quarter-moon, when he was dropped by a Halifax bomber from a base in Brindisi, Italy, as part of a bombing mission. According to Shaike Dan, the Germans had over

900 Royal Air Force officers and crew members in Romanian prisons; they had been shot down during massive air raids on the Ploesti petroleum facilities. He had promised the British that he would try to free some of these prisoners and lead them to Yugoslavia. This was the condition of his being parachuted into Romania.

Shaike Dan landed near the city of Arad, close to the Hungarian border. His only resource was a pocketful of gold Napoleon coins. It took him two weeks to reach Bucharest; two months later Soviet troops entered the city. Having established contact with a small local underground Jewish organization, Shaike Dan helped arrange the sailing of the *Toros* in November 1944 from the Romanian port of Constantsa to Istanbul. Aboard were 900 Jewish passengers, including 445 children. It was his first success in dispatching Romanian Jews to Palestine.

Shortly thereafter, Shaike Dan left Romania for Cairo. He stopped off in the Italian port of Bari, where he was introduced to Schwartz, who happened to be visiting the Joint office there. This was the beginning of a friendship— and Shaike Dan's special personal relationship with the Joint—that lasted thirty years, adding one more dimension to the ties that united the Palestinians and the Americans. Then, for Shaike Dan, it was back to Romania on Avigur's instructions, launching four decades of secret commuting between Tel Aviv and Bucharest and a lifelong friendship with Avigur as well.

At the time of Israeli independence in May 1948, Shaike Dan's connections in the Balkans played a vital role in the survival of the infant state. As part of Avigur's intelligence network, he was deeply involved in his program of acquiring weapons for the Haganah. It was his mission to persuade the Tito regime in Yugoslavia to allow Israeli pilots, flying combat aircraft purchased in Czechoslovakia and transport planes loaded with weapons, to refuel on Yugoslav territory on their way home. Working through his friends in the security service, Shaike Dan received authorization for the planes to refuel in Titograd in Montenegro; weapons and munitions would be shipped down the Danube from Slovakia to Belgrade and then sent on to Istanbul. "Without Yugoslavia," he said, "I don't know what the situation would be in Israel today . . . What Yugoslavia did for us is unbelievable . . . And always without receiving anything in return."

All in all, Avigur's planning for the final phase of the conflict and the postwar era was virtually impeccable. So were his choice of the Mossad's principal operatives in the field and his finely tuned system of giving them enough autonomy for on-the-spot decision making while closely supervising the overall effort from his Tel Aviv and Paris offices.

Still, the Mossad and the Brichah could not function in a vacuum, and it took an astonishing degree of both open and secret support for the Palestinian cause involving a wide variety of partners—including some very unexpected ones —to make it all work. In Turkey and the Balkans, the Palestinians enjoyed the full backing of the network of friends improbably composed of foreign diplomats, the Joint's organizers, pontifical envoys, British intelligence agents and Communist police chiefs. In Western Europe, the Joint and its Mossad and Brichah associates had the run of the territory because powerful figures in the U.S. government quietly favored their operations. Notwithstanding Britain's unyielding official opposition to illegal immigration to

Palestine, the British Army's Jewish Brigade (all of whose men secretly belonged to the Haganah) was incredibly free to work hand in hand with the Brichah in organizing the clandestine movements of Jewish refugees. This was possible because Jewish as well as non-Jewish Brigade officers privately sympathized with the Aliyah, concealing the undercover cooperation with the Palestinians from British military intelligence. Many other British officers in Europe were also generally aware of what was happening, and, acting as individuals, they became part of a conspiracy of silence protecting the illegal immigration.

In the end, individual actions by scores of people of many nationalities went far to neutralize the British government's opposition to Palestinian immigration and statehood, opening the way to ultimate Israeli independence. Human empathy—perhaps compounded by a residing sense of guilt over the Holocaust—became a more powerful force in day-to-day decisions affecting the plight of the Jews than official policies.

IX

Assignment: Italy

The war in Europe ended on May 8, 1945, with the Nazi capitulation. But victory there did not mean the end of Jewish suffering—even though lives were no longer in direct jeopardy—and it did nothing to open Palestine to the Jews. Now tens of thousands of Jewish refugees were filling the DP camps—a harrowing prospect after the years of concentration camps—with no place to go. In most cases, their homes and businesses and jobs in Eastern Europe had been destroyed and their loved ones were dead or missing. Fearing a new wave of anti-Semitism, they were reluctant to return to their native countries, which added another dimension to their resolve to stay in the DP camps. Palestine at the time was not a viable alternative; Britain had no intention of opening it up to the Jews.

Under the circumstances, the only solution was to make the DP camps so overcrowded as to render them humanely, politically and financially intolerable to the Allies in Germany and Austria, and to set up illegal immigration to Palestine. The strategy shared by Shaul Avigur and Joe Schwartz was to bring all these pressures to bear to the point where Britain would finally relent on legal emigration to the Holy Land. A new phase was opening for both the Mossad and the Joint, and they wasted no time adjusting themselves to the new conditions.

Schwartz's first recruit for the postwar period in Europe was Gaynor Jacobson, a thirty-two-year-old Jewish social worker and community leader from upstate New York. An affable and boundlessly enthusiastic man with blue eyes and wavy reddish-brown hair, Jacobson caught Schwartz's eye when he applied for an overseas job with the Joint. Jacobson would prove to be one of the most important and resourceful operatives in Europe, and he played a vital role in secret Jewish rescue operations in North Africa and the Middle East.

Jacobson had a most unusual history before he came to the Joint. He was born in Buffalo, New York, on May 17, 1912, the first of seven children of Morris and Rose Jacobson, who had emigrated from Latvia to the United States five years earlier. The full name on his birth certificate is Israel Gaynor Jacobson, Gaynor being the anglicized version of Gan-Or, meaning "Garden of Life" in Hebrew. But for political reasons he later reversed the order of his first and middle name. His father belonged to a Jewish socialist organization in Riga, where he managed a leather-goods store, but he was arrested by Czarist police for his political activities and sentenced to a life of forced labor in Siberia. He escaped after a few years with the help of funds provided by his brother and sister, who had already gone to live in the United States. Bribes for freedom and payoffs thus formed an early part of the Jacobson family history.

As soon as Morris was able to reach Hamburg from Siberia, the Jacobsons departed for the United States, making their way to North Tonawanda, New York, where Morris's brother, Israel, owned a successful cigar-making factory. After Israel's sudden death, Morris found a job in the Emblem bicycle factory in Angola, New York, a village of around 1,200 inhabitants twenty-one miles southwest of Buffalo, near Lake Erie. The "lone Jewish family" in Angola, the Jacobsons soon discovered racism—from personal attacks to Ku Klux Klan parades—in the ugliest possible forms. Gaynor is convinced that his Zionism was born as a result of it. "I will never forget," he remembered, "that youngsters at the age of three and a half and a little older, who attended the Catholic church, came down one Sunday afternoon throwing stones at me and calling me a Christ killer. I went in crying to my mother, asking what this was all about—I was three and a half too, just before kindergarten—and she sent me back out to fight with these youngsters, four or five youngsters. I go out and the thing subsided."

Thanks to his parents, Gaynor also acquired a sense of Jewishness. Though he attended the Angola public school, his parents "at a great expense to them" sent him every Sunday by trolley to Buffalo to a Jewish community religious school to receive religious education. Gaynor eventually graduated from the Angola high school in 1928 "with the highest marks," working summers on farms, in canning factories and for a hardware company. He had decided that he wanted to become a lawyer, and after finishing high school he traveled by bus to Brooklyn, New York, where his mother's cousins offered him a room in their Bay Ridge apartment while he tried to enroll at a college.

Gaynor managed to talk his way into an appointment with

Nicholas Murray Butler, the famous and feared president of Columbia University. Butler didn't make a habit of receiving impoverished sixteen-year-old Jewish students from upstate, but—inexplicably—he made an exception for Gaynor. Butler agreed to let Gaynor take evening courses at Columbia College toward a degree, since Gaynor was working (at a Jewish-owned paper company) during the day. Butler "was one of the few people who took me in consideration as a person," Gaynor recalled.

But after three years in New York, Gaynor was laid off by the paper company because of the Depression and had to quit Columbia. His parents were no longer able to earn enough to pay for the mortgage on the family house, and in 1932 the bank foreclosed. That same summer, after returning to Angola, Gaynor was invited to address the staff at a Jewish fresh-air camp, delivering a thundering talk entitled "The Coming Imperialist War." More to the point, Gaynor met there his future wife, a young camp volunteer counselor named Florence Stulberg.

Gaynor finally earned his bachelor's certificate and master's degree in social work from the University of Buffalo. In 1937 he was hired by the Jewish Welfare Society of Buffalo, and in 1938 he was hired as a family case worker by the Jewish Family Agency in Rochester, New York. He then became executive secretary of the Jewish Community Council of Rochester, and finally executive director of the Jewish Family and Children's Agency there. The person who accepted Jacobson's application at the agency was its executive secretary, Laura L. Margolis, whose own life would soon be linked to international refugee activities as well.

Jacobson spent his Buffalo and Rochester years deeply involved in every conceivable form of social and political activity, from urging young Americans to join the Lincoln

Brigade and fight on the Republican side in the Spanish Civil War to supporting China in its defense against Japanese aggression. He delivered regular weekly radio talks to counter racist and pro-Nazi propaganda broadcasts by the then famous Father Charles E. Coughlin, the Catholic radio priest of Detroit, and served as first vice president of the Rochester Branch of the National Association for the Advancement of Colored People at a time when relatively few American Jews worked with black organizations. "The rights of blacks," he said, "were somehow tied in my mind with what was happening with Jews in Europe."

In Rochester, Gaynor was also exposed to the problems of Jewish refugees, who were beginning to reach the United States from Europe. He had expanded his agency's Refugee Service, and in his annual report for 1942 on behalf of the Jewish Welfare Council, he noted that the city already had 700 refugees living there. By 1944, Jacobson's reputation in Jewish circles had spread to the point where the Joint contacted him that summer to see whether he would consider shifting to overseas refugee work. By then, Laura Margolis, his former Buffalo boss, had already signed up with the Joint. She first looked after Jewish European refugees stranded in Cuba (working with refugees from the *St. Louis* while the ship waited in Havana harbor), then ran the Joint's refugee protection program in Japanese-occupied Shanghai.

Schwartz flew from Lisbon to New York to recruit executives for the postwar phase—for which he wanted to be prepared—and Jacobson was his first conquest. There was a touch of the missionary and visionary about Jacobson when he signed up late in 1944 for the job of overseeing Jewish survivors of the Holocaust. Schwartz hired him virtually on the spot when they had their first meeting at the Joint's Madison Avenue offices in New York. Jacobson had only one reservation about accepting Schwartz's offer of a post in Europe: "In our first interview I explained that I was a philosophical Zionist and I told Dr. Schwartz that I could only work for the JDC if it meant that I could help to save Jews and that I could help Jews to go on to Palestine . . . I wanted him to realize that I had for some years believed that the only major solution to the Jewish problem of Europe, and wherever Jews were in danger, was to have a State of Israel, which would give unlimited acceptance to Jews in trouble . . . Joe put his arm around me and told me not to worry, and he shook hands with me on that deal. Zionism was not accepted within the JDC top leadership at the time —except, as I found out, by Dr. Schwartz. . . . Even within the ranks of the professionals who worked overseas you had those who were unfavorable toward a State of Israel, even though they were working with refugees in these countries."

The two men hit it off too in other ways, and Jacobson rapidly became a Schwartz favorite. Both were extroverted, both enjoyed people and liked to have a good time when they weren't working day and night. Schwartz was an intellectual, and Jacobson—a remarkably gifted sculptor—had an artistic penchant. Though their initial agreement was that Jacobson would take a year's leave of absence to help Schwartz with the European emergencies, he never again left international refugee work.

In November 1944, Schwartz rushed Jacobson to Italy, where his task was to set in motion the Joint's programs for the care of Jewish refugees emerging from concentration camps on the peninsula, as well as those moving down from Eastern Europe and the Balkans. Schwartz made it clear to Jacobson that immigration to Palestine, legal or otherwise, would be a very significant part of the postwar situation.

Meanwhile, in Tel Aviv, Avigur concentrated even more intensely on new emigration prospects from Europe. Several times a day, men handpicked from kibbutzim, Jewish Brigade units and urban plants and offices around Palestine were summoned to the Mossad's three-room office. They were told neither whom they would meet nor why they were being called; they were simply given the address of that obscure office on Allenby Street. Avigur wasn't taking any chances with British counterintelligence. His deputy, Ehud Avriel, and his assistant Moshe Carmil coordinated the traffic.

But compared with Schwartz, Avigur had a surprisingly casual approach toward his recruits. Years later, the Jerusalem *Post* described the recruitment of Yohanan Cohen, a twenty-seven-year-old kibbutznik who was called before Avigur in the summer of 1945:

> Cohen, who had arrived in Palestine from Poland eight years earlier, was asked if he was willing to return to his native country to help organize the Jewish survivors for the escape to Mediterranean ports. Which ports? Avigur didn't know, but that would take care of itself once the organization began functioning. How would he find and organize the Jews? That would be up to him. What were conditions like in Poland? Avigur didn't know. Cohen would be given a briefing when he got to Europe by members of the fledgling groups already there. But they didn't know much either. Cohen bought a grey suit in the OBG department store in Tel Aviv and got himself a back-pack. Three weeks later, he happened to be in Tel Aviv and stopped by the Histadrut building. "You're leaving tonight," he was told.

Avigur's recruits have told numerous such stories, but apparently there was method to this madness. Quite simply, he felt that emissaries who had to be carefully briefed beforehand would probably make useless Mossad operatives. It was sink or swim. In the end, most of the emissaries he picked by sheer intuition were unusually successful, and quite a few of them—like Ehud Avriel and Asher Ben-Natan—later became leading Israeli diplomats.

Advance plans charted separately by Schwartz and Avigur were nonetheless moving in the same direction. Soon their envoys would converge on Italian soil and open a new chapter in Jewish history.

Jacobson left for Naples sailing out of Newark, New Jersey, on a munitions-carrying Liberty ship that was part of a convoy escorted by the U.S. Navy. German submarines still infested the seas, but the ship arrived safely in Naples in early December. Schwartz, who had just reopened the Joint office in Paris, was delighted. Rome had recently been liberated by the Allies, and there were already at least 5,000 Eastern European Jews in DP camps throughout Italy. More turned up every day, and Schwartz feared an unmanageable situation.

The Joint had also assumed responsibility for rebuilding Jewish Italian communities, an ambitious task that involved more than 30,000 survivors. Jacobson was named deputy to Reuben Resnik, the Joint's director for Italy, who had come from Istanbul a few months earlier. At the time they were the only two Americans engaged in the Italian operation. But Resnik was a by-the-book director, and Schwartz was convinced that Jacobson would be a good deal more effective once he learned the rudiments of refugee work.

His mandate from Schwartz was "to work with Jewish communities to help them reestablish their homes for the aged, their children's homes, [and] . . . to get their synagogues going." Jews liberated from concentration camps and those who had escaped from behind German lines were to be placed in DP camps in Italy and treated as necessary. Of primary importance was the development of a program that would help them rebuild their lives and much of this would entail emigration. Happy to carry out these orders, Jacobson quickly began to work quietly behind Resnik's back—with Palestinian soldiers of the Jewish Brigade and with the Mossad.

Jacobson's most bizarre problem was Dr. Israel Zolli, the Grand Rabbi of Rome, who had survived the war under Vatican protection. Zolli pressured the Joint for funds to run his restored theological seminary, which trained religious teachers and rabbis. Two years later, he stunned the world by converting to Catholicism. Jacobson, to whom the Grand Rabbi routinely complained about insufficient funds from the Joint, recalled: "I was told by Catholic authorities that during the year prior to his official conversion, which took at least a year, he was fighting for a stronger [Jewish] seminary, for more and more official Judaism in Italy—and all the while he was going through conversion to become a Catholic."

Jacobson enjoyed considerable power in Allied-occupied Italy. As an official of the Joint, he belonged to the Inter-Governmental Refugee Committee, which, in turn, was part of the Allied Military Government. The committee was set up by the United States and Britain to try to coordinate refugee affairs, but it turned out to be rather ineffective. Like Schwartz, he was given the assimilated rank of colonel in the U.S. Army. That earned him the right to wear a military uniform, to have a jeep and military driver at his disposal, a secretary and access to Allied officers' hotels throughout Italy. In Rome, Jacobson's office was at the Military Government Headquarters and he stayed at the Flora Hotel, where he befriended British officers also billeted there. He had vital PX privileges, so he could buy American cigarettes, American canned foods and alcoholic beverages. Jacobson usually gave the food to Jewish Italian families.

Dividing his time between Rome and Naples, Jacobson worked closely with Jewish Brigade members of the British Army then stationed in Italy. In the field, they were the Joint's natural allies. As noted earlier, all of the Jewish Brigade soldiers secretly belonged to the Haganah; Avigur and other Palestinian leaders had urged them to enlist to gain modern combat experience. The British, of course, were aware of this, but politically they could not keep denying the Palestinian Jews the right to participate in the war against Hitler. What the British did not realize in time was that the Jewish Brigade in Italy was quietly controlled by Avigur and the Mossad, a fact Jacobson grasped immediately when he started dealing with its soldiers. That the British allowed members of the Jewish Brigade under their command to work hand in hand with the Mossad and the Brichah was one of the astounding incongruities of war. Jacobson did not rule out the possibility that British military intelligence simply never realized the extent of it. There is no known instance of British interference with the Brigade's Zionist conspiracies.

"Having the Jewish Brigade in Italy," said Jacobson, "meant that we literally had their resources—help with medical care, camp organization and children's homes, and I had confidence in the Jewish Brigade sincerely wanting to help our DPs." Brigade soldiers "were dedicated men who were cooperating to help get as many Jews out from behind enemy lines." Officially, the Brigade could not engage in all these pursuits, but "they found ways of having individuals being available to help."

The Brigade's commander was a British Army officer, a Jewish major named Aaron who always carried a swagger stick and managed to look the other way most of the time. But the key figure was a Palestinian sergeant, Mordecai Surkiss, a secret Avigur emissary who soon became the European commander of the Brichah. Jacobson's dealings with Surkiss—which would go on for years—began there in Italy and enhanced the cooperation between the Joint and the Palestinians.

Resnik, however, posed a problem. He was suspicious of the Brigade's motives and methods, and although the Joint "couldn't have met the needs of thousands of Italian Jews and displaced Jews" without the Palestinian soldiers, as Jacobson put it, he tried to challenge if not overrule their tactics. Resnik had little sympathy for a Jewish Palestine.

Jacobson's legal immigration activities in Italy began late in 1944 when the Joint suddenly obtained 900 British "certificates"—entry permits—for Palestine to be used for Jewish refugees filling up DP camps in Italy. This British decision was an early vindication of the theory held by both Schwartz and Avigur that rising DP populations in camps in Italy (and later in Austria and Germany) would create unbearable local pressures for national and Allied authorities. Immigration to Palestine was the only viable solution. Only non-Italian Jews were selected to fill this particular immigration quota. They would sail from the southern Italian port of Bari for Haifa.

Schwartz appointed Jacobson to oversee the operation, which included the selection of the emigrants. Jacobson set up his headquarters in Bari, and while he was thrilled with this new responsibility, the actual selection was a heartbreaking process. Many refugees had to be turned down. Jacobson asked the Jewish Brigade and the Mossad emissaries to help him assemble the lucky 900 emigrants, and he found an invaluable adviser in Asher Dominitz of the Jewish Agency, who joined him in Bari. Groups of American and British Quakers also assisted him.

In January 1945, Jacobson and his advisers began looking for candidates for the Mediterranean crossing in DP camps around Bari and Lecce and as far north as Florence. In Bari, the refugees were checked medically, issued travel documents and prepared for embarkation. Priorities, to meet Palestinian requirements, were for able-bodied young people and children; there were no facilities for the old and infirm. But there were virtually no intact families among these DPs. Most of them were Jews from Poland, Hungary and Yugoslavia who had been transported to Italy as part of the German Army labor battalions and were liberated there. There were survivors who had married each other in camps, orphans and children who had come to Italy from all over Europe. As Jacobson explained, children were safe in Italian concentration camps because "Italians didn't deport children to Poland like the other countries, and they didn't kill Jews in their camps." Many of these children were among the 900 who were to sail from Bari.

The ship was provided by the Allied Military Government, but the Joint footed much of the bill. Schwartz himself had come down to inspect the preparations, and on March 8, from Bari, he cabled the Joint's secretary, Moses Leavitt, in New York: "PALESTINE TRANSPORT 900 SCHEDULED DEPART MARCH 25 WILL COST 14 TO 15 POUNDS PER PERSON WHICH WE HAVE UNDERWRITTEN ORDER EXPEDITE MOVEMENT. YOU MAY CHARGE THIS AGAINST EMIGRATION APPROPRIATION."

The total cost was approximately $60,000. It was the first voyage funded by the Joint since the *Salah a-Din* brought 547 Jewish refugees from Constantsa, Romania, to Istanbul at a cost of about $1 million in August 1944. Earlier that year Schwartz had approved $3 million for sea rescue transportation from the Balkans to Istanbul; Jewish refugees could then legally proceed overland to Palestine. But now emigration funds were being switched for voyages from Greece and Italy as German forces fell back and escape patterns changed accordingly.

The Bari ship was the first one to sail legally from Italy, and it was followed by many legal and illegal crossings. Her departure fueled discussions in the Western press as to whether there had been a Holocaust. Jacobson recalled a conversation he had had one evening in Bari with American and British Quakers. "Yes, these people [the Jews] were miserable," they admitted, "but didn't I know that this was only a repetition of the false Belgian propaganda of World War I? No people could be guilty of the things that these people said; they were victims of propaganda themselves." That was in February 1945, Jacobson explained, and "good, well-meaning, hardworking Quakers had helped bring these people out of the camps, helped assemble them, and yet I was unable to convince them that this [the Holocaust] was so."

X

Sailing from Piraeus

B ari marked the end of Jacob-
son's assignment in Italy. He complained to Schwartz that
he could not go on working with Resnik because of disagreements over relations with the Jewish Brigade. As it happened,
the Joint needed a director in Athens to run the growing
Greek program, and Schwartz, who was delighted with
Jacobson's performance in Italy, promoted him immediately
to the new position.

Arriving in Athens on April 15, 1945, directly from Italy,
Jacobson found Greece still in the throes of war. The Nazis
were entrenched on the island of Crete, and in several areas
of the mainland a savage civil war had arisen between British-
supported right-wing political forces and Communist guerrillas. Moreover, the economic situation in Greece was dire,
with runaway inflation, hunger and homelessness.

Although there were fewer than 10,000 Jews in Greece in

1945 (out of a prewar Jewish population of 70,000), rebuilding the national Jewish community was no easy task. Working
closely with Greek Jewish community leaders, Jacobson
quickly realized that Mossad emissaries also operating in
Athens were eager to enlist the Joint's discreet assistance,
and were just as keen to organize illegal departures for
Palestine from the coast of Greece. In fact, the Mossad had
just transferred Ehud Avriel (still using his original name of
Ehud Ueberall) from Istanbul to Athens. The Jewish Agency
sent its own delegate, Jacob Chernowitz (later a leading
Israeli politician known under his Hebrew name of Jacob
Tsur), from Palestine. Medical teams from the Magen David
Adom, the Palestinian equivalent of the Red Cross, had also
been dispatched to Greece. The Mossad's top priorities were
to send orphaned Jewish children, brought secretly at night
to embarkation points in Magen David trucks, to Palestine
and to organize illegal voyages for the Jewish refugees who,
after the Nazi armies were dislodged, arrived from Hungary,
Romania and Bulgaria in rapidly growing numbers.

Jacobson willingly participated in the illegal immigration
projects. He acted as intermediary in arranging for ships
from UNRRA—the United Nations Relief and Rehabilitation
Administration—and in providing food and supplies for the
small caïques that perilously sailed the Aegean and the
Mediterranean en route to Palestine. His deputy, an American social worker named Belle Mazur, initially opposed
supplying the Mossad boats. She considered it illegal for the
Joint to engage in such undertakings, but Jacobson persuaded her otherwise. In the eight months he worked in
Greece, Jacobson estimated, roughly 3,000 illegal emigrants
sailed from the port of Piraeus. He made payments for the
vessels in drachmas borrowed from the Bank of Greece
against dollar deposits made by the Joint. Orphans always

had priority in the departures, and Jacobson recalled that some 225 children, with a group of adults looking after them, sailed aboard one of the illegal ships.

While in Greece, Jacobson developed "an unusual form of typhus" and his temperature soared to 106 degrees. He was treated by a young American Jewish physician attached to the UNRRA mission who had only sulfa drugs at his disposal. The drugs had no effect, and the doctor drove him to the British military hospital in Athens, where he was told he had only two days to live. Miraculously he recovered.

Released from the hospital, Jacobson accepted an invitation from the Joint's Judah Magnes to come and rest in Palestine. Because of his military status with the U.S. Army, Jacobson was able to fly on an RAF plane, and he stopped off in Cairo, where he visited some Egyptian friends. He proceeded to Tel Aviv, where he met his hosts, Golda Meyerson (later known as Golda Meir), the future Prime Minister, and Pinchas Lubianiker (also known as Pinchas Lavon), the future Defense Minister. They were key people in the Palestinian shadow government, and the attention they paid Jacobson was in recognition of his Joint activities in Italy and Greece.

On the night of October 9, 1945, Palmach commandos attacked the British Army's Athlit detention camp south of Haifa. There, 210 illegal Jewish immigrants whose ship had been captured by the Royal Navy were kept behind barbed wire. The raid was in response to the British government's refusal to grant the Jewish Agency's request, made immediately after V-E Day in May, for 100,000 immigration certificates for survivors of the Holocaust. The DP camps in Europe were filling up quickly, but the Cabinet in London took the view that the request was "ill timed" (though it was supported personally by President Truman) and that the best that could be done was to issue 2,000 certificates while seeking an agreement with Palestinian Arabs for monthly Jewish quotas of 1,500. But to the Palestinian Jews, this was a declaration of war, and it opened a new chapter—in which the Joint would be deeply engaged—in the struggle for the Jewish homeland.

Naturally, Avigur was among the top commanders in this offensive, and he helped plan the October assault on Athlit. Returning from his new command post in Paris for the raid, Avigur spent the night of the attack at the Haganah's Northern District Command operational center, hidden at the headquarters of the Haifa fire brigade along with the commander of intelligence of the Haganah, David Shaltiel, who directed the raid. It was a highly sophisticated operation, and most of the prisoners were freed.

The camp faced Mount Carmel, and the Haganah command selected Kibbutz Beit Oren atop the mountain as the staging area for the attack by a reinforced Palmach battalion. To prepare the prisoners for the liberation attempt, the commander of one of the assault units and five companions were sent beforehand to the camp, posing as Hebrew teachers who represented the Jewish Agency. The plan was for the inmates to climb up to the kibbutz before dispersing. In his after-action report, Nahum Sarig, the Haganah chief of the Athlit operation, described how it unfolded:

> The six Hebrew teachers—in fact, all instructors of judo—got into camp safely and went to work. At 2300 hours, the main force moved into position . . . On the signal of a blue flare, the attack began. Within seconds, the entire force was in position inside the camp, having overpowered the lone sentry in the guardhouse, who

was bound and gagged. With the help of our advance party, the prisoners had organized themselves in groups of ten, each under the command of one of their own men. Seven prisoners suspected by their fellow inmates of having been Nazi collaborators in Europe were tied and gagged and left behind in the camp infirmary. The column was on its way out of the camp minutes after we had penetrated it . . . Our trouble started when we began the ascent of the hills facing the camp. The immigrants were less fit than the highly trained Palmach soldiers and were unprepared for the difficult climb. To our amazement, many of them had taken some of their baggage. One of the groups wandered off in the wrong direction . . . We entered Beit Oren after having taken the necessary military precautions. One of the holding forces encountered a police vehicle . . . The police opened fire; it was returned. The police car overturned, a British officer was killed, and an Arab policeman was injured . . . When we were finally ready to move, I saw the headlights of an endless convoy of police vehicles approaching us from Haifa. Believing that all was lost and that the escape had already been discovered and reported . . . I directed [our] lead driver to move in the direction from which we had just come: to Athlit detention camp . . . At a curve that could not be observed from the more northerly road on which the policemen were traveling, the escapees jumped off the trucks, which continued freely on their way to Tel Aviv. The ruse succeeded.

The Athlit raid was Jacobson's first exposure to violence in Palestine. Ignoring the State Department's advice that all Americans leave Palestine at once, Jacobson stayed behind, discarding his uniform and pretending to be a kibbutznik. After two weeks, he returned to Athens, where he began to wind up his tenure in Greece. Schwartz suggested that he go home on leave before his next European assignment, and on his way to New York in December 1945, he stopped off in Paris. There, Schwartz casually told him he was being named country director for Czechoslovakia, one of the most important Joint operations in the world.

XI

Eretz Israel

While the Joint had been gearing up for major relief, rescue and emigration operations throughout Europe since the beginning of 1945, not even Joe Schwartz was fully prepared for what was to come. Having reopened the Paris office to serve as European and Middle East headquarters, Schwartz added new offices in Jerusalem, London and Brussels in addition to those in Istanbul and Lisbon. Saly Mayer, the Joint's financial genius, was busier than ever at his office in St. Gallen, Switzerland. Joint representatives fanned out to launch aid programs in Romania, Bulgaria, Yugoslavia, Hungary, Poland and Czechoslovakia. There were still Jewish European refugees in Shanghai as well, and Schwartz authorized the monthly budget there to go up to $150,000. Schwartz himself darted across Europe—from Paris to London, to Bari, Rome, Istanbul, Jerusalem and Warsaw—meeting Jewish community leaders and the authorities in the liberated countries to estimate potential needs.

In January, the Joint dispatched fifty tons of food and clothing to the liberated regions of Poland from the warehouses it had maintained in Teheran since 1943—the first such consignments. Additional shipments were being readied for Czechoslovakia, whose eastern provinces were now free of the Germans. From American Lend-Lease stocks in Teheran, the Joint bought large quantities of supplies for the shipment of 10,000 monthly parcels to the western Soviet Union and the Baltic states. In addition, shipments of Asiatic Soviet cotton garments were sent to refugees in the Balkans. Relief and reconstruction funds were also established for France, Belgium and Holland, where Jews were returning from Nazi incarceration. And, with its usual discretion, the Joint went on financing the main expense of transporting refugees to Palestine.

For 1945, the Joint's total expenditures in Europe soared to $25 million—roughly $300 million in 1991 dollars. To Schwartz, the logical sequence of the Joint's efforts was to locate Jewish refugees—or survivors—in Europe, to feed, heal, clothe and house them and then send them on to Palestine, if they wished to go. Schwartz was persuaded that, sooner or later, most of the Jews would opt for Eretz Israel.

But most of the Jewish refugees needed help to make their way to Palestine. Before long, the stretch of the Mediterranean between Palestine and the Italian and Greek coasts in the north became a fairly well-traveled route for the Mossad's specially outfitted small boats. It was a two-way sea lane, with boats bringing refugees from Europe through the British blockade and sailing back with Mossad operatives.

The most extraordinary among these operatives was thirty-eight-year-old Yehuda Arazi. Greatly respected by Avigur,

Arazi was a distinguished arms smuggler for the Haganah and an accomplished saboteur who had spent three years in the Balkans with British intelligence. He became the operations officer of the Haganah high command, and British counterintelligence hunted him desperately in 1945. Arazi was a man of many faces and mantles.

Born Yehuda Tannenbaum in Lodz, Poland, Arazi emigrated to Palestine in 1924. He earned a law degree and in the early 1930s served as an inspector in the Criminal Investigation Department of the British Mandate Police in Tel Aviv. He also operated secretly as a Haganah infiltrator, procuring weapons for the underground. But in 1934 the British caught on to Arazi and dismissed him. He then joined the Haganah intelligence service, using a job in the Haifa harbor as a cover. In 1936 and again in 1939, he went to Poland to buy weapons for the secret Jewish army. Avigur was in Poland on the second occasion for the same purpose, and was no doubt impressed by the arsenal Arazi had assembled: 225 light machine guns, 2,750 Mauser rifles, 10,000 grenades and two million bullets—a remarkable feat for an obscure Polish-speaking Jew from Palestine with no high-level connections. Arazi also succeeded in buying four Polish-built RWG trainer planes. The Haganah's first pilot, Aviron, learned how to fly on one of them. In addition, Arazi managed to procure the first machines to manufacture 9mm ammunition in Palestine, and in Finland he purchased 100 Suomi submachine guns. The Nazi attack on September 1, 1939, caught Arazi in Warsaw, but he escaped through Romania, Yugoslavia and Italy.

Arazi was held in such high esteem that British intelligence decided to let bygones be bygones and persuaded him to run sabotage operations against the Germans in the Balkans, which he did with aplomb. But by 1942 Arazi had tired of it and returned to Palestine to resume his Haganah activities. Working again for Avigur, he conducted illegal immigration missions in the Middle East and North Africa, in order to bring in military-age men to Palestine to strengthen Haganah ranks. Arazi also stole weapons from British Army bases and railroad trains in Syria and in March 1943 led a raid on a supply base for British paratrooper and intelligence units at Mount Carmel. His booty included hundreds of machine guns and rifles and quantities of ammunition. But the raid also marked the end of his Haganah career in Palestine. The British put a price on his head and Arazi vanished underground in July.

He then underwent plastic surgery to change his appearance, and he grew a beard as he waited for his next opportunity. In 1944, after the Allied invasion of Italy, he flew to the peninsula as a Polish copilot aboard a British aircraft captained by an English Jewish officer. There he surveyed the Italian situation. He made his way back aboard an illegal immigration vessel, and Avigur decided that Arazi should remain indefinitely in Italy in charge of the illegal immigration program. He sent him back via Cairo for safety reasons. As soon as he reached Italy, Arazi made two basic decisions. First, immigrants would be assembled only with the aid of Jewish Brigade soldiers who had access to trucks and supplies. Second, refugees could be successfully transported aboard very small vessels to escape British detection.

Arazi started construction of these ships immediately. The "little boats" could sail back to Italy with Mossad agents and Haganah radio operators for the communications network Avigur planned to set up in Europe. Most of Arazi's boats were designed to accommodate and sleep four passengers, but they often carried as many as 80 refugees (the British seldom bothered to stop and check them). Some of the vessels were schooners under 250 tons, and between May and December 1945, a dozen of them delivered 4,400 illegal immigrants to Palestine. During his two years in Italy, Arazi succeeded in sending over twenty ships with 11,415 immigrants.

Arazi also concentrated on creating the clandestine radio network for the Mossad. Transmitters and receivers were built in secret workships in Palestine, and parts were acquired locally or sent over by Arazi on one of his boats. Arazi discovered that in Italy almost anything could be traded for liquor, and one bottle of whisky could buy enough parts for a transmitter. The Haganah consequently ordered all Jewish Brigade soldiers to surrender their weekly ration of a bottle of gin and a bottle of whisky to a special "liquor bank" to conduct Mossad barter operations. At one point, a single case of whisky bought a detailed map of maritime minefields along Italian coasts from the Italian Admiralty. In time, secret wireless stations were set up in every port used by the Mossad—or to be used in the future. Each Mossad boat also carried a transmitter to communicate with land points and other Mossad vessels.

Arazi then organized an internal European radio network with stations in Paris (where Avigur's daughter Ruth worked as an operator), Marseilles, Athens, Milan, Naples and Antwerp. Naturally, the European wireless system was linked with Mossad and Haganah headquarters in Tel Aviv. Two Jewish specialists of the Royal Engineers unit and the "liquor bank" were responsible for this miracle of undercover technology. The Mossad also organized its own telephone communications among European capitals with the use of code. As masses of refugees began moving across Europe, often guided by the Brichah, the Palestinian commanders knew at all times what was happening. *The New York Times* reported in January 1946 that "the Jews moving from Poland to Germany seem to have a better system of communications even than the American Army."

Arazi had landed in June 1945 on the southern Italian coast from Egypt aboard one of the Mossad's small boats that he had helped design. With the greatest ease he wore a British Army sergeant's uniform. (The Mossad had access to the British uniforms of the Jewish Brigade and manufactured their own along with soldiers' paybooks and other items of forged identity.) Arazi was to act as commander of the Haganah and Mossad in Italy.

Arazi's main objective was organizing illegal immigration, and his primary operational instrument was the 462nd Palestine General Transport Company, stationed in Milan. When he arrived in Italy he made immediate contact with its sergeant major, Eliahu Cohen, a founder of the Palmach commandos in the Haganah. He used Jewish Brigade veterans to set up a fictitious British Army unit. His "soldiers" would drive up to arms depots in various Italian towns, submit forged requisition papers and load their trucks with arms and ammunition. The arms were then transferred at night from Italian ports to the schooners Arazi used for illegal immigrants, and sent on their way to Palestine.

Arazi also sent groups of his "soldiers" to Germany and Austria to explore the possibilities of emigration from the camps there. Early in June 1945, a platoon of the 462nd moved up to Tarvisio near the Austrian border, and several soldiers crossed into a nearby camp which held about 100 refugees. By coincidence, a Brichah group from Romania, hoping to establish contacts with the Jewish Brigade, reached the Tarvisio area at the same time as Arazi. As a result of these meetings, a Jewish Brigade delegation traveled to Bucharest, where it convinced the Brichah to send 15,000 refugees from Romania, Hungary and Austria to Italy for transport to Palestine. To track down refugees and channel them toward Palestine, Arazi came to depend on the Brigade. As we have seen, the British, who expended so much effort in blocking Jewish immigration to Palestine, allowed the Brigade virtually total freedom to do as it pleased when it came to the activities of its soldiers.

Simultaneously, Joint representatives began establishing *their* ties with the Brichah. This marked the start of a great cooperative effort over the next three years involving Jewish soldiers, the Mossad, the Brichah and the American Jews.

XII

Great Battles, Great Decisions

The Joint's involvement in the European refugee problem was formally recognized when Joseph Schwartz was invited, in July 1945, to participate in a U.S. government mission appointed to investigate the DP camps in the American Zones in Germany and Austria, with special attention to the "many Jewish survivors of Nazi persecution." President Truman authorized the mission in response to charges from many Jewish community organizations and newspapers in Europe and the United States that the American Army was treating Jewish DPs as brutally as the Nazis had. There was no actual evidence of such brutality, but this was a highly charged political issue and the President thought it prudent to act.

The mission was headed by Earl G. Harrison, dean of the University of Pennsylvania Law School and former Commissioner of Immigration. It was Harrison who proposed that Schwartz accompany him. The two men visited a number of the DP camps, and the report drafted and issued by Harrison in August 1945 was extremely critical of the U.S. Army.

Harrison stated, for example, that Jews were made to wear SS uniforms, received insufficient food and faced hostility from non-Jews in the camps. "Many Jewish displaced persons," Harrison wrote, "are living under guard behind barbed-wire fences, in camps of several descriptions (built by the Germans for slave-laborers and Jews), including some of the most notorious concentration camps, amidst crowded, frequently unsanitary and generally grim conditions, in complete idleness, with no opportunity, except surreptitiously, to communicate with the outside world." Though at the time there were only 50,000 Jews out of a total of 1.5 million DPs in Germany and Austria, Harrison proposed that Britain immediately admit 100,000 Jews to Palestine. This was the same figure recommended in May by the Jewish Agency and rejected by Britain's new Labor government. It's not entirely clear why Harrison resurrected the idea. The Israeli historian Yehuda Bauer speculated that Schwartz suggested it, which would be plausible given his pro-Zionist bent. The British again turned the proposal down.

Bauer noted that "one of the main effects of the report was the entry of the JDC into the camps." To Schwartz it also meant a chance to play a greater role in shaping immigration patterns. He had told a Joint audience in October 1944 that "Palestine raises many vital and important problems as to the role the JDC is going to play."

For Shaul Avigur and the Mossad, the Palestinian role was the one they had so long waited to play in a decisive way.

Avigur was the supreme chief of the Mossad for illegal immigration and the de facto European chief of the Haganah and the Brichah. Nahum Kraemer acted as the official Haganah commander in Europe, and Mordecai Surkiss of the Jewish Brigade was the European Brichah commander. But both of them deferred to Avigur when it came to key decisions. For all practical purposes, Avigur was the most important Palestinian. In his immediate circle of trusted advisers, he also had Ehud Avriel, summoned from his Balkan assignments, and his friend Ruth Aliav-Klieger, who had served brilliantly in Bucharest and Istanbul.

By late 1945, Avigur was firmly established in Paris, running a number of parallel and often overlapping operations. All of them were still in the initial stages and he lacked adequate resources to proceed as rapidly and effectively as he desired. Impatient to accelerate the flow of refugees to Palestine, Avigur had entered into preliminary, but increasingly frequent discussions with his old acquaintance Joe Schwartz, who now ran all the European operations for the Joint from Paris. Schwartz, encumbered with emergency relief problems, could move only gradually toward accommodating Avigur's needs. Much, therefore, depended on Ruth Aliav-Klieger, who in the very short time since her arrival in Paris had established such impressive contacts with General Eisenhower's Supreme Allied Headquarters that she was able to dispatch nearly 4,000 illegal Jewish refugees to Palestine aboard two U.S. Army troopships. But British protests put an end to her use of U.S. shipping.

The other colossal task facing Avigur was the procurement of arms for the Haganah. With Britain's refusal, despite the end of the war, to open Palestine's gates to Jewish refugees let alone consider a State of Israel, it was a foregone conclusion that the Jews would soon have to fight both the

British and the Arabs if they were ever to achieve a homeland.

"We must bring tens of thousands of survivors to Palestine," Ben-Gurion wrote to Ehud Avriel. "We must create new kibbutzim in the desert and on the frontiers, and we need the people to build them. The survivors of the Holocaust are the ones who will be happy to join us. We must train them in the use of arms even before they reach Palestine. . . . And we shall bring the arms we need to defend ourselves when the inevitable showdown comes. These are the tasks. The remnants of Europe's Jewry are with us. . . . The time has come for great battles and for great decisions."

It was up to Avigur to find and bring the arms to Palestine. He and Nahum Kraemer were directly responsible for the purchase of arms—the weapons procurement project codenamed Rechesh—and they were endlessly imaginative. One of Avigur's most successful ideas was to purchase, through various intermediaries, stocks of British Army weapons left behind after the war, mainly in Belgium and Italy. It was a long time before the British Army realized how the Jews obtained their arms.

In France, Avigur's men cheaply purchased captured German arms from the extant Resistance movements. French military and police authorities under Charles de Gaulle, who had resented the British for many wartime slights, were particularly cooperative in easing the passage of clandestine Jewish arms convoys to the ports, asking no questions when the ships sailed. French officials also helped the Haganah locate and rent great estates and châteaux in the south for its military training camps, which also doubled as rest camps for Jewish children awaiting emigration. Most of these camps were run by Laura Margolis, the Joint's refugee expert from Shanghai, who now worked for Schwartz in Paris. Her husband, Marc Jarblum, headed the Federation of Jewish

Societies in France, an organization of Eastern European Jews that assisted refugees from the East. They became close friends of Shaul Avigur. Laura was deeply involved in illegal immigration, and Marc used his friendships with police authorities to obtain transit visas for prospective voyagers to Palestine. It was harder and harder to tell the Joint and the Mossad apart.

To pay for the weapons, the Haganah raised funds in the United States, Palestine and even Germany. Teddy Kollek (the future and celebrated mayor of Jerusalem for over a quarter century), who conducted intelligence work and arms procurement for the Mossad, helped to set up the Friends of the Haganah, Inc., in New York, which underwrote many of the arms purchases. Thus, not only did the American Jewish community help European Jews escape to Palestine; it also paid for weapons that they used to defend themselves. As Golda Meir remarked years later in her memoirs: "For all the years preceding the establishment of the State of Israel, [Shaul Avigur] was, in effect, our underground minister of defense."

Europe, 1945-1950

XIII

No Place to Go,
No Place to Return

While peace came to Europe
in 1945, the birth of the State of Israel, or any promise of a
Jewish homeland in Palestine, still seemed remote. Britain
maintained strict limitations on Jewish immigration to Palestine, presumably out of concern for its relationship with
the Arab world, and there could clearly be no Jewish state
if Jews remained a minority.

Sovereignty continued to be a matter of more or less
theoretical debate even among Jews themselves; it certainly
wasn't on the Allies' agenda as the war wound down. Even
if the British had thrown open the gates to the Mandate
territory, the numbers of immigrants would have been
relatively small due to the limited resources for relocating
them. It's a near miracle that the Mossad, aided by its
American friends, was able to bring to Palestine as many

Jews as it did during those years—115,000 between 1943 and 1948.

A whole new reality emerged after V-E Day—that of the displaced persons. Millions of starving, homeless and disoriented DPs were let loose across liberated Europe, creating problems and pressures the victorious Allies had never anticipated. At the end of 1945, about 7 million DPs roamed Western Europe, 7 million more were in the Soviet Union and Eastern Europe and there were 10 million freed German war prisoners. After the nightmare of the Holocaust, the ever-rising tide of Jewish refugees, with no homes to which they could or would return, faced yet another horror. The only Allied policy at that juncture—and for the next few years—was to keep the DPs alive. There were no long-range plans.

Schwartz had rushed to liberated Central Europe from Paris the moment hostilities ended. He saw firsthand the incredible human toll the Holocaust had taken. He also discovered that out of the 7.5 million Jews inhabiting Europe before the war, 6.25 million had been killed or had died. Until then, no one had realized the magnitude of human destruction. Schwartz flew back to New York and addressed the Joint's executive committee on June 20, just six weeks after the Nazi surrender. In a confidential report, he briefed his associates on the catastrophe, warning them that if American Jewry failed to provide the resources, the survivors would perish:

We have a situation in Europe today which gives us very little reason for optimism. We have a continent on which five-sixths of the Jewish population has been exterminated. We have a continent on which there are some 1,250,000 Jews left—Jews who are living under the most distressing conditions. It may be said, using a Biblical phrase, that there is not a Jewish home in Europe today in which there is not one dead. And there are many Jewish homes in which there is not one living. Everybody is mourning for a father or a mother who has been deported and of whom no news has been heard, in mourning for children who have vanished, in mourning for some dear one and near one who will never be heard from again. There are children—thousands of them—who are without father and mother, and without anybody to look after them.

Describing the condition of Jews returning from Nazi death camps and from exile in Soviet Asia, he wrote:

They come in from those boats—boats that start their journey in Odessa, come through Naples and then into Marseilles—and then they find their way into our Paris office. They are literally without anything. They are without clothing, they are without shoes, they have no place to spend the night. They haven't a sou in their pockets. They have nothing to look forward to . . . I must tell you that many of them are swollen with hunger. Many of them cannot walk a step. Many of them need immediate medical attention and medical care. They cannot be put on their own. They cannot be told to shift for themselves. People are coming back who had been given up for dead. They come in walking like ghosts, like shadows, not realizing that they are back in their home country. It is no longer a home country to them: their families have disappeared; they don't know

where there is a place which they can call their own or
a home.

To aggravate the problem, Schwartz reported, Jews were
turning on Jews in liberated Europe:

> You have divisions, you have splits; you have people
> who accuse one another—because these years of occu-
> pation have worked tremendous hardships on all of
> these communities. . . . Jews have become divided, just
> as the general community has, into Jews who were active
> in the resistance and Jews who are accused of not having
> been active in the resistance, and even of being collab-
> orationists. . . . Then, too, you have differences between
> native Jews, between German Jews and Polish Jews,
> between Communist Jews and Zionist Jews.

The immediate problem was some 200,000 stateless Jews
who originated in Eastern Europe but refused to be repatriated. There were Polish Jews, Yugoslavian Jews, Lithuanian Jews, Latvian Jews and 30,000 Hungarian Jews "with
no place to go, no place to which to return."
The prospects for European Jewry were bleak, and
Schwartz concluded his appeal for funds from the American
Jewish community on a somber note:

> They are living on a sick continent. They are living on
> a continent that is facing starvation; on a continent
> which, during the past winter, actually froze because
> there was no fuel; on a continent on which there is no
> transportation, no coal, no employment to speak of, no
> raw material; on a continent in which . . . the anti-
> Semitic virus has taken hold. There is anti-Semitism in

Europe today. The seeds that Hitler has sown . . . have
taken root.

Schwartz was right about the "anti-Semitic virus," but he
may have underestimated both its potential and the Jewish
response to this historical phenomenon—the Holocaust notwithstanding. While there were only 50,000 Jews among the
1.5 million refugees in DP camps in the immediate aftermath
of the war, there were some 7 million additional DPs and
refugees who were crisscrossing Western Europe. The Jewish
numbers began to increase alarmingly after Schwartz delivered his report in New York. Fearing new outbreaks of anti-
Semitism, tens of thousands of Jews were streaming from
Poland, Romania and Hungary into Austria, Germany and
Italy seeking a safe haven. By the end of 1946, a quarter of
a million Jews filled 72 of these camps—with no place to go
and little to sustain them.

As Schwartz and Avigur anticipated, the rapidly deteriorat-
ing situation of Jews in Europe would reopen the question
of Palestine. It required no leap of the imagination to see in
the closing months of 1945 that unless the Jews of Europe
were permitted to emigrate to the Holy Land in considerable
numbers—perhaps as many as the 100,000 proposed by the
Jewish Agency and the Harrison Commission—they would
perish in the DP camps or succumb to the horrendous living
conditions in Eastern Europe, particularly in Romania and
Hungary, where famine reigned.

The U.S. Army and, to a lesser extent, UNRRA (which
was to be phased out of Europe at the end of 1946) provided
limited emergency relief—mainly food—to refugees in the
camps. While the Joint was able to supplement their aid to

maintain the daily minimum caloric intake, its help could not last indefinitely. Over half a million Jews had survived in Romania and Hungary (in Hungary, only 300,000 had survived out of a prewar Jewish population of 800,000), and the bulk depended on food supplied by the Joint, the only relief agency operating in these countries. In the first six months of 1945, the Joint expended nearly $5 million (over $50 million in 1991 dollars) on food for Jews in those two countries. In addition, the Joint shipped fifty tons of food to Poland every week.

The situation was further complicated by the growing refusal of Jews in DP camps to be repatriated, and the U.S. government would not force the issue—especially as Communist regimes began taking over Eastern Europe. Washington's policy was not to make Jews return against their will—a Geneva Convention requirement to protect refugees—and most of them did not wish to be sent back. And there were still thousands of Jewish orphans, saved during the war by Christian families or Roman Catholic monasteries and convents, who needed new homes.

The conventional wisdom, shared by the Joint, was that Jews returning from the Soviet Union would welcome resettlement in such areas as the former German territories of Lower Silesia. And although the Joint offered to help bankroll it, it soon became evident that for a variety of reasons, ranging from fear of anti-Semitism to Zionist sentiments and a general foreboding about the future in Eastern Europe, Jews in general had little interest in rebuilding their former communities.

Since no other country in the world—including the United States—was prepared to receive Jews in great numbers, there was no viable alternative to the Palestine solution. Nevertheless, the new Labor government in Britain, and notably

Foreign Secretary Ernest Bevin, who came to power in July 1945, made it perfectly clear that it planned no change in its restrictive immigration policies. This left the Jews, as it were, to their own devices, and it forged a Jewish linkage with Palestine of unprecedented strength. The more Jews there were in Palestine, the greater the chances of an independent Jewish state. It was an old idea whose time had come.

The tragedy was that it took Britain so long to come to terms with history and reality and relinquish Palestine altogether. Not a minute before the official deadline on May 14, 1948, did the British allow Jews to enter the country freely. So many lives and so much grief could have been spared if the British had relented.

In the aftermath of the war, European Jews could depend only on the extraordinary alliance that quietly developed among their own young militant Zionists, secret emissaries from Palestine and American Jewish organizations. It took hundreds of millions of dollars to finance the great rescue enterprise; 200 dedicated American men and women helped run it from day to day.

XIV

The Brichah

Parallel American and Palestinian operations were launched to extricate hundreds of thousands of men, women and children from Eastern Europe and transport them to Palestine through the British blockade. It was an extremely difficult and risky venture, but it was believed that the pressures created by masses of Jewish refugees in camps in Germany, Austria and Italy and, to a lesser degree, in France and Belgium were bound to force the United States and Britain to reach a political solution.

Four principal partners organized this vast underground operation, which was conducted in an extraordinarily informal yet extremely efficient fashion. First, there was the Brichah. Created by young Eastern European Zionists in the closing period of the war, the Brichah had primary responsibility for assembling, protecting and transporting Jews across Europe to points of embarkation for Palestine. Next were the soldiers of the Jewish Brigade, who helped the Brichah to start the initial migrations by Jews. Then Avigur's Mossad set up the Palestinian network of emissaries (mostly European-born) who were sent in growing numbers to the Continent to coordinate illegal immigration and handle the maritime transport arrangements. After 1945, the European command of the Brichah was shared by Avigur's emissaries, as were the most important Brichah country commands. Avigur, working out of Paris, was the overall boss, but national Brichah commanders enjoyed wide autonomy to achieve their goals.

The fourth underground partner was the Joint, which functioned both as an overt relief organization that fed hundreds of thousands of starving Jews and as an impressively sophisticated private intelligence agency. The Joint provided the cover for Brichah operations throughout Eastern Europe—wherever the Joint had reopened its offices—that made it possible for the Brichah "boys and girls" to function. The Joint also paid the Brichah's living and operational expenses (Brichah activists received no salaries), organized and supervised large railroad transports of Jewish refugees across Eastern Europe and staffed major frontier crossing points with its American or local employees.

Austria was the central transit region for Eastern European refugees. Asher Ben-Natan, who served there as Brichah commander from late 1945 to mid-1947—and afterward became Israel's first ambassador to West Germany—played a leading role. Indeed, the entire immigration and independence objective would have collapsed had it not overcome powerful obstacles in moving the arriving Jews into Germany and Italy. Ben-Natan's command was located in Vienna, but he had regional units in Linz, Graz, Innsbruck and Salzburg. "Salzburg's role was to get the people into Germany or into the French [occupation] Zone of Austria," he said. From the French Zone the refugees could be smuggled over the mountains into Italy.

During Ben-Natan's assignment over 200,000 Jews passed through Austria on the road to freedom. A personable and elegant man, the twenty-five-year-old Ben-Natan worked undercover in Vienna as a correspondent for Palestinian and American news agencies. Assuming the code name Arthur Pier (his name at birth was Arthur Piernikarz), Ben-Natan used charm, guile and threats on Austrian officials and on American, French and British military officers to keep the Jews moving. If masses of Jews were bottled up in Austria, where they were considered undesirable in any case, waves of refugees would back up in Hungary, Czechoslovakia and Poland, and the overall movement would grind to a complete halt.

The goodwill of Allied officers was, of course, vital, and Ben-Natan cultivated it with great success. Captain Stanley K. Novinsky, head of the U.S. Army's Displaced Persons Section in Salzburg, sympathized with the operation and lent his help. "Novinsky was of Polish origin," Ben-Natan recalled, "an anti-Semite by birth, but who, being faced with the problem of Jewish refugees, became a very close friend of ours. He virtually became a member of the Brichah." Novinsky went so far as to issue Ben-Natan a document stating that he was accompanying a prisoner around Austria. This enabled Ben-Natan to go virtually anywhere he wanted— even to the United States. As Ben-Natan put it, "the prisoner whom I was guarding was myself."

Ben-Natan fought every inch of the way to assure the continued movement of Jews. When French authorities in

Austria closed their border to Jews coming from the American Zone (apparently under British pressure to prevent Jews from moving on to Italy and then to the Mossad ships), Ben-Natan chose confrontation. Rounding up 500 young Zionists at the Saalfelden DP camp in the American Zone near the French frontier, Ben-Natan ordered them to march across the boundary and lie down on the road if challenged by the French military. The French brought in light tanks, and the Jews, as instructed, lay across the road. But at that moment two Joint officials in U.S. Army uniforms appeared and began negotiations with the French commander. In the end, the 500 youths crossed the border. There were many "repeat performances," according to Ben-Natan, and the French looked the other way to avoid further confrontation.

On another occasion, French authorities in Austria stopped a trainload of 350 refugees that the Brichah and the Joint had sent from the American Zone to France. The refugees, who had already received French transit visas—Mossad organizers having claimed that the Jewish families had visas for a South American country—were to sail to Palestine aboard an illegal ship from a French Mediterranean port. But in Innsbruck, where the train halted briefly, French officials canceled the transit visas when they discovered that there were no South American visas. They then ordered the train back to the American Zone, while Ben-Natan persuaded his American friends not to allow the train reentry because it had left "legally." The French forced the refugees to disembark, whereupon Ehud Avriel telephoned Ben-Natan from Paris and urged him to "take them back . . . we have got trouble here." Ben-Natan countered: " 'No. Never go back. We don't go back. If we do it once, we'll have to do it again.' . . . A few hours later, Avriel called me again and said, 'Take them back. . . . This is an order!' I said, 'I don't accept any orders,' and I hung up the phone." The French had no choice but to move the refugees by truck to a camp in their zone. The refugees dispersed, and finally reached their destination.

In the spring of 1946, Ben-Natan met with Shaike Dan on the Slovak-Hungarian border. Shaike Dan warned Ben-Natan that huge numbers of Jews wanted to leave Romania via Hungary for Austria. "Are you able to handle it?" Shaike Dan asked. Ben-Natan replied: "Any number you can send, send them. This is our responsibility." Later he recalled that "there was never a question of us agreeing to stop the flow of refugees because of any problems we may have had."

One of the problems Ben-Natan faced was the infiltration of British "spies" among the refugees arriving in Austria. He recalled one incident as follows:

> One day when a transport came from Romania, the commander of the transport gave me a small slip of paper, which said, "So-and-so is a British spy . . . Get rid of him." So I went to Salzburg to see a Major Lifschitz of the Counterintelligence Corps and said, "I've got a foul apple here in this transport. I've got to put him on ice." He said, "I'll handle it." So this chap was arrested by the American authorities and was tried. He got two years in jail. Do you know for what? For crossing the border illegally!

When he was planning operations, Ben-Natan's imagination seemed to know no bounds. His Vienna activities included organizing a group who searched for Nazi criminals, the first such expedition, he believed, to hunt for Adolf

Eichmann. Ben-Natan managed to track down Eichmann's deputy, Dieter von Wisliceny, in a prison in Bratislava, where he was awaiting execution, and was able to interview him because "the prosecutor in Bratislava was a Jew and he got me into the prison." Wisliceny told Ben-Natan that Eichmann's chauffeur was in prison in Vienna, and the chauffeur in turn came up with the name of Eichmann's girlfriend near Linz. With the help of the Austrian police, Ben-Natan then obtained from her a photograph of Eichmann—none were available at the time—and soon learned the whereabouts of Eichmann's wife and two children. "The idea was proposed to kidnap the children and force Eichmann out of his hole somewhere," but "an order came from Paris not to do it because it might have endangered our whole Brichah operation."

The Brichah depended upon the Joint's financial assistance for its operations, but occasionally, Ben-Natan admitted, the Brichah misused it. "We had trucks in Salzburg with Joint license plates, and we had people in Joint uniforms, which the Joint didn't know about, or did know about and closed both eyes."

Until the spring of 1946, the collaboration among the Joint, the Brichah and the Mossad was still informal in character. Policies were improvised and decisions tended to be made on an ad hoc basis. But the new postwar policies of the big powers and, above all, the dramatic developments concerning the fate of European Jewry demanded a clearer definition and direction to this alliance.

Politically, the turning point in the history of the Palestinian question came in April 1946, when the Anglo-American Committee of Inquiry, charged with investigating the Palestinian and Jewish refugee problem, recommended that 100,000 victims of Nazi and Fascist persecution be allowed to emigrate to Palestine that year, if possible. It was Britain's Labor Party Prime Minister, Clement Attlee, who proposed the formation of the committee to President Truman.

It became painfully obvious, however, that the wartime Allies were at loggerheads over the issue. The United States openly favored a significant relaxation in immigration controls; Britain maintained its opposition to it. The British government also disagreed with the committee's view that "all of the Jews, or the bulk of them, must necessarily leave Germany, and still less Europe." The British government insisted that the Jews had a reasonably promising future on the Continent, which obviated the need for emigration to Palestine. Presumably, Attlee and his Foreign Secretary, Bevin, assumed that the six British and six American members of the Committee of Inquiry, all of them private citizens, would uphold the British assessment. This assumption proved to be another of Britain's catastrophic errors of judgment in the postwar period.

As it happened, the committee reached diametrically opposed conclusions. After touring the DP camps, the committee was convinced that most of the Jews had no future in Europe and that they earnestly desired to live in Palestine. Consequently, the committee urged the British government to grant 100,000 immigration certificates—the same figure the Jewish Agency had requested immediately after V-E Day and which Truman had endorsed in late 1945. But Attlee and Bevin once more turned down the immigration proposal. Neither side would compromise, and the stalemate continued. It seemed that tens of thousands of men and women with blue Nazi concentration camp serial numbers tattooed on their arms were now condemned to the DP camps in

Europe. The Committee of Inquiry also went to Jerusalem, but it refrained from making a recommendation on the question of Jewish statehood; in fact, it even accepted the need for an indefinite continuation of the British Mandate.

Yehuda Bauer, the Czech-born Israeli historian, theorized in a private conversation in 1989 that British policy on Palestine stemmed from the concern over disintegration of the British Empire at that juncture. "The only way remnants [of the empire] could be preserved was by keeping the central link, which was the Suez Canal and its immediate neighborhood. . . . That could only be held if the Arabs were kept sweet . . . and Arab pressures on the British were tremendous in 1945 and 1946. The British argument was: 'We can't afford to antagonize the Arabs.' "

In Bauer's view, London was guilty of a complete miscalculation. Had the British accepted the 100,000 immigrants recommended by the Committee of Inquiry, they "could have prevented effectively the rise of the State of Israel." It would have "taken the steam out of the Zionists' demands centered in the DP camps in Central Europe," and would have raised the number of Jews in Palestine from 650,000 to 750,000, and "that would have been the end of that."

Instead, the British feared that opening the gates to Palestine would lead to a major war with the Arabs. Their restrictionist policy played into the hands of Ben-Gurion, and the resulting pressures, particularly on American policy, Bauer believes, led to the United Nations General Assembly vote for Palestinian partition—and consequently the birth of Israel.

The fiasco of the Anglo-American Committee of Inquiry thus helped coalesce proponents of illegal immigration, and the Joint's operations in Europe entered a new phase.

———

The Brichah and the Mossad were now firmly entrenched on the Continent. Out of the Eastern European Survivors, which was organized in Poland in 1945 by survivors of Polish and Lithuanian anti-Nazi uprisings—including the young poet Abba Kovner—and Jewish returnees from Central Asia, the Brichah grew into a continental network of hundreds of young men and women. They served as leaders of refugee groups stealing across borders, couriers carrying instructions and money and organizers of prospective illegal immigrations to Palestine.

The Mossad, supported by the Jewish Brigade and its Merkaz la-Gola (Diaspora Center) Jewish refugee relief organization in Fiuggi, Italy, had over fifty emissaries—called *shlihim* in Hebrew—directing and coordinating Brichah activities under Avigur's command in Paris. The first emissaries, such as Yehuda Arazi (whom the American journalist I. F. Stone described as the "Jewish Garibaldi"), Ruth Aliav-Klieger and Ehud Avriel, were joined by outstanding operatives like Ben-Natan, Levi Argov and Elhanan Gafni. Efraim Krasner Dekel, the forty-two-year-old Haganah chief of intelligence (whose official job in Palestine was head of the National Fire Brigade), followed Mordecai Surkiss as the first Brichah commander in Europe. Convivial and good-humored, Dekel, though similar to Avigur in other ways, neither acted nor looked the part of a top intelligence operative. Before leaving for Europe, Dekel raided a British Army command in Sarafand to steal and copy secret documents outlining British plans for a crackdown on the Haganah and the Mossad. He was able to return them without arousing British suspicions.

In addition to its superb radio and telephone communications and the services of Brichah couriers, the Mossad in Europe counted on the quiet cooperation of Jewish U.S.

Army chaplains and of Rabbi Philip S. Bernstein. Bernstein, who held the rank of major general, advised commanders of American occupation forces in Germany on Jewish affairs. He was part of a crucial link between the Jewish militants, the American authorities and the DP camp leaders. Bernstein's contacts with American civilians engaged in refugee problems—Jacobson had known Rabbi Bernstein in Rochester—were also vital. All in all, a formidable mechanism now existed in Europe to challenge the British over Jewish access to the shores of Palestine.

The Mossad's pride was its Operation Documents, which could produce perfect passports and protection certificates from any country in the world, including the Vatican— military travel orders, soldiers' paybooks, birth, marriage and death certificates and any other piece of paper required to save or move one or more Jews. The Mossad forgers sometimes made sport of their work, issuing identification cards with Hebrew names like Ashrei Yoshvei Beitecha (Happy Are They Who Dwell in Thy House), Mizmor Ledavid (Psalm of David), or documents with impressive initials such as Y.Tz., which stood for Yidishe Tzores (Yiddish for "Jewish Troubles").

Now it was the Joint's turn to become totally engaged in the Jewish illegal immigration enterprise, virtually formalizing the evolving relationship with the Mossad. Schwartz, having built a new Joint structure in Europe, assured the physical survival of hundreds of thousands of Jews through the supply of food, medicine and clothing. The Joint maintained offices and American representatives throughout Eastern and Western Europe, in addition to fully staffed operations in the DP camps, where more than 2,000 local employees were assigned. The Joint even had a program in the Soviet Union, where it spent $500,000 on penicillin purchases in 1945, because the Soviets were not yet in a position to manufacture the antibiotic at home.

Once the Joint was firmly reestablished on the Continent, Schwartz concentrated his efforts on leading the Jews out of Europe. After touring Eastern Europe, he was appalled by the resurgence of anti-Semitism, "so prevalent that any Jew with a beard or who 'looked Jewish' took his life in his hands when he went outdoors in the evening or got on a train." At the Joint's annual meeting in New York in 1946, Schwartz remarked, "A Jew in Warsaw today is a curiosity. People look around in surprise when they see a Jew walking on the streets. The attitude of the general population seems to be 'What, is he still alive?' " In fact, the Jews in Poland presented a major problem: of the 80,000 who remained, 70,000 required "some kind of assistance." In Hungary, the situation was even worse. It was "practically impossible to find the necessities of life."

Back in Paris, during his frequent meetings with Avigur, Schwartz continued to assess all aspects of Jewish life in Europe. Together, the two men calculated what would be required to launch the largest possible illegal immigration movement, and specifically, what role the Joint would secretly play with the Brichah and the Mossad.

Their conclusions—and their handshake—constituted the Paris agreement of April 1946 and marked the start of an unprecedented undertaking to save the Jews. Needless to say, they signed no papers and left no written record of their accord. Notwithstanding the enormous sums of money that would be involved, it was a matter of absolute mutual trust. They had no doubts that American Jewry would come up with the resources. Neither Schwartz nor Avigur, however, could have anticipated how soon their decision would have to be implemented on an emergency basis.*

Ephraim Dekel, the Brichah's European commander, who worked directly with the Joint, wrote in his book *B'riha: Flight to the Homeland* that "the JDC . . . quickly decided to extend to Brichah any financial or 'official' assistance it might need," and that "it was the general consensus that for most of Europe's surviving Jews the only answer was Palestine, and that if Brichah could get them there, Brichah was deserving of support." Dekel stated further that "funds from the Joint helped pay [the refugees'] way past suspicious border guards and, when necessary, to secure their release from arrest," and that "the JDC aided Brichah . . . by bringing its influence to bear on Brichah's behalf whenever that was needed."

Funds from the Joint helped refugees bribe border guards, secure their release from arrest, and they also financed the acquisition of ships by the Mossad for the illegal Mediterranean crossings. Crews were provided by Palyam, the naval arm of the Palmach commandos, and at least 200 American volunteers were counted among the sailors.

It has been estimated that 250,000 Jews traveled the Brichah routes, making it "the largest organized illegal mass

* Yehuda Bauer greatly underestimated the scope of the Schwartz-Avigur deal when he wrote in his book *Out of the Ashes* that the Brichah activists' operational expenses "were covered, often unwittingly but eventually with full knowledge, by the American Joint Distribution Committee as 'transit' expenses for transport, food, and basic lodging." Moreover, Bauer is unfair to Schwartz in suggesting that it was the Jewish Agency that had asked the Joint to "give direct support" to the Mossad—Schwartz needed no prompting from Jerusalem—and in stating that the Joint agreed to do it "from a pragmatic point of view; fewer Jewish DPs in Europe would mean less expense for the Joint." Bauer acknowledges that between 1946 and 1948 the Joint authorized many millions of dollars to secretly fund the Mossad's immigration activities, although "there is no documentary evidence of it." In fact, confidential minutes of the meetings of the Joint's Administrative Committee in New York, which actually dealt with financing, provide such evidence.

movement in modern times," as Bauer put it. By all accounts, the Brichah could not have kept these lanes open without the support of American Jews, as represented by the Joint. Ironically, perhaps the highest compliment to the operation was paid by the British government when in an official statement issued on August 12, 1946, it described the Mossad as "a widely ramified and highly organized movement, supported by very large financial contributions from Zionist sources . . . whose organizers maintain a closely knit network of agents in the countries of eastern and southern Europe, by whom considerable numbers of displaced Jews are moved from points as far distant as Poland down to the Mediterranean seaboard." The statement chose not to mention the Joint by name and failed to say that among the financial contributions from "Zionist sources" were the Central British Fund for World Jewish Relief and Canadian and South African Jewish communities.

Meanwhile in New York, the Joint's board of directors was far less enthusiastic about the accord Schwartz had worked out with Avigur. Most of its members resented the fact that their European chairman failed to consult them beforehand. While most of them liked and admired Schwartz and were accustomed to his fairly cavalier ways, this time, the board felt, he had gone too far. In confidential messages sent in early May to Paris, the board vetoed, in effect, Schwartz's deal with Avigur.

But there was more to this negative reaction than simple annoyance with Schwartz's methods. The majority of the board members were not Zionists; some were actually anti-Zionist—for example, William Rosenwald, whose brother Lessing J. Rosenwald was a leader of the American Council for Judaism, an organization dedicated to opposing the creation of a Jewish homeland in Palestine. At the time, there was a broad split in the American and Palestinian Jewish community over the homeland issue. In fact, Schwartz was the only senior Joint executive who was regarded as a fervent Zionist. In spite of his reports, the board (curiously like Britain on this point) still believed in the spring of 1946 that European Jews wanted to return to their ancient roots on the Continent rather than risk migrating to Palestine. In the words of one member, the board preferred legal immigration to the approach taken by "freebooters" like Joe Schwartz.

To Schwartz, the rejection of his agreement with Avigur signified that his integrity and honor, to say nothing of his continued policymaking freedom, were at stake. The evening he received the critical messages from headquarters, he dined with Laura Margolis Jarblum, one of his most trusted advisers, who oversaw the Joint's French operation. Schwartz told her of the board's response, and his own ultimatum: "Either we can do it—or I'm out." The next day, May 10, Schwartz cabled his resignation to Moses Leavitt, the Joint's secretary and one of its most powerful figures. Schwartz chose to send his cable to Leavitt's residence rather than to the Joint's office, presumably to maintain confidentiality— and to leave his options open.

Jarblum recalled that it was "touch and go." But Schwartz felt he had to stick to his position as a matter of principle; he realized that to renege on the agreement would undermine—if not destroy—Avigur's master plan for moving the Jews out of Europe. His instinct was perfect. The resignation caused alarm among key board members, all of whom understood at once the harm the Joint's reputation would suffer, in view of Schwartz's worldwide prestige. On May 12, Edward M. M. Warburg, chairman of the board, and Paul Baerwald, one of the most influential members, sent separate cables to Schwartz in Paris rejecting his resignation. Schwartz interpreted this response, of course, as official authorization to keep the Joint in business with the Mossad and the Brichah; his judgment was never questioned again.

Less than a year later, the same board voted to make $1 million available to Schwartz "for the purposes of financing immigration to Palestine." While this authorization was duly recorded in the "Highly Confidential" minutes of the Administrative Committee's meetings, the exchange of cables pertaining to Schwartz's resignation is nowhere to be found in the Joint's archives. The matter was hushed up. Warburg, who served as the Joint's board chairman for twenty-two years, remembered telling Schwartz in his cable: "Forget it . . . Of course we back you . . . I love you anyway." Looking back in 1990 at the 1946 episode, Warburg acknowledged: "Joe was miles ahead of the Joint—he made good Jews out of American Jews."

With the complete support of the Joint, Avigur could now develop his strategy. Jacobson, whom Schwartz had just named the Joint's director for Czechoslovakia, stopped off in Paris for a meeting with Schwartz and Avigur and recalled the Mossad's strategic plans as follows:

What [Schwartz] had in mind was that Czechoslovakia would be a major, if not *the* major, outlet for Polish and other Eastern European Jews who needed to get to the American Zones of Germany and Austria and to Italy —for most of them to go eventually to Palestine when that could take place. But they had to get out of these trouble spots where incidents and minor pogroms were taking place . . . and an army of Ukrainian and Polish pro-Nazis [were] committing atrocities against Jews in Poland while trying to overthrow the government there.

Although at that stage only a few hundred people were crossing daily from Poland to Czechoslovakia, larger numbers from Eastern Europe were expected.

Jacobson would be integral to Avigur's plan. Avigur insisted that Jacobson meet with Brichah personnel in Poland to familiarize himself with the entire region. Jacobson was to hold the official post of Joint director in Prague, but "a group of people working for Avigur would be a sub-department of the Joint." That way the Brichah would be allowed by local authorities to operate in Czechoslovakia.

Under the Schwartz-Avigur deal, the Joint paid the Brichah directly for food, transportation and other expenses for the refugees. As was customary, Saly Mayer in Switzerland transferred the funds for clandestine operations—also Joint money—to the chief Mossad representative in Prague. This spared the Joint embarrassment should an operation go sour.

But just as the Mossad geared up, the British struck back. On June 29, 1946, the day Israelis remember as "Black Saturday," British forces arrested hundreds of Jewish Agency, Haganah and Mossad leaders across Palestine in surprise raids. This attempt to stamp out illegal immigration once and for all occurred after London had rejected the Anglo-American Committee of Inquiry's proposal. British counterintelligence had discovered that the Mossad and its friends were preparing to respond on a major scale. Moshe Sharett, Golda Meir and all of the other members of the

Jewish Agency executive committee were detained. Luckily both David Ben-Gurion and Shaul Avigur were in Paris and they eluded the British dragnet. Haganah commander in chief Moshe Sneh also managed to flee in time.

The mass arrests did not put an end to the Jewish defiance. Whereas the Mossad was able to send only 20 vessels with 5,422 refugees to Palestine in 1945, the movement gained considerable momentum after the Schwartz-Avigur alliance. Rather than screen the Palestinian coast with the Royal Navy, the British shifted tactics. By August, illegal transport ships were allowed to enter Haifa, where refugees were apprehended and deported to camps on Cyprus, then a British colony. Undaunted, the Mossad continued to dispatch ship after ship. Between 1945 and 1948, 32 vessels were seized in Palestinian ports and 52,000 immigrants were interned in Cypriot camps; they stayed there until Israeli independence in 1948.

XV

Czechoslovakia:
The Avenue of Escape

If any single event in the post-war period can be said to have determined the mass Jewish exodus from Eastern Europe to the DP camps in the West, it is without doubt the pogrom in the Polish city of Kielce on July 4, 1946. A quiet city between Warsaw and Cracow, Kielce had only 200 Jews out of a pre-war Jewish population of 30,000. Violence erupted when a nine-year-old shoe-maker's son reported to the militia that Christian children were being murdered in cellars for ritual purposes. Almost instantly, a bloodthirsty mob surrounded the headquarters of the local Jewish committee. Forty-two Jews were killed and scores were injured.

The Kielce pogrom came in the wake of smaller riots and individual killings of Jews in Poland and Slovakia, and it triggered panic-stricken waves of Jews fleeing from Poland, primarily to Czechoslovakia. In Poland, Kielce was the final signal to run for one's life. Between July and November 1946, approximately 90,000 refugees escaped from Poland to the West. On some days as many as 3,000–4,000 refugees tried to enter Czechoslovakia at a single frontier crossing point.

This massive migration drastically changed the entire refugee picture in Europe. From Czechoslovakia refugees had to be rapidly moved to the DP camps in Germany, Austria and Italy. In less than four months, the Jewish population of the camps in Germany, Austria and Italy swelled from some 50,000 to over 175,000.

Most refugees fled through Czechoslovakia from Poland, and in much lesser numbers from Romania and Hungary. Some moved directly from Polish territory in the north to Stettin and then into Germany. Only a small percentage, however, succeeded in reaching Palestine at the end of their flight. The rapid deployment of Brichah, Mossad and key Joint personnel and supplies in early 1946, especially in Czechoslovakia, put in place a mechanism to deal with emergencies like Kielce that Schwartz and Avigur were convinced would develop sooner or later.

Moreover, it was discovered that the numbers of children in the Jewish camps were rising at an astounding rate. In his Joint executive committee report, Schwartz noted that just after the liberation in 1945, there were no more than 5,000 Jewish children in the camps between the ages of fourteen and eighteen. By the end of 1946, there were 24,000 children, mostly under fourteen, representing a "marked increase in the birth rate in Jewish communities . . . practically all over Europe," he observed. "Jews have a great desire to return to some kind of normal living: they are getting married and they are having children." After so much death, the birth rate exceeded the experts' calculations and projections.

On another level, the Kielce pogrom served to vindicate Schwartz and Avigur's long-held belief that most Eastern European Jews would, if they could, emigrate to Palestine. Apart from the fact that Eastern Europe and the Soviet Union had a long history of anti-Semitism (which resurfaced, alarmingly, with the collapse of Communism in the late 1980s), a special situation arose in Poland in 1945–46.

Hundreds of thousands of Jews returning from labor and death camps in Germany and from Soviet exile devoted themselves immediately to locating their missing relatives and their former homes and businesses. Not surprisingly, original owners laid claim to those properties that had survived the war. But those locals who had taken them over during the intervening war years just as naturally refused to surrender them.

These conflicts surfaced quickly and soon proliferated into daily clashes, which culminated in pogroms. Yehuda Bauer calculated that in the first nine months of 1945, 351 Polish Jews were "murdered on trains, kicked out of trains, or thrown out of running trains by the Polish population." In Cracow in August 1945 many Jews were murdered and their property destroyed in a large pogrom; after a visit to Warsaw in 1946 Jacobson reported that the only rabbi he could locate there was "clean-shaven" to avoid attacks on himself and his family. Wearing a beard and side curls marked a man as a Jew.

In addition, Polish Jews at the time were divided between loyalty to the new Communist regime (there were Jews in key posts in the government brought from Moscow) and the opposition, just as they were split among themselves between pro-Communist and anti-Communist Zionists. Inevitably, these ideological confrontations set off new rifts among Zionists. Moshe Sneh, the Haganah commander in chief, began sliding precipitately toward the Communist ideology of the Soviet Union, while Shaul Avigur, his archenemy, subscribed to Ben-Gurion's more moderate left-of-center Mapai (Labor) Party.

Through luck as much as design, an amazing cast of characters—Eastern European Jews, Palestinian emissaries and the ubiquitous American Joint representatives—was assembled in 1946, chiefly in Czechoslovakia, when the refugee onslaught from Poland began. Avigur and Schwartz had earlier concluded that Prague, astride the main east-west routes, was the natural Brichah operational center for Europe. Consequently, Czechoslovakia became a top priority in terms of the anticipated refugee flows.

Measured by the actual expenditure of the Joint's funds, Hungary had the largest single Eastern European program in 1946. Indeed, 100,000 Hungarian Jews were being fed daily at the Joint's public kitchens. But politically it was Czechoslovakia that truly mattered as the only great avenue of escape for the Jews bottled up in Poland. Besides, out of 370,000 Jews in prewar Czechoslovakia there were no more than 50,000 left, including inmates returning from the Auschwitz and Terezin concentration camps. With a reasonably good economic situation in the country, Czech and Slovak Jews were not a major concern.

Gaynor Jacobson's assignment in Czechoslovakia called for patience, equanimity and delicate diplomacy with the highest levels of the Czechoslovak government, the U.S. Army in Europe and the State Department. His job required constant discretion in his dealings with the Brichah and the Mossad, an ability to get along with Communist secret police chiefs and recalcitrant ultra-Orthodox rabbis, imagination and a talent for improvisation. Jacobson needed considerable political as well as physical courage, and with his deep sense of humanity, good nature and dedication, he was up to the task. All these qualities served him brilliantly when the Kielce crisis exploded—and long afterward.*

The Joint had reopened the Prague office immediately after liberation in 1945. Under the first two American directors, Harry Viteles and Harold Trobe, its efforts were directed toward helping the Jewish community in Czechoslovakia rebuild after the war, setting up farm producers' cooperatives in Slovakia, feeding Jews where necessary and aiding individuals in processing legal emigration abroad (though not to Palestine). The Prague office was a low-profile operation until Jacobson arrived in late April 1946.

With the official Joint-Brichah connection following the Schwartz-Avigur deal, the Brichah "boys and girls" actually became local employees of the Joint's Prague office and therefore enjoyed the full protection of the Americans. The still non-Communist Czechoslovak government turned out to be enormously helpful during the great exodus, but it rigidly insisted on the legal status of all those engaged in refugee activities. In all likelihood, the Czechoslovak authorities were unaware that most of the Joint's "local employees" were Brichah activists also working in Poland, Austria and elsewhere. There was no need for Jacobson to explain the Joint's work chapter and verse. The Czechoslovak government asked no questions and quite possibly chose to look the other way. In the end, Jacobson provided a foolproof cover for the Brichah in Prague and a first-rate, modern American "private" intelligence operation. Without this link,

* Today, more than forty years later, Jacobson is still idolized in Israel by his Palestinian and Eastern European Brichah partners; many of the latter have become Israelis and have reached ambassadorial and other top positions. When Jacobson visited Israel in the 1980s, the Mossad hosted a reception for him that was attended by virtually all of Israel's former super-spies and Mossad directors.

the Brichah would not have been able to conduct all of its invaluable rescue and migration operations.

The Joint's Prague offices occupied a massive gray six-story building, formerly headquarters of the city's Jewish community organization in old Prague. Located on Josefovska Street No. 7, a dead end leading to the Vltava River, it faced the baroque church of St. Joseph and stood around the corner from a synagogue. Jacobson's office was on the top floor, where his Canadian secretary, Lillian Benjamin, tried to maintain a semblance of order. Jacobson, who tended to be slightly eccentric, insisted on bringing his German shepherd, Lord, to the office. Lord had been given to Jacobson by a defecting Jewish soldier in the Soviet Army who claimed that the dog had killed a Nazi trooper to protect him.

Jacobson's staff was supplemented by Adolf Beneš, a Czech who had reopened the Joint office after the occupation and who had encyclopedic knowledge of local politics. Aaron Berkowitz, a young Slovak who had lived in the United States and held an American passport, served as Jacobson's interpreter. As a courtesy, the Czech government granted Jacobson diplomatic status, including CD plates for his car and jeep, which gave him great freedom of movement and access. Jacobson also retained his assimilated rank of colonel in the U.S. Army, another advantage in postwar Europe. And it was fortunate that the American ambassador in Prague at that time was the Joint's old friend Laurence Steinhardt, who had served as ambassador to Turkey in 1943–44.

The Joint's departments dealing with legal emigration and legal affairs were located on the fifth floor of the Josefovska Street building. The entire fourth floor was assigned to the Brichah "department," officially called "Immigration Office

No. 2." Here Brichah and resident Mossad operatives, acting under the Joint cover, directed all phases of illegal immigration in and out of Czechoslovakia. The Brichah contracted with Czechoslovak railways for trains to transport refugees from border to border, assigned guides and escorts to border crossings to lead the refugees and provided food, shelter and clothing for them. In one corner of the fourth floor, the Brichah housed its passport and visa forgery section—a vital adjunct to its operation. Without this link, the Brichah would not have been able to conduct all of its invaluable rescue and migration operations.

As elsewhere in Eastern Europe, the Brichah organization in Czechoslovakia was essentially democratic. There were no real bosses, except the country commanders often appointed by Avigur in Paris. The political makeup of the Brichah was also diverse, inasmuch as volunteers ranged from right-wing to left-wing Zionists, from Reform to ultra-Orthodox religious communities. Inevitably, there were different opinions on every subject—schisms that remain alive in Israel to this day. In retrospect, it is remarkable how effectively these Brichah factions worked together when it came to the formidable and most important task of shepherding hundreds of thousands of scared and destitute Jews across much of Europe.

The chief Mossad delegate in Prague was Moshe Govsman, a stocky, blond, blue-eyed Palestinian who also acted as deputy to Ephraim Dekel, the European Brichah commander. Govsman, who was a veteran of the Palmach commandos of the Haganah, was really a financial wizard, and he was able to practice his true vocation to his heart's content for the Brichah.

Because of the immense fluctuations in currency rates in Eastern Europe immediately after the war, the U.S. dollar could fetch ten or more times the official rate on the black market. Govsman was thus in a position to enormously increase the Joint's purchasing power. (In Prague, the spread was between 50 korunas at the official rate and 800 at the black.) Huge fortunes were made by professional black marketeers all over Europe, but even respectable institutions—such as the Joint—became almost openly involved in the currency black market. It was simply impossible to conduct rescue and relief operations at the artificial exchange rates established by local governments. In fact, in many countries the Joint formally negotiated with the government for a special dollar rate, "splitting the difference."

Levi Argov was another key Mossad-Brichah operative who worked closely with Jacobson. A twenty-nine-year-old Czechoslovak-born kibbutz farmer who had emigrated to Palestine in 1939, Argov returned to Prague on Avigur's orders. Argov had served as a commander in the Jewish Settlement Police, and on V-E Day landed, disguised as a Jewish Brigade soldier, in Taranto, Italy. Avigur's orders, characteristically vague, were to "see what you can do to help the Jews" in Eastern Europe. Argov made his way to Budapest and then to Bratislava, the capital of Slovakia, where he established a Brichah organization. Just across the Danube from Austrian territory, Bratislava was a crucial point in illegal immigration, as the refugees streaming into Austria from Poland, Romania and Hungary had to pass through it.

Argov, like Govsman, was also a financial brain. He convinced Schwartz and Saly Mayer to abandon their system of supplying Eastern European Brichah movements with local currency (based on the official exchange rate) and to provide them with dollars instead. Once a month, he traveled to Switzerland from Budapest or Prague, each time bringing back between $300,000 and $400,000 in Joint funds, which was then divided among Brichah organizations in Czechoslovakia, Hungary, Romania and Austria for sale on local black markets.

Argov had the extraordinary idea of using József Cardinal Mindszenty, head of the Roman Catholic Church in Hungary, as a source of local currency for the Brichah. As he described it: "Mindszenty gave me money in pengös in Budapest, as much as I wanted, without signing anything, and I put it in dollars in his account in a Swiss bank." The Joint approved of this mutually advantageous deal. It enabled Mindszenty and the Church to transfer their money from Hungary, already falling under Communist domination, to accounts in the West, while, as Argov puts it, "it was a better way to bring money from Switzerland to Hungary without risk." Otherwise, Argov said, "I had to smuggle the money." The cardinal's Hungarian currency was spent primarily on food for hungry Jews in Budapest—sometimes up to 4,000 people had to be fed each night. In all likelihood, Mindszenty, who paid the Brichah a 15 percent commission on the transfers, knew how his money was being used. For one thing, Argov had met Mindszenty through a Jewish religious leader in Budapest. And, as Argov said, "such things you can do only if you have confidence."

The floating Mossad contingent in Czechoslovakia, all of whom were in constant contact with Jacobson, included Elhanan Gafni, a Czechoslovak-born operative also sent by Avigur. Gafni spent much of his time at Polish border crossings. He recalled one occasion when he spotted an elderly Jew walking into Czechoslovakia with a fiddle under his arm. "Because we had asked the people to put all their baggage on carts, I told him he shouldn't be carrying the violin. But the man said, 'My violin is very dear to me,' and

I was so proud to see how the Jewish people liked their instruments, the kind of people they are. Then he asked, 'Do you know why it's so dear to me? Well, it's full of greens . . . dollars.' "

Bubu Landa, a gregarious and resourceful Slovak whose parents died in a Nazi concentration camp, was another key member of Jacobson's team. Landa was involved in all aspects of the operation, from surveying border-crossing points to complex negotiations with Soviet and American military commanders and Czechoslovak refugee organizations. His job with the Joint was a cover for his Brichah activities.

When Soviet forces liberated the Terezín concentration camp in mid-1945 and the military commander decided that 400 to 500 young Polish Jews should be repatriated to Poland, it was Bubu Landa who succeeded in convincing the Soviet major that the survivors were really needed in Palestine. With the assistance of a cooperative Czech Repatriation Office representative, they reached an agreement (which Landa signed on behalf of the Joint) that provided for the transport of the Terezín group to the American Zone of Germany. From a U.S. Army officer he had befriended, Landa obtained a document stating that the Army would assume responsibility for transferring the refugees to the Joint so they could then be transported to Palestine. Sylvia Neulander, a young woman representing the Jewish Agency, was able to furnish enough blank British immigration certificates for the Terezín group. The Czech railway provided Landa with a train, and the Polish Jews were duly turned over to the U.S. Third Army in Pilsen.

———

The Joint and the Czech Repatriation Office had had the foresight to establish a small camp in the town of Náchod before the Kielce pogrom. North of Prague and just below the Polish frontier, Náchod, which had only 20 remaining Jews out of a prewar population of 300, was an ideal entry point. Polish Jews had begun to enter Czechoslovakia there in fairly limited numbers, taking advantage of its position as a railhead, which enabled them to catch a train and keep going.

Jews in Náchod contacted the Joint and the Czech authorities for assistance, and the Brichah was alerted to the possibility of larger-scale activities there. The Czech Repatriation Office set up its small camp with two barracks in late 1945 to assist and feed the arriving refugees. The Polish Brichah began concentrating potential refugees around Katowice and in the small town of Klodzko, some ten miles east of Náchod. A one-lane road linked Klodzko with the Czech border, meandering through the mountains. About 5,000 Jews passed through Náchod in 1945, with the local chapter of the Red Cross handling most of the traffic.

Bubu Landa made it a practice to visit Náchod more frequently in the spring of 1946, currying favor with the local officials and citizenry. Other Brichah emissaries, such as Leale Schlinder, a young Polish orphan, and the American Joint representative Anne Liepah were assigned full-time to Náchod.

Jewish refugees coming through Náchod had one extraordinary advantage: Pick and Beck (nobody seems to have recorded their first names for posterity), natives of Náchod and close friends, were the first Jews to return from Auschwitz to their hometown. They quickly became the leaders of their minuscule Jewish community, soon rebuilt their lumber business and within a year were highly influential citizens who worked out of an oak-paneled office.

When the first Polish Jewish refugees began crossing into Czechoslovakia, the two friends, both tall, impressive men in their late thirties, decided that it was their responsibility to help them. They had informed the Joint in Prague that they would assist the refugees "as long as they were coming one here, one there, and so on," Landa recalled. But as the problem grew, the Joint, in cooperation with the Red Cross and other Czechoslovak government agencies, took over the work at Náchod.

Jacobson remembered Pick and Beck as "very clean-cut, well dressed, very gregarious." Though Pick and Beck had initially provided lodging for the refugees, as well as rations of dark bread, salt and garlic, the Joint soon had to start giving them funds to pay for food and train transportation to Bratislava, from where the Jews entered Austria. At that stage, the Czechoslovak border police at Náchod did not interfere with the refugees, but Polish guards on the other side were occasionally trigger-happy, and Pick was in charge of bribing them when required with Joint-supplied American cigarettes. Eastern Europe, mercifully, was full of Picks and Becks.

Indeed, bribery was part of daily life in Eastern Europe; Soviet soldiers there and in Austria were the principal beneficiaries. The Joint traditionally provided American cigarettes, vodka (they didn't care for whisky) and "merry" young women to encourage Soviet border guards to look the other way as refugee convoys passed by. Mordecai Surkiss, the first European Brichah commander, estimated that between 1945 and 1947 approximately $500,000 in gold and U.S. currency was expended *monthly* to pay off Soviet commanders on the Austrian-Slovak frontier (then in the Soviet Occupation Zone) and the Austrian-Hungarian border to enable Jewish transports to enter Austria.

However, there were also Soviet Jewish officers who helped the Brichah for nothing, often exceeding their authority in order to let Jews pass. One Soviet colonel who commanded the garrison in the Austrian city of Graz ordered—at Surkiss's request—the mayor to make two local hotels available to Jewish refugees. Soldiers from the Jewish Brigade then smuggled the refugees over the border at night into Italy. Another senior Soviet officer quietly tipped off the Brichah in Austria that a train would be available to bring Jews from the Slovak border to Vienna after a vehicular bridge over the Danube had been placed off-limits to Jewish refugees by the Soviet authorities. The officer told a Brichah commander, "What's the matter with you people? Can't you read? The military order says you cannot use *this* bridge but it says nothing about taking trains over other bridges." Even some non-Jewish Soviet officers acted in a helpful manner toward escaping Jews, offering discreet advice to the Brichah.

U.S. Army officers up to the highest level could usually be depended upon for support, and the Jewish chaplains maintained close contacts with the Brichah. As the American journalist I. F. Stone, who traveled extensively with the illegal refugees, wrote at the time, "the U.S. Army is the best friend the Jews have in Europe today." French officers in the French Occupation Zone were often on the side of the Jews too.

Only the British had turned themselves into the enemy of the Jews. Under strict orders to nip in the bud Jewish illegal immigration to Palestine, British military intelligence spent much valuable time chasing the Brichah and the Mossad. By mid-1946, with waves of fleeing Jews breaking over Europe, it became open warfare.

XVI

Covert Cooperation

The success or failure of the great Jewish exodus of 1946 hinged, first and foremost, on the goodwill of the Czechoslovak government. Politically, it was a very difficult year for the first postwar coalition government in Prague, but many high-ranking officials in both Communist and non-Communist camps put their careers and lives on the line to save Jews. In Prague's treacherous political environment, Jacobson, with his diplomatic acumen, attractive personality and astounding luck, carried off an extraordinary performance.

In 1946 Czechoslovakia was slowly evolving toward Communist rule. As a result of a 1945 compromise between Czechoslovak leaders of the London-based government-in-exile and Communist leaders who spent the war in Moscow, a National Unity government was formed under President Eduard Beneš, who had been ousted when the Nazis invaded his country in 1939. Ždenek Fierlinger, a left-wing Social Democrat from Moscow, was the Prime Minister, but the real power was held by Fierlinger's deputy, Klement Gottwald, a Moscow Communist. Václav Nosek, a Communist who sat out the war in London, headed the Interior Ministry, which included the secret police and the frontier guards.

But the most visible and internationally influential Cabinet member was Foreign Minister Jan Masaryk, son of Tomáš Masaryk, who had founded the Czechoslovak republic after World War I. Masaryk was an intimate friend of President Beneš; having served in the exiled London government and having frequently visited the United States, he had countless personal friends in Britain and America.

On May 26, 1946, just a month after Jacobson arrived in Prague to take over the Joint's office, Czechoslovakia held its first free parliamentary elections. Surprisingly, the Communist Party won a plurality. In an alliance with Fierlinger's Social Democrats, the Communists obtained the control of 51 percent of the parliamentary seats. Beneš therefore was obliged to appoint Gottwald as Prime Minister on July 3 (just one day before the Kielce pogrom). But Beneš kept Masaryk as a top adviser. Because of his fine international connections, the Communists wished to retain Masaryk, certainly until their coup d'état in 1948. This decision was a great relief to Jacobson, who had become Masaryk's close friend. Jacobson had immediate access to Masaryk, even to his bedroom in the ministry's Czernin Palace, where Masaryk did much of his work.*

---

* It was a heady time in Czechoslovakia, before the Communist coup ended a brief honeymoon of democracy. For the Jacobsons, who lived with their two infant daughters (and Gaynor's German shepherd) in a luxury villa in Prague's Vinohrady district, it was an opportunity to build marvelous contacts through the arts and their personal brand of diplomacy.

Prague was always rich in musical life, and it attracted great artists from all over

On his first official call in Prague, Jacobson outlined for Masaryk his plans and goals in Czechoslovakia concerning the local Jewish community and foreign Jews in transit. He omitted specific mention of the Brichah and illegal immigration. Masaryk assured him that he would be personally responsible for the free passage of Jews and for their welfare while in Czechoslovakia. Masaryk advised Jacobson to take out additional political insurance by establishing contacts with the Communists, who were extremely influential in the government even before the May elections. He arranged for Jacobson to meet Gottwald, who then served as Deputy Prime Minister. It was a relationship that proved to be crucial when the Communist chief was promoted to Prime Minister in July. Masaryk also made a point of introducing Jacobson to Vladimir Clementis, a Slovak Communist who was Deputy Foreign Minister and who was later executed in the Stalinist purges in Czechoslovakia. Jacobson went so far as to call on President Beneš at Hradčany Castle to explain his mission. Beneš, he reported, heard him out in "a most friendly fashion."

But the most important contact, Masaryk told Jacobson, was with Zoltán Toman, the Communist Deputy Interior Minister in charge of the State Security Department and, as such, the country's top policeman. Nosek was a mere figurehead as Interior Minister; it was Toman who controlled Czechoslovakia's frontiers with his special border units. To-

---

the world. Leonard Bernstein visited the Jacobsons and practiced on their grand piano. Yehudi Menuhin, the great American violinist, also came to the villa and he practiced there too, accompanied by his sister on the piano. On one occasion, Schwartz turned up in Prague, and Moshe Sneh, the Haganah commander in chief, joined Leonard Bernstein and other friends for an evening of music and storytelling at the Jacobsons'.

man also kept an eye on the foreigners in the country through his secret police, the StB. He had a reputation for toughness, and because Jewish refugees tended to reach frontiers without documents of any kind, Jacobson was concerned that they would be kept out of Czechoslovakia. "If Toman is on your side," Masaryk advised Jacobson, "the frontiers will be open to your Jews."

Toman was born Ascher-Zelig Goldberger in the village of Sobrance near the Ukrainian border in 1909, five years before the outbreak of World War I. He became a Communist as a teenager after having experienced widespread anti-Semitism. "I made myself a Communist," he maintained. When he was thirteen, a village youth "came to me and said, 'You stinking Jew,' and he hit me in my face, and I fell down." Arriving home, bleeding, Toman asked his father to denounce the attacker to the authorities. But his father replied, "Now, my son, we are not going there," and when he asked why, the reply was: "Because we Jews have been born to suffer." Toman became convinced that "the Jewish question can be solved only through Communism."

Toman was the fourth of eight children of Chali and Rosa Thoman Goldberger. When he decided later to drop the name of Goldberger, young Zoltán made up the new one from his mother's maiden name, Thoman. Zoltán was a common Hungarian name, and friends later called him Zolo. At fifteen, he got a bank clerk's job and worked for three years while studying at night for a teacher's certificate; at that point, Toman aspired to teach. But he also devoured Marxist literature and in 1928 he joined the Communist Party youth organization at the age of eighteen. The Communist Party was legal in Czechoslovakia between the wars, and by then Toman already firmly "believed in the dictator-ship of the proletariat."

His ambition was to attend the university, and after a stint of recruiting at home for the Communist Party, he traveled to Prague. The first place he visited there was the Communist Party headquarters, where he met, among other top leaders, Klement Gottwald, the party chairman. Toman received his law degree in Prague in less than five years, a record in those days, and then he moved to Skalica, a Slovak town near Bratislava, where he went into partnership with a Nazi lawyer who was bedridden and virtually paralyzed. "I was one of the best-paid lawyers in Czechoslovakia," he remem-bered. Toman remained in Skalica until the Germans oc-cupied Czechoslovakia in March 1939. He had married at the university a fellow Communist, a Polish Jew named Tesla Gutman. But by then the Nazis had outlawed the Communist Party.

In May 1939, the Tomans fled to London, where they joined the Czechoslovak Communist Party section. With his political refugee status Toman was allowed to work, first as a houseman for a rich Jewish Austrian woman, then as a bookkeeper at the Lyons tearoom chain. When the Beneš Czechoslovak government-in-exile and the Communists reached a coalition agreement in London, the party picked Toman to serve as the social works director in the reorganized Cabinet.

It was in London that Toman met Masaryk; he told him that after the war Czechoslovakia would be the "bridge" between the Soviets and the West. Masaryk replied, "Yes, with our bodies we shall be the bridge and the Russians will walk over us with their boots."

Later, in Moscow, Gottwald startled Toman with an ac-count of a top secret meeting with Stalin and a small Eastern

European leadership group, who were told that "the war is nearing its finish, and you are going back to Czechoslovakia and to the other countries as leaders of the Communist Party." Toman was even more surprised when Gottwald confided, "I am telling this to you because it has been decided that you will be the head of security in Czechoslovakia—you will be the head of all security because you are an intelligent, clever person, and a flexible one."

With a small Soviet Army detachment, Toman traveled by car to Czechoslovakia in the snowy winter of 1945. He reached Košice in Slovakia in early spring, and arrived in Prague immediately after Soviet forces liberated the city in May. His wife joined him within days. Toman's first task as chief of security was to organize the Communist militia, and in due course he became the First Deputy Interior Minister.

In the spring of 1946 Masaryk arranged a meeting between Toman and Jacobson at the Interior Ministry. What Jacobson did not know at the time was that Toman himself was Jewish. In fact, few people knew this, and Masaryk chose not to tell him.

Jacobson learned of Toman's heritage through an amazing coincidence. Shortly after he arrived in Prague, he met a Czech Jewish community leader by the name of Imre Rosenberg. Rosenberg, who was on the verge of leaving for a two-month honeymoon in Palestine, offered to rent Jacobson his house in Prague for the period of his absence. Jacobson, tired of his room at the Alcron Hotel, agreed. He was then introduced to Rosenberg's wife, Aranka, who was Jewish and, as she told Jacobson, Toman's sister.

Toman's Jewish origins clearly had everything to do with his attitude toward the wandering Jews. Masaryk had told

Jacobson that he would resign as Foreign Minister if Jews were denied entry, but fortunately Toman's influence obviated such an action, although the Czech-Polish frontier was occasionally closed for short periods. Toman had the authority to shut the borders to the Jews, but he chose to keep them open even under the most trying of circumstances. Indeed, Toman deserves full credit for the rescue of at least 200,000 Jews who traversed Czechoslovakia on their way to the West and to Palestine.

At their initial meeting, Jacobson sensed that "something clicked between us." It was the most important encounter of his entire tenure in Czechoslovakia. Neither the Mossad nor the Brichah could aspire to such high-level access: it could only be the Joint and Jacobson. Toman interrupted Jacobson's description of the plight of the Jews by admitting, "You're telling me a story I already know everything about." The Jews, Toman continued, had already suffered enough, "but something similar could happen again," and Toman felt compelled to do whatever was in his power to help them. There would be "no problem" with Jews in transit, he informed Jacobson. Toman then told his secretary to "send the following order to all the commanders of the border police: that Jews without any documentation should be allowed to enter Czechoslovakia. It is enough for the person to say, 'I'm Jewish.' " And so, Toman recalled, "the Jews arrived, and our friend Jacobson took care of them. I gave the order; I didn't ask anybody." In fact, Toman claimed, he did not inform anybody in the government of his decision, not even Gottwald, the Deputy Prime Minister and chairman of the Communist Party.

Much of Toman's power derived from his position as First Deputy Interior Minister. As he later put it, "I had the files on everybody," including the Gestapo wartime files on inmates of Nazi concentration camps, as well as on Czechs who collaborated with the Germans.* His principal responsibilities, in the first postwar government, were foreign espionage, counterintelligence and internal security. He was concerned with security inside the Communist Party and, as one who had experienced anti-Semitism firsthand, launched his own private campaign against anti-Semitism in the top echelons of the party. But his youthful idealism would soon be betrayed. It became the foundation for his actions regarding the Jews—and the price he paid for them.

* Among the collaborators were the Communist poet Julius Fučik, eventually killed by the Nazis, and the general secretary of Beneš's own party.

XVII

The Flood Through Náchod

When Jacobson asked Toman in the spring of 1946 for special treatment for Polish Jews who were trying to enter Czechoslovakia without travel documents, he was thinking in terms of several hundred people monthly, at most. He had no idea of the eventual magnitude of the onslaught. This was the result of two separate migratory movements.*

* Before they ironed out their deal, refugees had been entering Czechoslovakia with forged documents of every description. But this was neither easy nor foolproof. One ingenious ruse was the "Greek bluff."

The Brichah had learned that non-Jewish Greeks from Nazi concentration and labor camps were being repatriated, often in a chaotic fashion, and the idea occurred to someone that since many Jews have fairly dark complexions, they should be made to pass for Greeks. Accordingly, the Brichah document forgery shops began churning out papers identifying the bearers as former German prisoners returning home to Athens or Salonika. The "Greeks" were warned by their Brichah guides that during the crossing of border areas, the only language they were allowed to speak was Hebrew, if they knew it, because the border police

By late 1945, Polish Jews who had been deported to Central Asia by the Soviets after the occupation of eastern Poland in 1939 were allowed to return home. The Soviets simply wanted to be rid of them. The new Communist regime in Poland, several of whose key leaders were Jewish, thought the returnees could (and should) be absorbed into the "People's Republic." Counting the children born during exile, between 150,000 and 200,000 Jews—hungry and desperate—migrated from the East into Poland, returning to find whatever they could from the past.

Despite efforts to help them resettle, however, they were generally not welcome back in Poland. Most of them spoke Yiddish or Russian—not Polish—which further alienated them. Moreover, they were surrounded by hundreds of thousands of Poles from peasant backgrounds who had been transferred to Silesia when the Soviets annexed eastern Poland. It was a highly unstable state of affairs that sympathizers in America, and even in Palestine, failed to comprehend fully.

In his report to the Joint executive committee in May 1946, Schwartz described the predicament of the Polish exiles: "Some of them said to me: 'We have spent years in Russia. We have worked very hard; we have been called upon to perform the kind of labor to which we were not accustomed. It was a hard life during those war years in Russia. But we had one thing: we had personal security. We felt safe; we were not afraid to walk out on the streets at night. And now we come back to Poland—to our own country—and we find that we are constantly in danger, that

---

would assume it was Greek. Polish, Russian and Yiddish were forbidden; those who spoke no Hebrew had no option but silence. Known as Operation Z, the Greek ploy succeeded until the Czechoslovaks agreed to let Jewish refugees travel without documents and no questions were asked.

our lives are imperiled, that we cannot wander out into the streets of an evening.' "

In addition to these returnees from the East, a second prospective disaster concerned the 20,000 Polish Jews released from German concentration camps. They too had hoped to locate homes, businesses and families. But they found virtually nothing to assure them of any kind of reasonable future in Poland. The surviving Jewish community of about 60,000 souls could offer them no optimism.

The principal difference between Jews returning from Central Asia and those from Germany was that the latter were much more aware of the options available to them. Whereas the "Asians" had survived literally in isolation, the Jews from the concentration camps and the DP camps—on the whole much better educated to begin with—knew that Palestine could, sooner or later, be a solution for them. In broad terms, they knew about illegal immigration; some had been in contact with Jewish Brigade soldiers and even with Brichah activists.

Soon after returning to Poland, most of these survivors concluded that their best course of action was to try to go back to the DP camps in Germany. From there they hoped that the route to Palestine might open up. With or without Brichah assistance, the refugees began filtering out of Poland into the Stettin area on the Baltic—formerly German territory—in an attempt to reach Berlin and the American Zone. Another route was to move from Silesia through Wroclaw (formerly Breslau). Others tried to cross into Czechoslovakia over the "green borders" in the Carpathian Mountains and the Tatra chain or through the regular frontier crossings.

But the easiest route from Poland was still through Náchod. According to Yehuda Bauer, the exodus "gained

momentum" in March and April 1946, with Zionists accounting for a significant percentage of it. Schwartz reported to
the Joint's executive committee that in May 1946 "only 3,000
Jews left Poland for Germany," but the numbers jumped to
10,000 in June—and this was still before Kielce.

The Joint faced a tremendous responsibility. Tens of
thousands of Jews had to be shepherded back to Poland
from the Soviet Union and distributed in various localities.
New homes had to be improvised, new quarters found and
hospitals had to be set up for the many sick returnees.
Moreover, provisions had to be made for thousands of
children. And all of this "had to be done primarily with the
resources that the JDC was placing at the disposal of the
Polish Jewish community." The Poles were so grateful that
President Bolesláw Bierut, a Communist, decorated Schwartz
with the Order of Polonia Restituta, the highest civilian
award. But after Kielce, the bottom suddenly fell out of the
whole Polish situation, and the Joint had to concentrate on
the panic-stricken flight of the Jews from Poland.

Almost immediately after the July pogrom, masses of Polish
Jews began pouring across the border to Náchod. There was
railroad service from Náchod to Brno in Moravia, to Bratislava, and, with luck, to Vienna. Since there was no railway
connection from the Polish side to Náchod, the refugees
streamed from Kłodzko and points north to the border by
any means possible. Most came by truck or horse cart and
then walked the last few miles to the actual frontier. The
highway from Kłodzko to Náchod runs through a valley of
farm villages and small mountain health resorts, and in the
summer the trip was not too exhausting. Others tried to
enter the American Zone in Germany through Aš on the

Czech-German border. But the U.S. Army wasn't quite as permissive as the Czechs, so that route was infrequently used.

The border facilities at Náchod were extremely limited, and as soon as word of the mounting exodus reached Jacobson in Prague, he began sending out reinforcements. Brichah emissaries and Jacobson's own staff members joined forces with the handful of Czechoslovak officials in Náchod. But no one was prepared for the frightening number of refugees, which increased from 1,000 per day to a high of 3,800. Another staffed crossing was opened at Broumov, which also had a railway station, some fifteen miles away.

Jacobson believed that the failure of Poland's Roman Catholic primate, August Cardinal Hlond, to immediately condemn the Kielce pogrom exacerbated rising fears among the Jewish populace. Even though Polish authorities executed nine of the rioters convicted of murder, Jews still fled at an alarming rate. The Brichah's Mordecai Surkiss, who went to Kielce two days after the pogrom, found the situation "very bad."

Jacobson and Czechoslovak officials decided to transport the refugees to Bratislava by trains provided by Czechoslovak authorities. The Czechs were concerned about an epidemic, so before boarding, the refugees were registered by name, checked medically, fed and even clothed, if necessary. Each train, however, had a maximum capacity of only 1,000 passengers, and as a result, growing numbers of refugees ended up spending the night in Náchod and Broumov. Exhausted, some without a place to rest, "they fell on the floor sleeping, mainly women and children. Men often had to stay up all night," Jacobson recalled.

Dorothy Greene, an American psychiatric social worker assigned to the Joint's Prague office, was dispatched to Broumov, where she became the co-director of the refugee operation. The camp in Broumov had a capacity of 1,000, but one week it had to accommodate 2,600 because the borders en route to the American Zone had been temporarily closed. In a letter to the Joint's headquarters, Greene described the situation of the returnees from Central Asia: "Here it is a matter of supplying immediate needs only. They are almost destitute for clothes and the food situation is a daily problem. Hours are long. We have no regard for time . . . Groups come here completely disorganized and the whole cry is, 'I want, I want, I want . . .' "

The human dimensions of the exodus were staggering. Hasidic Jews compounded the overcrowding by refusing to travel after sundown on Friday because of the Sabbath, thereby adding a day to their stay at the border. "They wouldn't even give you their name to make a list because you shouldn't write on the Sabbath," Bubu Landa recalled. Some refugees "behaved like savages, fighting their way to get on the train . . . They were frightened and aggressive. . . . But the impression we had was that these people were running from hell."

Through Náchod alone, 17,903 Polish Jews crossed in July, 32,441 in August, 15,682 in September, 5,682 in October, and 2,017 in November, for a five-month total of 73,725 at just one border. Approximately 90,000 Jews left Poland through all exits during 1946, and Schwartz warned his executive committee in closed session that another 100,000 Polish Jews might follow, leaving "only a handful" in Poland. In the meantime, the Joint had to supplement the food the Czechoslovak authorities were providing the refugees.

Food was so scarce at the borders that the Joint had to help supply basic rations, sometimes taking it from stocks reserved for the Czech Jewish community. Because the trains from Náchod stopped at Brno in Moravia, hot meals—

subsidized by the Joint—were served by local Jewish families to the refugees there at night. The Joint also fed the refugees in Bratislava before they crossed into Austria. The Austrian Brichah finally assumed responsibility for meals in Vienna —with the Joint's funds. All told, the Joint had to make emergency purchases of 25 million pounds of high-calorie foods for the new refugees.

Jacobson's operation ran so low on funds that he rushed to Vienna to meet with Schwartz to plead for a higher budget. Schwartz consented, and cabled New York for more money. The Administrative Committee voted immediately to appropriate $425,000 "for the emergency needs of the Brichah." This allowed Jacobson to borrow from Prague banks for the most urgent local food purchases.

With the Polish exodus and the mass support of Jews in Romania and Hungary, the Joint spent $18 million for supplies (approximately $200 million in 1991 dollars), for a record total of $58.9 million in 1946. By all accounts, the Czechoslovak government—from Beneš and Masaryk to Gottwald and Toman—acted with extraordinary goodwill to smooth the Jewish passage through their country, although problems did crop up here and there. Regrettably, Prague was treated shabbily by UNRRA, whose representatives reneged on their commitment to reimburse the government for the cost of rail transportation for the Jewish refugees. At the end of the exodus, Czechoslovakia, which never asked for a prepayment for the trains, was owed $1 million. The bill remained unpaid forty-five years later.

Notwithstanding the benevolence displayed by the Czecho-slovak government, the Jewish exodus was an exceedingly delicate, sensitive and difficult operation. Not the least of the problems was the British diplomatic and intelligence offensive against illegal Jewish emigration to Palestine.

After the Kielce exodus Philip Nichols, the British ambassador in Prague, voiced the first official protest against the active role played by Czechoslovakia in facilitating the mass movement of refugee Jews, who, he knew, were bound to wind up in DP camps and would then press for emigration to Palestine. Nichols demanded Jacobson's expulsion from Czechoslovakia. Masaryk, naturally, rejected the request with indignation, and then hastened to inform Gaynor amid peals of laughter.

Next, for wholly different reasons, protests were delivered by Soviet ambassador Valerian Zorin (whose chief function in Prague was to prepare a Communist coup d'état) and by American ambassador Steinhardt. Because of special relations between Communist parties, Zorin handed his protest to Prime Minister Gottwald, bypassing Beneš and Masaryk. The Soviets complained that Czechoslovakia was improperly allowing Jews to emigrate from sister socialist countries. But what seemed to bother Moscow was that the movement involved Jews released from Central Asia who now were trying to reach Palestine.

Gottwald, in turn, complained to Toman that he had never been informed of the order to let Polish Jews freely enter Czechoslovakia without travel documents. Indeed, nobody in the government hierarchy knew about the order until Zorin and Steinhardt made their formal protests. But Toman succeeded in convincing Gottwald that if the frontiers were closed to the Jews, it would seem as if Czechoslovakia was succumbing to British and American pressures, which sought the same objective. In the strange world of Communist logic, Toman won the day. The Soviets dropped the subject—but the NKVD, the Soviet secret service, remembered that Toman had issued the order.

Almost immediately, Toman was embroiled in another squabble with the Soviets—and the NKVD. Late in 1946 Interior Minister Václav Nosek told him that "the Russians claimed that we have camps filled with Jews here, and that these Jews have arms." Toman admitted there were camps containing Jews. When Nosek asked why he hadn't been informed, Toman replied, "Is it not enough that I have this problem? Should I burden you with it? After all, you have a Jewish wife." But he denied that there were weapons in the Jewish camps, and when Nosek said that Soviet officers wished to inspect the camps, Toman replied that they could go in two days. Nosek then claimed that Toman "sent people from the ministry there to hide the arms, and when the Russians went to the camps they couldn't find any." In fact, the camp refugees were being trained—with Toman's permission—by Haganah instructors to use rifles and machine guns in preparation for their emigration to Palestine.

Around the same time in 1946, Toman listened to Haganah and Mossad envoys plead for authorization to purchase arms in Czechoslovakia, a leading manufacturer of weaponry. The Haganah's permanent undercover representative in Prague, Felix Doron, and Mossad deputy chief Ehud Avriel had come to the Interior Ministry on a secret mission to propose the deal. Toman, who had the power of decision on arms sales, decided in favor of the Palestinians with the concurrence of Gottwald, Nosek and General Ludvik Svoboda, the Defense Minister. "They all agreed," he recalled, "and Soviet objections didn't come until much later." Toman seemed to be deliberately taunting the Russians.

Toman's clash with Ambassador Steinhardt had its own

element of vindictiveness. Toman seemed to be out to punish the American ambassador for a stance he considered anti-Semitic. It irked Toman that Steinhardt, as a Jew, carried out instructions from Washington that were not completely pro-Jewish. According to Toman, Steinhardt not only protested in the name of the United States government that Jews were flowing through Czechoslovakia and into the American Zone, a claim to which Beneš pleaded ignorance; he also recommended that Toman be removed from his post "because the Jews are always in favor of the Jews, and you should have there a Christian, not a Jew."

Masaryk then informed Toman that Steinhardt wanted him to close the border with Poland. Toman, however, insisted that the ambassador produce a written protest, and when it was submitted, he asked for a copy and arranged to have the top secret document privately photographed. Toman called Steinhardt and, dispensing with pleasantries, said, "I'm going to send the National Guard and they will take you out of your office, and like a sack of potatoes we shall throw you out."

Toman summoned Maurice Hindus, a French Jew who was a well-known foreign correspondent for the New York *Herald Tribune*, and explained the situation. He then handed the incredulous journalist a copy of Steinhardt's letter, and added, "But if you tell anybody that you got this note from me, my life is in danger." Hindus's story was published and Steinhardt made such a fuss about it that President Beneš instructed Prime Minister Gottwald to have Toman's organization seek out the traitor who had leaked the document. Two weeks later Toman phoned Gottwald to report that a U.S. embassy employee bore responsibility, "but I can't tell you the name. You have to accept that I am the only one who knows this man."

The Soviets, meanwhile, continued to press for the closing of the border. Gottwald and Nosek ordered Toman to comply, but he ignored them, using an old schoolboy's excuse: "I had so much work to do that I forgot it." Finally, Nosek gave him an ultimatum: "You are playing with your life. Please close the frontiers." In the absurd world of Communist politics such bizarre situations often arose among top leaders, and this time Toman obeyed and closed the Polish border. Thousands of Polish Jewish refugees began to back up on the other side, and Toman—working quietly but closely with Jacobson and Schwartz—turned to a new strategy which verged on high-wire acrobatics.

Toman urged Masaryk, before the Foreign Minister left for the United States in July 1946 (two weeks after Kielce), to persuade Gottwald to reopen the frontier. The next day Toman himself issued the order, having sent this message: "Dear Klement: Yesterday at eleven o'clock in the evening, Masaryk phoned me to say that he had visited you because he wanted you to open the frontier, and you agreed to it. Because of this, I opened the frontier." Gottwald, who had been sick in bed, called Toman for a confrontation, but, in the end, he let him keep the borders open.

Toman speculated that if a non-Jewish Communist had held his government post, Jacobson would have been refused outright in his request to let Jewish refugees enter Czechoslovakia without documents. "The Jews were not liked by the Communists," Toman explained. "The Communists didn't even like my giving Jews clothing and food. The majority said, 'We have to think of how to solve the problems of our people,' and Jews were not generally considered 'our people.' " Had the Jews been bottled up in Poland, Jacobson believed, "there would have been more incidents, more pogroms, and more Jews would have died . . . it was very explosive."

On July 26, three weeks after Kielce, the divided Czechoslovak government ironed out a compromise of its own. The Cabinet took the formal decision to leave the frontier open, but the refugees would be allowed to remain only a minimal time in the country. The Western governments were asked to help with a solution for the refugee problem, and UNRRA was solicited to help pay for the rail transportation already being provided within Czechoslovakia. The Cabinet was informed that day that the Joint had agreed to come up with nearly $250,000 in new funds for refugees. As Yehuda Bauer described it, the Joint's action "was a decisive factor in influencing the Communist vote at the Cabinet meeting." It was a major victory not only for Toman and his Joint friends but for the whole future of illegal immigration— and, quite possibly, for the future of Israel.

The refugee movements were entirely spontaneous, and not even the Brichah could have started or stopped them. The Joint, however, remained deeply involved during the entire period in high-level policy discussions and negotiations with governments and military commands—an unprecedented situation for a relief organization.

At the height of the exodus, for example, Jacobson was invited by General Joseph T. McNarney, the U.S. Army commander in chief in Europe, to brief him on the unfolding events. Late in 1946, Jacobson, rather than Ambassador Steinhardt, was charged by General McNarney with proposing to Prime Minister Gottwald (and to Toman) a plan that would enable 10,000 Jewish refugees from Poland en route to American-run DP camps in Germany to spend the winter in Czechoslovakia's Sudeten region to alleviate the human pressures in the camps. Gottwald agreed in principle (after lengthy negotiations which lasted through the winter) once McNarney committed himself in writing to take the refugees back in the spring. But in the end the idea was dropped as impractical. As matters stood at the close of 1946, there were 250,000 Jewish displaced persons in Western Europe—with no place to go.

XVIII

Special Interests

The sheer magnitude of the exodus from Poland and the endless political issues and dilemmas it had brought to the fore were not the only aspects of the challenge that faced the Joint and the Brichah during that incredible summer of 1946. Solutions had to be found for special Jewish religious requirements that often defied patience and imagination. A particular problem concerned thousands of ultra-Orthodox rabbis, rabbinical students and faithful who poured into Czechoslovakia among the refugees demanding treatment and care. Some of the rabbis had up to twenty-two children in their families.

At one point, there were as many as 700 rabbis and thousands of yeshiva students who succeeded in breaking away from the Joint-organized railroad trains en route to Vienna and who decided to stay indefinitely in and around Prague. Under the terms of Jacobson's understanding with

Masaryk and Toman, this was illegal: *all* refugees were to be moved out of Czechoslovakia as rapidly as possible. Concern therefore developed at the Joint office that the rabbis and their followers might upset the delicate arrangements for the free passage of Jewish refugees.

Most of the rabbinical groups—believing that there was no future for them in the Soviet Union or in Communist Eastern Europe—hoped to emigrate to the United States rather than to Palestine. They were under the mistaken assumption that American visas would be forthcoming in Prague. Moreover, some of the ultra-Orthodox organizations engaged in bringing their adherents out of Eastern Europe, such as the Vaad Hatzalah, had also promised to provide them with relief and financial assistance. But since they too had very limited funds, the burden fell to the Joint.

In the meantime, different religious groups simply could not tolerate one another for reasons of doctrine, dogma or interpretation. "We assisted two hundred rabbis and their families for several months outside of Prague," Jacobson recalled, "and we set up a kosher kitchen for them and met all their needs. . . . I quickly learned there was a difference between Orthodox and Orthodox. When we set up a kosher kitchen, I had permitted one Orthodox group, the Mizrachi, to run the kosher kitchen. We then had delegations of rabbis threaten to tear the place down if we didn't get those 'Reform Jews' out of the kitchen! They had to have a 'glatt kosher' kitchen. So we set up 'glatt kosher' kitchens."

The Joint also had to set up kosher kitchens along the Polish border so that observant Jews could receive kosher food. Freda Cohen, the American Joint representative at the Broumov frontier crossing, remembered that "everything had to be kosher on the border. We took care of all their needs." But, Jacobson pointed out, "the rabbis would never accept food until others were fed first."

Next, word got around that the Joint had decided to increase by 50 percent the relief payments to the rabbis and their families. Schwartz, himself a former rabbi, had concluded that "they should get a little bit of a differential treatment." This decision led so many bearded men to claim they were rabbis that the Chief Rabbi of Prague finally said to Jacobson, "Listen, something's wrong here; there seem to be too many rabbis." Schwartz, who happened to be in Prague, appointed Jacobson's wife, Florence, to be a "supervisor" of the rabbis, to determine whether they really were clergymen. He suggested that she check their *smichas*—rabbinical degree certificates—but inasmuch as Florence was not a *smicha* specialist, the problem remained unsolved. Jacobson therefore proposed that a "board of rabbis" be named to check rabbinical credentials, but this too failed. "The local rabbis could not check out the Eastern rabbis. The Eastern rabbis said they had different standards, and wouldn't recognize the Czech rabbis because 'they don't have our standards of Orthodoxy.' "

At that point, the Czechoslovak government complained to Jacobson that "there were too many Eastern European Jews with beards walking around in the streets, and the Czech people resented that." Jacobson recalled that "we were asked to hurry up their departure because it wasn't making for good relationships." The Orthodox, however, turned to their counterparts in the United States, who protested the Joint's efforts to move the rabbis out. At that juncture, Jacobson had grown so desperate that he had the Brichah lead a group of 1,000 Orthodox rabbis who had settled in Prague to the nearest western border. In a letter of October 1946, Henrietta K. Buchman of the Joint's New York office explained to the rabbi of the Orthodox Agudas Chasidei Chabad congregation in Brooklyn: "We have assisted hundreds . . . in Prague who were brought out mainly by the Aguda and the Vaad Hatzalah without the permission of the government, thereby hindering the whole movement of Polish refugees through Czechoslovakia. . . . This has irritated the government officials, who give this as one reason for closing the borders."

In the first week of October, the Joint in Prague had provided special aid and transportation for eleven Yeshiva groups. Because the Vaad Hatzalah's European office was in Paris, Florence Jacobson, who then worked full-time in the Joint headquarters in Prague, had to negotiate for French transit visas so that the Orthodox could be on their way out of Czechoslovakia. It was an endless string of complications.

The Joint in Prague also had to assume financial and operational responsibility for 488 Jewish children and 101 accompanying adults whom the Chief Rabbi of Palestine, Yitzhak Isaac Halevi Herzog, brought from Poland on August 25, 1946.

The Polish-born Yitzhak Isaac Halevi Herzog (who had served for twenty years as Dublin's Chief Rabbi) had extraordinary contacts around the world, including Ireland's Prime Minister, Eamon de Valera (which resulted in the decision by the neutral Irish to ship kosher meat to Jews in European DP camps). In 1941, Yitzhak Isaac Halevi Herzog had persuaded Japan, which was still at peace, to accept 6,000 Polish Jews from Soviet-occupied areas. But his overriding concern after the war was to extricate Jewish children who were survivors of the Holocaust from Europe, and this mission took him from capital to capital.

Early in 1946, Rabbi Herzog conferred with Pope Pius XII in the Vatican and Prime Minister Alcide de Gasperi in Rome, with Queen Wilhelmina of the Netherlands, the Prince

Regent of Belgium, Britain's Prime Minister, Clement Attlee, the Archbishop of Canterbury and de Valera—all in quest of support for locating an estimated 10,000 Jewish children in non-Jewish homes throughout Europe and effecting their departure for Palestine. Chaim Herzog, the Chief Rabbi's son, who served later as President of Israel, said that his father "didn't get to first base with the Pope," but he fared better with Monsignor Roncalli, the Apostolic Delegate in Turkey, whom he had known in Istanbul.

Rabbi Herzog was able to identify about 1,000 Jewish children in Poland. He obtained the consent of Polish authorities during visits to Warsaw and the promise of transit visas from France and Belgium. Then he received a commitment from the Joint to finance the entire operation.

Rabbi Herzog's undertaking touched some of the most sensitive and emotional dilemmas to emerge from the war: whether surviving Jewish children should be left with the Christian families who had saved their lives and had raised them or returned to a Jewish environment. This philosophical issue was never settled and there was much heartbreak as Rabbi Herzog organized his group of young emigrants in Poland.

In the end, Rabbi Herzog was able to take 488 children and 101 adults; they traveled on a Red Cross train to Prague. But the French visas had not arrived. Rabbi Herzog left after two days, leaving the children in the care of the Joint and the Jacobsons. Ultimately, the visas came and the youngsters reached France under the auspices of the Joint.

With all of these responsibilities, the Joint's budget in Czechoslovakia for 1946 soared to nearly $5 million, not including the "secret" funds from Switzerland for the Brichah, the Mossad and special expenses, such as Rabbi Herzog's venture, which was financed by funds originally allocated for other countries.

XIX

Bridge to the West

Once the refugees were in Czechoslovakia, the most convenient point for crossing into Austria was Marchegg, just half an hour from Vienna. Refugees were brought by bus or truck from Bratislava to the Slovak border village, where they easily walked across a wooden footbridge spanning the March River, a tributary of the Danube. This linked Devínska Nová Ves on the eastern bank and Marchegg on the western bank. While the Soviets often stopped refugees on the main bridges over the Danube, they never interfered with traffic over the little bridge. In 1946 alone, some 100,000 refugees used the March River bridge. The Brichah set up barracks with a capacity of 300 in Devínska Nová Ves for stopovers in the event that the refugee traffic was backed up.

But a disaster occurred during the extremely severe winter of 1946–47 when ice floes on the March River tore the little bridge down. Refugees then had to be ferried across the river in barges several miles south, but this was risky and caused a giant logjam on the Slovak side. Indeed, without the March River bridge, the whole Czechoslovakian operation could have come apart.

The secret police again acted as the Brichah's guardian angel. Levi Argov, the Brichah commander in Bratislava, had maintained close contact with the head of the Slovak Communist security forces, and when the March River bridge went down, an officer named Bertig made an offer: "Build a bridge, and we will send a customs man and a border policeman. . . . And it will be only for the use of the Brichah. Nobody else will pass on this bridge."*

Argov, Dekel, the Brichah's European commander, and Jacobson rushed to the March River to look over the situation and concluded that there was no alternative but to replace the bridge. On the Brichah's behalf, Dekel offered to erect a new bridge—funded by the Joint—and the two border towns agreed. Work began at once, and the bridge was back in operation two months later. Some 75,000 more refugees crossed it on their way to Austria.

Once the Jews were in Austria, many chose to cross the Alps, from the French Occupation Zone to Italy and the DP camps there. This journey, too, was dangerous, especially in the winter. Austrian Brichah guides led the way, as entire

---

* In the early 1950s, the bridge was pulled down completely to prevent traffic through the Iron Curtain. A chain-link fence was erected to run the length of the border, and the villagers on the two sides of the river could no longer communicate. After Communism collapsed in Eastern Europe in 1990 and the Iron Curtain was literally torn down, the bucolic mood returned to the site of the former bridge. The fence was gone, villagers rowed back and forth in their little boats and storks flew freely between the two countries, bringing food for their nests atop the concrete pylons that once held the fence together. But forty-odd years later, no villager on either side remembered, even vaguely, the refugee armies of Jews crossing their bridge.

families moved at night through the deep snow, sometimes in the middle of a storm in the high mountains. Old people and children were carried on men's backs. Brichah escorts were partial to British uniforms as a protective disguise, and it was the task of the Jewish Brigade to provide them. The trip across the mountains sometimes took up to five hours, but it was the final section of the human pipeline that had begun on the Polish border.

In 1947, the Náchod crossing point from Poland into Czechoslovakia was permanently closed to refugees. But during 1946, 209,667 Jewish refugees found their way to freedom through it.

XX

Exodus '47

"The fact of the matter is that the Jews are on the march. The trouble is that they have nowhere to go."

This was Joseph Schwartz's view of the state of European Jewry in early February 1947. The flight of the Polish Jews had filled up the DP camps in Germany, Austria and Italy to a record level of 250,000 refugees. Unless these Jews were allowed to emigrate somewhere—anywhere—there was the danger of a permanent and intolerable refugee camp situation in the heart of Europe. The U.S. Army ran the camps, but it could not handle the task forever. Already it had asked Congress for $300 million in additional funds just to keep them going. And inevitably, the despair and the breakdown of morale among the camps' inmates created a highly volatile situation. There were 50,000 more Jewish refugees in temporary asylum elsewhere in Western Europe.

In Eastern Europe, more Jews plotted to escape as well, driven by famines in Hungary and Romania and fears of anti-Semitism and Communism, and often moved—the young in particular—by Zionist sentiment. At the outset of 1947, the Jewish population of Romania was 400,000, and that of Hungary, 200,000; in Poland, at least 100,000 Jews remained.

All told, then, one million Jews in Europe awaited a solution, if not a miracle—and soon. In the meantime, they had to be fed, housed, clothed and given medical assistance.

The only existing central organization in the world attempting to cope with the vast nightmare was the Joint. No government was willing or prepared to shoulder the full responsibility for the Jewish refugees in Europe, not only because it was expensive but also because it raised a basic international political problem: the question of how to deal with Britain over Palestine. UNRRA was going out of business altogether, and the Jewish community in Palestine— though it was rich in political and operational ideas—lacked the financial means even to help make a dent in the problem. As for the Joint, it had only $75 million available in 1947, having appealed to American Jewish communities for $122 million. Budget requirements for 1948 stood at $98.5 million, and the Joint hoped American Jews would continue to contribute huge sums. The number of American Joint staff members in Europe jumped from 200 to 300 between 1946 and 1947.

In his presentation to his country directors at the start of 1947, Schwartz was quite blunt. The problem of the Jews was that "they do not want to go back where they came from and they do not want to stay where they are." In Romania, Schwartz remarked, "150,000 Jews would emigrate tomorrow if they had a chance," though he was doubtful that they would go to Germany to spend several years in a DP camp. The same situation, he argued, was true of Hungary. Schwartz had entirely abandoned the notion that Eastern European Jews should be assisted in rebuilding a life in their countries of origin, and he suggested that "the second fear which the Jews of Eastern Europe have today is that they soon will not be able to leave, that the laws restricting the movement of population in those countries will be similar to those of the Soviet Union and that movement will become absolutely impossible for that reason."

The number of Jews in DP camps was not only a problem for the Joint; it was an international quandary. Schwartz then went public with what had been his private policy all along. "The only solution for the problem of the Jews in Germany is emigration to Palestine, if possible. . . . It should be the policy of the Joint to push for emigration possibilities; to put pressures on governments and on international bodies and to try to find a solution for this problem of Jewish homelessness."

But what Schwartz chose not to say was that the Joint— and the Mossad—were already looking into secret arrangements for "buying" Jewish freedom from the Romanian and Hungarian regimes for dollars. For the first time since its creation during World War I, the Joint was systematically moving away from its tradition of being a purely apolitical body and concentrating only on relief. Schwartz's quiet dealings with Avigur and the Mossad on illegal immigration had already broken the old mold; now it was accepted by the American organization. The Joint's Administrative Committee approved $1 million "to be utilized by Dr. Schwartz . . . for the purpose of financing immigration to Palestine."

To test and challenge the British, Avigur decided to take more than 4,500 refugees out of DP camps in Germany and transport them illegally to Palestine. This was the first time the Mossad had turned to the camps' populations for illegal immigrants. But the Palestinian Jews evidently wished to score a political point and call the world's attention to the appalling situation of the Jewish displaced persons. The Joint was involved in such operations in a variety of ways, and the most famous venture was that of *Exodus '47*.

The commander of the *Exodus* enterprise was Joseph ("Jossi") Harel, a sixth-generation Jerusalemite and a member of the Haganah from the age of seventeen. The slim, blue-eyed professional soldier joined the Aliyah Bet as soon as it was created in 1939—he had known Avigur for at least two years prior to that—and he went through seamanship and navigation courses to prepare for his naval role with the Mossad.

In August 1946, Avigur dispatched Harel to Athens aboard a small, 20-ton diesel-powered boat. Harel took along two valises containing gold coins worth $250,000 to pay for two ships the Mossad wanted to buy for transporting illegal immigrants from the Balkans. Harel assumed that the money came from the Joint's funds, having been transferred from Schwartz to Avigur.

After nineteen days at sea, Harel reached Piraeus, where he picked up the two vessels, which had been sunk by German aerial bombing during the war and salvaged from the bottom of the harbor. The 1,800-ton *Anna*, immediately renamed the *Knesset*, was intended by Harel to carry 4,000 passengers; the 600-ton *Athena* was to take about 1,000 people. It was sheer folly to overload the ships to such an extent, but that was how illegal immigration was conducted in those days when seagoing vessels were virtually unavailable.

Harel and Benjamin Ulshalmi, a fellow Palestinian officer,

Náchod, Czechoslovakia, 1946. "Infiltree trains," furnished by the Czech government, transport Jewish refugees from Náchod to Bratislava *(Photo courtesy of the American Jewish Joint Distribution Committee Archive)*

Náchod, Czechoslovakia, 1946. In the wake of the Kielce pogrom, Jewish refugees line the street at the JDC-run emergency reception center in Náchod *(Photo courtesy of the American Jewish Joint Distribution Committee Archive)*

Salzburg, Austria, 1948. Refugees in a UNRRA DP camp *(Photo courtesy of the American Jewish Joint Distribution Committee Archive)*

Prague, Czechoslovakia. Joseph Schwartz and Edward Warburg, Chairman of the JDC, confer with Czech President Eduard Beneš *(Photo courtesy of the American Jewish Joint Distribution Committee Archive)*

Prague, Czechoslovakia, 1947. A convivial evening at Gaynor Jacobson's home celebrating the International Music Festival, 1947. From left to right: Frank Pollak, Jiri Singer, Leonard Bernstein, Odnapassoff, Gal, Hugo Weisgal, Gaynor Jacobson, and Joseph Schwartz *(Photo courtesy of Gaynor Jacobson)*

Budapest, Hungary, 1949. Gaynor Jacobson, Joe Schwartz, and Dr. Geza Szulc visit the Tarbut Hebrew School *(Photo courtesy of the American Jewish Joint Distribution Committee Archive)*

Piraeus, Greece. Jewish
refugees arrive in
Piraeus, a way station on
the journey to Palestine
*(Photo courtesy of the American
Jewish Joint Distribution Committee
Archive)*

Piraeus, Greece. 674 refugees submit their passports for inspection aboard
the SS *Mediterranean*, chartered by the Jewish Agency to transport Jews to
Palestine *(Photo courtesy of the American Jewish Joint Distribution Committee Archive)*

Shaike Dan

Joseph J. Schwartz

Moshe Govsman

Gaynor Jacobson

Shaul Avigur

Raphael Spanien

Laurence A. Steinhardt

Brichah operatives

Moroccan Jews.
Operations Framework
in the 1950s and
Yahkin in the 1960s
eventually rescued
most of the ancient
Jewish population *(Photo
© Gerda Bohm; courtesy of the
American Jewish Joint
Distribution Committee Archive)*

Teheran, 1951. Kurdish
Jews, fleeing from
persecution in their tribal
areas in northern Iran,
settle in JDC refugee
camps *(Photo courtesy of the
American Jewish Joint Distribution
Committee Archive)*

Aden, 1949. Jewish
refugee prepares for
Operation Magic Carpet
*(Photo courtesy of the American
Jewish Joint Distribution Committee
Archive)*

Aden, 1949. Thirty thousand Arabian Jews were airlifted to Israel aboard
Joint-chartered planes *(Photo courtesy of the American Jewish Joint Distribution Committee
Archive)*

Yemenite Jews, tightly
packed aboard DC-4s
specially built for
Operation Magic
Carpet *(Photo courtesy of the
American Jewish Joint
Distribution Committee Archive)*

Jewish priests in the Ethiopian village of Gomamge dedicate a new synagogue built by the JDC in 1988 *(Photo courtesy of Donald Robinson)*

Ethiopia, 1988. Falasha
women in the village of Teda,
Gondar region
(Photo courtesy of Peggy Myers)

moved the two ships to Bakar on Yugoslavia's northern Adriatic coast to outfit them for passengers, putting in bedding, bunks, kitchens, toilets, public-address systems and ventilation. The Yugoslavs were so helpful, Harel recalled, that "we couldn't have done it without them." About 4,000 immigrants were then brought to Bakar from Yugoslav camps by Shaike Dan, the wartime paratrooper and now the Mossad's chief Balkan operator. The immigrants were from Romania, but Shaike Dan kept them in shelters in Belgrade and Zagreb until it was time to sail.

The Joint and local Yugoslav authorities provided food for the Harel mission, "good American food: pineapple juice, milk, Spam, everything you wanted." Most of the provisions had been picked up in Athens. But the bread had rotted, so Yugoslav officials in Bakar used up all the available flour for baking bread, and gave it to the convoy. The town was left without bread for a week.

Harel and Ulshalmi had planned to run the British blockade along the Turkish coast up to the Syrian coast and then sail south past Tripoli and Beirut to reach the Palestinian shore. But they were spotted by RAF bombers and two Royal Navy destroyers, which followed them to the port of Haifa. Inside the harbor, British boarding parties fought their way aboard the Mossad ships, firing tear gas at the crew and the refugees, and then placed all the 4,000 immigrants aboard three prison vessels for the short voyage to Cyprus and the detention camps. Harel was released early in 1947 and went to Italy to help with arms shipments for the Haganah from a small port near Milan. But almost immediately Avigur telephoned him for a meeting at a Milan café. "We have another ship that has just come to Portofino," Avigur informed him, "near La Spezia. Her name is *President Garfield.*" It was the start of the *Exodus* odyssey.

The *President Garfield* was a 2,000-ton pleasure ship that

used to ply the Chesapeake Bay and normally carried 120 passengers. But she was able to cross the Atlantic, and Harel decided the small ship could take 4,500 immigrants, which was just as foolhardy as the earlier voyage from Yugoslavia. Harel sailed the vessel from Portofino to Sète, a French port on the Mediterranean west of Marseilles, where she was fueled. Then he took her to Port-de-Bouc, near Sète, to receive passengers. Avigur and his people had brought 5,000 immigrants in twelve railroad trains across France from the DP camps in Germany, but departure was delayed because French officials insisted that each passenger have a visa of some kind. A Costa Rican consul, located in Marseilles, loaned the Mossad his visa stamp for quick processing of the passports, at five dollars per traveler.

The *President Garfield* left Port-de-Bouc at dawn on July 11. A radio message from Palestine ordered that she be renamed *Exodus '47*. By the time Palestine was in sight four days later, Harel had collected a British cruiser and five destroyers.

On July 17, boarding parties of Royal Marines stormed their way aboard *Exodus '47*, which was anchored off Haifa. There was a terrible fight, and the ship began to take on water. *Exodus '47* was escorted into Haifa harbor on July 18, where Harel unloaded the bodies of three men killed, along with the wounded. *Exodus '47* was impounded and burned.

While observers from the United Nations Special Committee on Palestine (UNSCOP) stood by, the British forced the immigrants aboard three prison ships headed back to Port-de-Bouc, to "punish the French." Avigur, however, did not see this as just one more defeat: the way the British in Haifa manhandled the Jewish refugees had had a powerful impact on the UNSCOP observers. Indeed, politically it served the Israeli cause better in the long run than the arrival of 4,500 more Jews in Palestine.

When the prison ships reached Port-de-Bouc on August 2, the French decided not to let the Jews disembark—in order to annoy the British. The refugees became political pawns. In Paris, Schwartz was immediately informed of the situation; the ships were running low on food and medical supplies. Laura Margolis Jarblum, head of the Joint's operations in France, organized a truck convoy of provisions and rushed down to the coast with it. Her husband, Marc Jarblum, who had close contacts among the French authorities, made sure she was protected by them.

The ships sailed on to Hamburg, then in the British Occupation Zone, and the immigrants were sent back to the camps on September 7. But the steadfast refugees began their exodus all over again, escaping from the DP camps that night for Italy.

If politically beneficial, the aborted *Exodus '47* episode proved detrimental to the Jews' overall morale. Camps and Jewish communities became scenes of desperation; the growing anti-Semitism in Germany only aggravated the situation. On October 15, Moses Leavitt, the Joint's secretary, reported to the executive committee that "the morale of the Jews in Germany has dropped to the lowest point since last winter."

The UNSCOP report that followed in the wake of the *Exodus '47* saga laid the foundations for the United Nations vote for the partition of Palestine. Schwartz's friend Moshe Sharett, the foreign affairs planner for the Jewish Agency (and Avigur's brother-in-law), had asked Schwartz to appear before the committee. UNSCOP, undoubtedly impressed by Schwartz's testimony and by what they had witnessed in Haifa and Germany, recommended that "approximately 150,000 Jews" held in DP camps "be dealt with as a matter of extreme urgency for the alleviation of their plight and of the Palestine problem."

Another extraordinary by-product of the *Exodus '47* incident was the JDC Administrative Committee's "highly confidential" discussion on October 20 of a proposal by Rabbi Abba Hillel Silver. Rabbi Silver, a leading voice in the American Jewish community, proposed that the Joint provide $6 million over the next few months for secret arms purchases for the Haganah. The Joint had previously stayed out of the arms business, but the board designated its chairman, Edward Warburg, and three other members to discuss the proposal with Rabbi Silver and Moshe Sharett, who was engaged in frantic diplomatic footwork at the United Nations. Then, surprisingly, the Joint's board agreed—in secret. "Accelerated collections" were ordered in the payment of pledges made during fund-raising campaigns. Even a 10 percent increase in the collections, the members said, might yield the $6 million for the Jewish army. Mossad and Jewish Agency emissaries began to fan out across the United States to raise money for arms and to acquire them.

At the same time, however, great problems continued to loom over Eastern Europe, and the Joint was under immense pressure to try to solve them.

XXI

The Only Help in Hungary

From the Joint's point of view, Czechoslovakia was a means to an end. The extant Jewish community was relatively small—just over 50,000—and it had commensurate aid from the Joint. In contrast, Hungary had close to 200,000 Jews, 150,000 of whom lived in Budapest, including 50,000 elderly survivors of the ghetto. It was a large community and for the most part destitute; Hungary suffered from devastating postwar famines resulting from weather-inflicted crop failures. The Joint was the only aid agency in the world represented in Hungary—helping Hungarians, no matter what their faith. Moreover, the Joint spent $600,000 annually for supplies for Christian and later Communist children's homes, old-age homes and clinics. As Jacobson put it, "In Hungary, there were no UNRRA activities, so we were the big outstanding welfare folks." The

Joint assumed responsibility for looking after the Jews and building a new social infrastructure for them.

Jacobson left Prague for Budapest in August 1947 to assume his post as director for Hungary. Hungary was the Joint's largest single operation in the world, and it cost roughly $8 million for 1947. Previously, Joint programs had been run by a Hungarian Jewish community group, and Jacobson was the first American authorized by the postwar Hungarian regime to serve as country director in Budapest. It was almost as if Jacobson were responsible for running a small nation single-handedly.

When Jacobson arrived in Budapest, the Joint was busy financing the daily feeding of tens of thousands of Jews— and non-Jews—in soup kitchens around the country. Most of the Joint's budget was allocated for food purchases. But it also funded farm and urban cooperatives. In addition, it maintained three hospitals (including a 700-bed Jewish hospital in Budapest, a 350-bed general charity hospital and a maternity hospital), a chain of clinics, orphanages with thousands of children and a full-fledged department store stocked with clothes donated by Joint-sponsored "SOS" charity drives in the United States. The donations posed a bit of a problem, "because many Americans sent high-heeled shoes and party dresses," Jacobson said. But the Joint's department store, directed by the talented Tibor Waldman, had tailors and seamstresses, and the clothing was altered accordingly. In bleak postwar Budapest any kind of clothing was at a premium, but Jacobson claimed that "the best-dressed people in the city were our clients who used this department store."

The Joint was beginning to see that pride played an important role in survival. When Schwartz addressed his country directors at the 1947 Paris meeting, he stressed the urgency with which shoes were needed throughout Europe. "If the JDC sent over a million pairs of shoes in the next six months they would not meet the requirements of the Jewish children in Europe today," he said. "But you come to the question of climate and habit and tradition. When I go to Romania they say, 'Look, a Swiss shoe. Maybe in Switzerland they wear shoes like that, but here nobody will wear it.' Someone tells me he wants reconstructed shoes, and when I was in Poland, they said, 'What the Swedish Army cannot use you will pass on to us? With patches and new soles? You cannot do that to us. We are a proud people.'" Americans had to learn to be culturally sensitive in their charity.

While the overall Joint program in Hungary was supervised and administered by Jacobson and a locally recruited headquarters staff of twenty-five to thirty people, each operation was run on a day-to-day basis by local employees of the Hungarian Jewish Relief Committee, a community organization funded by the Joint. But the government ruled that all employees of the Relief Committee were technically the Joint's employees (presumably to control them better), and Jacobson found himself in late 1947 personally responsible for the activities of over 3,000 individuals. Suddenly Jacobson was head of the largest nongovernmental organization in Hungary. And he predicted—correctly—that the Hungarian authorities would one day accuse his organization of espionage.

To keep an eye on the Joint, the government installed two top Communist officials from the Interior Ministry and the Social Welfare Ministry on the floor below the Joint's offices, "controlling every piece of paper . . . and every activity, attending every meeting I went to . . . they knew everything that was going on. They had to be paid by the Joint," Jacobson joked.

Indeed, the Joint paid for almost everything imaginable in Hungary, from food for Jews and non-Jews to discreet payments of millions of dollars to the Hungarian Communist Party to spring Zionist leaders from prison and allow them to emigrate to Palestine. "We had soup kitchens for single elderly people," Jacobson recalled, "and soup kitchens for families. But we also had a soup kitchen that served only starving Hungarian artists, writers, poets, actors and actresses who were mainly non-Jewish."*

Jacobson and Schwartz were convinced that the failure to feed non-Jews in a hungry society was an open invitation to anti-Semitism. But Jacobson was subsequently charged with violating Hungarian laws because the Joint's soup kitchens also fed the starving Romanian Jews, including Orthodox rabbis, when they turned up in the country. In collaboration with the Haganah, the Mossad and the Brichah, the Joint's Hungarian operation also provided cover for camps where 10,000 young Hungarian Jews trained in weaponry for the day they arrived in Palestine and joined the underground army.

The question of Jewish emigration from Hungary—legal, illegal or semi-legal—was extremely complicated, one of the most difficult issues Jacobson faced in Budapest. Unlike

* Jacobson's closest friend in Budapest was the Hungarian sculptor Zigmund von Strobl, who encouraged Jacobson to use his atelier to pursue his sculpting avocation. Strobl had been one of the last students of Auguste Rodin in Paris, and he was internationally famous. He was married to a Hungarian Jewish woman, and he was among the last Hungarians to insist on being seen publicly with Jacobson when the campaign against the United States and the Joint was unleashed in 1949. Strobl had sculpted George Bernard Shaw's bust in the 1920s (Shaw described it in his *Thirteen Self-Sketches* as probably better than the one Rodin had done of him), and immediately after Budapest's liberation from the Nazis he did a magnificent statue of Raoul Wallenberg. But the Soviets would not allow the Wallenberg bust to be displayed publicly, and Strobl was forced to change it into a tribute to the Hungarian Air Force. Nevertheless, the elderly sculptor made a point of showing Jacobson the statue and identifying Wallenberg as the inspiration.

Poland, Hungary did not allow its Jews to leave freely, and they could not cross the frontier into Austria at will. The Brichah was able to extricate small groups, often children, through Romania and Yugoslavia to board the Mossad's illegal immigration ships to Palestine, but the flow was only a trickle. In fact, there were Romanian Jews fleeing across the "green border" into Hungary because they thought— erroneously—that this was the best route to the West.

As a matter of officially stated policy, the Joint neither encouraged nor discouraged Jewish emigration. It believed in the Hungarian Jews' right to emigrate if they wished. Jacobson repeatedly made this point to Budapest's Communist mayor, Zoltán Vas, a Jew (born Weinberg) who became Minister of the Five-Year Plan soon after they met. Vas was Jacobson's best channel into the Communist hierarchy, possibly because he realized that the Joint was Hungary's largest single source of dollars and an important importer of industrial machinery for the Jewish producers' cooperatives.* Through Vas, Jacobson was introduced to key Communist leaders with whom he could negotiate terms for the emigration of Jews and the freedom of Zionist leaders: László Rajk, who was first Interior Minister and then Foreign Minister, János Kádár and Mátyás Rákosi.† Jacobson was the only American in Hungary with such access.

Rákosi, who was of Jewish origin, was the general secretary of the Communist Party and the most powerful man in Hungary. Vas had told Jacobson to call on Rákosi before meeting Hungary's figurehead President, Zoltán Tildy. To

---

* American dollars were exchanged for forints in Budapest according to a complicated formula whereby the Joint and the Communist Party split the difference between official and black market rates.

† Rajk was executed after a show trial in September 1948 in the first of the Stalinist trials that terrorized and decimated the Eastern European Communist leadership over the next four years—almost until Stalin's own death in March 1953.

Jacobson's surprise, the bullet-headed Rákosi, who spoke English quite well, seemed to take to him and they met with a certain regularity to discuss emigration and the Joint's programs in Hungary. Jacobson felt sufficiently at ease with Rákosi to tell him that the Joint was providing the fleeing Romanians with food and shelter in Hungary because it was "a basic human need."

Jacobson negotiated payments with Rákosi for the legal departure of some 300 Zionist youth leaders who had been imprisoned by the Hungarian authorities late in 1948. The price was $1 million for the group, and part of it was delivered by the Joint in the form of machinery for producers' cooperatives, in addition to the machinery that had already been provided for Jewish organizations. The Hungarians also agreed to let 5,000 young Hungarian Jews leave legally. Jacobson was later accused of having actually 10,000 of them, a charge he doesn't deny. "I felt that, given my cooperation with the Mossad, it wasn't my job to hold them to 5,000 instead of 10,000." These were the same youths whom Haganah instructors had trained in weaponry in camps throughout Hungary.

Still, the regime treated Jacobson with velvet gloves. Within a year of his arrival, he and Schwartz were awarded the highest Hungarian civilian decorations in recognition of the Joint's humanitarian programs. He socialized with Vas, who attended the Passover Seder at the Jacobsons' luxurious Budapest villa in 1948, and even Rákosi came to parties at the Jacobson home. At a reception for a prominent Hungarian diplomat, Rákosi confided, "You know, Jacobson, I like you as a person. Most American representatives are agents or spies. That's why I kicked out all the other American organizations. I don't know if you are or not, but I'll have to be careful with you." Jacobson later saw this as a warning.

XXII

The End of
Illegal Immigration

The political, diplomatic and armed struggle over Palestine came to an end on November 29, 1947, opening the way for the birth of the State of Israel and seemingly removing the need for illegal immigration. This was not only the fulfillment of the Zionist dream; it was the potential solution for the 250,000 Jewish refugees in European DP camps and for tens of thousands of Jews elsewhere who wished to live in Palestine.

Following the failure of a British-organized Arab-Jewish conference in January 1947, the British government concluded that it was time the Palestinian issue was shifted to the United Nations. On April 2, a special session of the UN General Assembly in New York, at Britain's initiative, had organized the United Nations Special Committee on Palestine.

After three months in the field, the majority of the eleven-nation committee recommended that Palestine be partitioned into an Arab and a Jewish state, with Jerusalem as an international city under UN supervision. Canada, Czechoslovakia, Guatemala, the Netherlands, Peru, Sweden and Uruguay were in favor of it; India, Iran and Yugoslavia held out for a federal state; Australia abstained. There is no question that the committee's exposure to the DP camps, and to the Palestinian blockade battle, notably the *Exodus '47* affair, moved it toward partition and therefore a solution to the refugee problem.

But the General Assembly still had to endorse the recommendation by a two-thirds majority as a political but nonbinding decision. There are reasons to believe that Britain was confident that partition would be defeated in the General Assembly vote. This, presumably, would have confirmed the validity and legality of Britain's Palestine policy, including restrictions on Jewish immigration.

The British calculated that the Soviet Union and its satellites, Arabs and their friends and many Roman Catholic nations would vote against the resolution. They assumed the Russians would want to court the Arabs.

But the partition resolution was approved by 33 votes in favor, 14 against and 10 abstentions. The United States and the Soviet Union joined in supporting partition in what was one of the most important postwar international decisions. Washington's announcement on October 11 that it would support partition and increased immigration to Palestine did much to sway opinion for an affirmative vote. No outsiders knew at the time how hard the State Department had fought against it in monumental internal battles—until Truman made the decision.

Although it was generally accepted that Israel would win independence within months—unless something wholly unanticipated altered the course of events—a final drama remained to be played out in the great battle of illegal immigration between the Mossad and Britain. Both camps were determined to fight to the last moment. And this ultimate engagement in the illegal immigration war turned David Ben-Gurion and Shaul Avigur into open adversaries.

At issue was the question whether two Mossad ships with nearly 15,000 illegal immigrants should sail from the Black Sea to Haifa during December 1947 as an act of defiance and an affirmation of Zionism. Avigur and the Mossad insisted on the sailing, but Ben-Gurion and the Jewish Agency executive feared that despite the General Assembly's favorable vote in November, this venture could damage chances for Israeli independence. The United States opposed the sailing, wanting to avert dangerous confrontations.

The ships, the *Pan York* and the *Pan Crescent*, were 5,000-ton Panamanian-flag banana boats, which the Mossad had acquired in the United States from the United Fruit Company. Avigur, of course, kept Schwartz informed of the Mossad's activities; the boats were purchased—it was believed—with a hefty contribution from the Joint. Jossi Harel, the captain of *Exodus '47*, was put in charge of the new naval operation. The *Pan York* was moved to Venice, where a British frogman tried to sabotage it with explosives, which detonated, but the ship was quickly repaired. The *Pan Crescent* was sent to Marseilles, and the two ships awaited further instructions.

In Romania, Shaike Dan obtained permission for the emigration of 12,000 Jews (he paid in cash for "exit permits," a euphemism for bribes to government officials), and the *Pan York* and the *Pan Crescent* sailed to the port of Constantsa to be refitted. From Tel Aviv, Harel and several associates flew to Prague, and were then transported in November by the Brichah—without any documents—through Austria and Hungary to Bucharest and finally to Constantsa, where Shaike Dan awaited them. But due to the powerful pressure of the British government, Romanian authorities asked the Mossad to find another port of embarkation. Shaike Dan had no trouble persuading Bulgaria's Deputy Prime Minister, Traicho Kostov, who had previously dealt with him and the Mossad, to grant permission for the *Pan* ships to leave from Burgas, the Bulgarian port on the Black Sea. Shaike Dan and the Brichah teams then began rounding up the prospective immigrants in Romania using nine trains to transport them to Burgas, where the two ships were now ready to set sail. About 15,000 refugees arrived in the port. The *Pan* ships normally carried about 600 passengers each, but 7,500 were put aboard each vessel.

The struggle over the sailing began in earnest in early December. The British were aware of American sensitivity to any Communist design, and the Foreign Office convinced the U.S. State Department that the ships would be bringing 10,000 handpicked pro-Soviet Communists to Palestine. From New York, the chief Palestinian diplomat, Moshe Sharett, advised Ben-Gurion that this charge had to be taken seriously—even though it was false—for fear of losing crucial American support in the pre-independence days.

But Avigur was opposed to any concessions to the British, and on December 9 he flew from Paris to Tel Aviv for a meeting of the secretariat of the Mapai (Labor) Party to argue for his position. Supported by the top Mossad officers in the Balkans, he set a departure date of December 14. Ben-Gurion recorded in his diary that at the meeting Avigur warned the Mapai session that any delays would "endanger the Zionist movement not only in Romania but throughout Eastern Europe." The 15,000 waiting to sail from Burgas, he added, would not survive the winter without subsistence of any sort. Failure in Romania at that stage, Avigur emphasized, would jeopardize confidence in Palestinian leadership and would complicate illegal immigrations of Jews from the Middle East and North Africa.

Ben-Gurion, on the other hand, had always been opposed to Avigur's strategy of bringing in large boatloads of refugees, preferring small groups to avoid confrontations. Even if he agreed personally with Avigur and Shaike Dan, he pointed out, "I would go along with our colleagues in America" for political reasons.

Avigur urged Ben-Gurion to send Shaike Dan to New York to explain the Mossad point of view to Sharett and his colleagues. Shaike Dan refused to get trapped in a diplomatic impasse. Sharett then flew to Geneva to confer with Avigur, and a compromise was finally worked out between them. The ships could sail, but if the British so desired, they would go only to Cyprus. Avigur conceded, but only because he now planned to "flood" Cyprus with Jewish refugees, thereby forcing the British to dismantle their detention camps and let the Jews into Palestine.

On the morning of December 28, 1947, the *Pan* ships set sail with 15,500 refugees. Avigur radioed Harel with a citation from Genesis 32:28: "You have striven with God and man and have prevailed." Harel, meanwhile, was concerned that British pressure might lead the Turkish authorities to prevent his ships from passing through the Bosporus to reach the Mediterranean from the Black Sea. Because the Bosporus is an international waterway, ships could be stopped if sanitation conditions were not up to international standards; Harel suspected the British would try that ploy. Mossad emissaries in Istanbul had given the Turkish military commander and the governor material "incentives" not to interfere, and it was agreed that the ships would sail through the Bosporus on Saturday afternoon, when no one would be in the Turkish offices to respond to British demands if the vessels were spotted.

The *Pan York* was Harel's flagship, and at two in the afternoon she reached the Bosporus. They were stopped by Turkish officials, but Harel was ready for them with "coins, gold watches, gold pens, everything gold," and the ships resumed their journey. On December 30 they entered the Aegean Sea, only to find themselves surrounded by two British cruisers and a screen of destroyers. For hours, Harel negotiated via radio with the British admiral commanding the task force. In the end, he agreed to take his ships to Cyprus, but only after he raised the ship's flag and renamed the *Pan York* the *Independent*.

At Famagusta in eastern Cyprus, the 15,500 refugees disembarked and proceeded to the camps. It was January 1, 1948. The British promised to send 750 refugees monthly to Palestine, but, Harel recalled, "on May 15, Israeli independence day, the same ships brought 30,000 people from Cyprus to Israel." The final trip was the largest shipment of Jews by sea and, Harel noted wistfully, "was the end of illegal immigration."

XXIII

The Birth of Israel

Nineteen forty-eight was a year of promise, challenge and victory for the new State of Israel; indeed, for Jews around the world. Israel's birth, however, came amidst traumatic pangs—political and military—that threatened its immediate survival.

While the November 1947 General Assembly partition vote called for Britain to terminate its mandate over Palestine on August 1, 1948, the diplomatic edifice quickly began to crumble. On March 5, the partition plan failed to win the necessary seven-vote majority in the UN Security Council, the only organ that had the power actually to enforce partition (the General Assembly was confined to recommendations), although the United States, the Soviet Union and France were among those supporting it. Faced with a stalemate and an inevitable crisis in Palestine, Britain decided to wash its hands of the whole affair and withdraw on May 15, two and a half months ahead of schedule.

At that juncture, a secret drama, unprecedented in American history, unfolded inside the Truman administration. The President remained committed to partition and Israeli independence, but most of his top advisers turned against him, arguing that it would not be in the U.S. national interest and warning that it would probably force an armed American intervention in the Middle East. The CIA was joined by the intelligence agencies of the State, Army, Navy and Air Force departments in a formal assessment that partition was impossible. Loy Henderson, the head of the State Department's Near East Bureau and an Arabist, was opposed all along to the idea of a Jewish state. Dean Rusk, the new director of the Office of United Nations Affairs, thought that the situation had changed so much since the November vote that new solutions should be devised.

Support began to coalesce in the State Department for placing Palestine under a United Nations trusteeship on the grounds that it was incapable of governing itself in the foreseeable future. The Jewish Agency now had every reason to wonder whether its new state would ever survive; the imposition of an embargo by the United States on shipments of arms to the Jews in Palestine added to the sense of foreboding descending on the Jewish diplomats.

Nevertheless, David Ben-Gurion and his Jewish Agency colleagues were determined to proclaim Israeli independence on May 15, the instant Britain ended the mandate rule. A furious battle broke out in Washington over the issue of U.S. diplomatic recognition of Israel. Truman proposed to do just that, to make America the first nation to recognize the Israeli state. But Truman encountered a formidable opponent in Secretary of State George Marshall, who had taken a stand against augmented Jewish immigration to Palestine four years earlier. The President had boundless admiration for Marshall—he regarded him as the "greatest living American"—but he disagreed with him on principle and turned down his recommendation for a Palestinian trusteeship. Moreover, Truman had made a personal commitment to Chaim Weizmann, the Zionist leader, to recognize Israel.

The battle over Israel came to a head on May 12—with two days to spare for the United States to make a decision —at an Oval Office meeting at the White House. The principals in the dispute were Truman and Clark Clifford, Truman's trusted counsel on domestic affairs, and, on the other side, General Marshall and Under Secretary of State Robert Lovett. After Lovett and Marshall presented their arguments against Israeli independence, Truman asked Clifford to list the reasons in favor of it—and of an immediate American recognition. Even at the time it was generally known that the President and his Secretary of State disagreed over Israel, but the depth of Marshall's fury at Truman was revealed only forty-three years later when Clifford quoted him in his memoirs, published in 1991. Marshall told the President, "If you follow Clifford's advice and if I were to vote in the election, I would vote against you." This was, of course, an election year, and Truman was the underdog in the contest with the Republican challenger, Thomas Dewey. Truman's foes contended that he supported Israel to garner Jewish votes, a notion Clifford considers wholly absurd. History, in the end, vindicated Truman's judgment on Israel.

As planned, David Ben-Gurion proclaimed Israeli independence on May 14, to be effective at midnight, Israeli time, and eleven minutes later the White House announced that "the United States recognizes the provisional government as the de facto authority of the new State of Israel."

On the following day, the Arab states of Lebanon, Syria, Jordan, Egypt and Iraq attacked Israel. Israel had only the most rudimentary army, which evolved from the Haganah, and virtually no air force. For weeks it was touch and go. At one point, the Egyptians were twenty-five miles from Tel Aviv, but in the end the Arabs lost the war mainly because of their own military errors. Still, Israel sacrificed 6,500 lives—1 percent of its population in 1948.

After armistice agreements negotiated by the United Nations (Iraq was the only country to refuse to sign one), Israel emerged as a precarious geographic entity of 7,847 square miles, formed by a narrow coastal north-south wedge between Lebanon, the Gaza Strip and the Sinai Desert (held by Egypt), and by the Negev Desert adjoining the kingdom of Jordan in the east. West Jerusalem was Israeli, East Jerusalem was Jordanian. Jordanian West Bank territories jutted as bulky salients into Israel; at its most narrow point —between Jerusalem (the capital) and the Mediterranean— the country was less than thirty miles wide. Because of its continued vulnerability to the Arabs, the geographical position of Israel was a military and strategic nightmare for the Israelis. But after centuries of waiting it *was* their independent state.

Among those who died in the 1948 Arab-Israeli war was seventeen-year-old Gur Meyerov, the son of Shaul and Sara Avigur, killed on July 13 in Sajrah, near the family's home of Kibbutz Kinneret. Gur had belonged to a Kinneret commando unit and in all likelihood was shot by Syrian troops. Shaul and Sara later wrote a memoir of their son, titled simply *With Gur*. In it, Shaul describes how he learned of his son's death from a friend who brought the "terrible" news to his hotel room in Geneva early the morning after.

Avigur had been in Europe acquiring arms for the Haganah. Then came a telegram that Gur was buried at Kinneret, and Avigur went down to Lake Geneva, to sit there and to make an "accounting." "Is this the reward that blind fate—is it really blind?—prepared for me in its mystery at this time?" he asked. "I am going to return to a Kinneret without Gur in it. It is like missing a living organ, and I don't have a God in heaven to raise against him a helpless fist." The next day, Avigur went to the Mossad's Geneva office to "continue working" on his arms assignment. A week would elapse before he could go home to Kinneret.

XXIV

Darkness over Eastern Europe

Just as light shone over the Holy Land, darkness descended on Eastern Europe with the final consolidation of Communist rule in the region.

On February 25, 1948, the Beneš coalition government was ousted in a Communist coup and Czechoslovakia became a "people's democracy." Klement Gottwald, the Prime Minister and head of the party, was now the man in power. The independent-minded Toman in the Interior Ministry had been pushed aside in preparation for the takeover; no doubt his insistence on keeping the Polish border open for the transit of Jewish refugees was among the reasons for neutralizing him. In late 1947, Toman had lost control of the security services, which were handed over to his immediate subordinate. Then he was demoted from his post as First Deputy Interior Minister. Toman still oversaw intelligence —except it was intelligence "outside the country."

On March 10, Jan Masaryk, the Foreign Minister who dreamt of making Czechoslovakia a bridge between the East and the West and who had helped Jewish refugees escape from Poland in cooperation with Toman, was found dead in the courtyard of Czernin Palace, four stories below the window of his ministerial apartment. He had agreed to remain temporarily in the new Communist government, but that lasted less than two weeks. More than forty years later, it is still a mystery whether he was murdered or committed suicide.

Toman was arrested shortly thereafter. He could have fled Czechoslovakia to avoid imprisonment, but his wife refused to leave. His sister Aranka was arrested at the same time, and she ended up spending twelve years in prison.

Toman was taken to the first-floor jail of a Prague courthouse, but he received no explanation for his arrest. As he put it, "Nobody took notes on me." After ten days, a police officer informed him that his wife had committed suicide. Toman assumed she was killed by security agents, but he never knew why. Their son, Ivan, was nearly two years old at the time, and Toman would never see him again. "He's in a good place," he was told.

Toman was put to work cleaning jail toilets, presumably on orders from Interior Minister Nosek. He managed to escape through a window in the prison corridor while the guards were distracted, and walked out into the broad daylight. When it was dark, he went over to the Jacobsons' old villa, hoping that the Joint's new director in Prague, an American named Jules Levine, would help him. But Levine was scared and told Toman to leave. He even refused to lend Toman twenty korunas so he could eat and get around the city. A Czech friend was more charitable and took Toman to his dacha outside Prague. Toman stayed for a week, eating "only onions and bread . . . because he had nothing else to give me."

Toman made his way back to Prague, where a cardiology specialist offered assistance since Toman had allowed his brother to emigrate from London to Czechoslovakia. He provided Toman with a forged identity card, and Toman traveled by train west to Karlovy Vary. He then set out on foot for the West German border, but he got lost in the woods. A peasant told him that a creek about two hundred yards away formed the frontier. Miraculously, there were no guards in sight when Toman crossed into Germany over a partially destroyed bridge. Ironically, it turned out to be a short distance from the border city of Aš, through which tens of thousands of Jewish refugees had streamed to freedom two years earlier—because of Toman's orders to keep the frontier open.

Toman went from Germany to France, and in Paris he called Interior Minister Nosek to inquire about little Ivan. Nosek urged him to return and resume his former job. When Toman refused, the minister warned: "As long as you keep your mouth shut, your son will be alive. . . . As soon as you start to talk, your son will have to die."

Toman decided to join his brother in Venezuela, where he later started his business and made his fortune. He remarried, but he is still haunted by the fate of his son at the hands of the Communists.

The tide began to turn for Gaynor Jacobson as well. In March 1948 he received a message in Budapest from the Joint office in Prague. Work in Czechoslovakia, Jacobson was told, would be in jeopardy unless he returned to clear up allegations that he had helped Toman escape from jail.

Jacobson made the mistake of complying, and he flew to Prague, where he was met at the airport by a Dr. Goldsmith, whom he knew to be a Communist implanted in the Joint's office.

Goldsmith told him that the interview with Czechoslovak authorities would be held at Prague's Pankrac prison. Jacobson still felt that he had "nothing to fear." But once inside the prison, he was submitted to hours of interrogation by senior security officials. Jacobson insisted that he could not possibly have been involved with the Toman escape because he was not in Prague or West Germany at the time, but in Budapest. He showed his passport to prove it. Had he been involved with Toman's escape, he explained, he wouldn't have bothered coming back. Jacobson left Pankrac in mid-afternoon, and no one stopped him on his way out.

When he saw Ambassador Steinhardt later at the American embassy, Steinhardt had an aide call the airlines and told Jacobson: "You go in my car and get out of this country as fast as possible . . . They made a mistake. They would never have you come to Pankrac prison and then release you this way." A member of the embassy staff put Jacobson on a plane for Budapest that afternoon. "By that time," Jacobson concluded, "I was a little alarmed."

Jacobson still enjoyed friendly relations with the Hungarian government in 1948. He was in Budapest when Israel gained independence in May, and he congratulated Ehud Avriel, who had become the Israeli ambassador accredited to Hungary, as well as to Czechoslovakia, where he continued to supervise arms purchases for the new Israeli Army.

But as 1949 rolled around, tremendous pressures mounted in Budapest. Stalinist hard-liners began a lethal struggle inside the Communist Party, and soon Americans were openly denounced as "imperialists." In June, the American legation (it had not yet been upgraded to embassy status) advised Florence Jacobson to leave Hungary with her two small daughters, and they did so almost immediately. Jacobson believed he could go on running the Joint's program, which he considered essential to the Hungarians.

In the autumn of 1949, Rajk was executed and Cardinal Mindszenty was arrested. Jacobson heard their "confessions" over the radio and began to worry about his own safety. Most of his Hungarian friends and contacts avoided him. When the Joint opened a new clinic at Budapest's Jewish Hospital with the most modern equipment, sent over from the United States, a ceremony was held in the presence of senior Hungarian officials. The Health Minister exclaimed: "Look at this beautiful hospital. Look at its equipment. . . . This is proof that the People's Democracy is functioning well!" Other speakers repeated this refrain. When Jacobson's turn came, he said through an interpreter that he was glad the People's Democracy was proud, but he himself was especially proud that it was the American Jewish Joint Distribution Committee that had sent the equipment. American Jewish funds kept the hospital going, he reminded the gathering, and it practiced American medicine. "There was a hush when I finished," Jacobson recalled.

Before leaving in late October on a short trip home, Jacobson was concerned enough to request an audience with Rákosi. Jacobson told him that he had heard disturbing rumors and he hoped nothing unpleasant would happen on his return to Budapest. Rákosi was no longer "the warm, friendly person he had been in the past, but I thought he was agreeing that I had nothing to fear by coming back." For the first time, Jacobson faced delays getting his Hungarian exit visa.

Driving back from Vienna to Budapest on December 15,

Jacobson was stopped ten miles inside Hungarian territory by three cars "full of armed security people," who proceeded to arrest him and take him to the secret police headquarters at 60 Andrassy Street. Jacobson was held on "suspicion of espionage," and it was cause for serious worry. On November 18, the Hungarians had arrested Robert A. Vogeler, an assistant vice president of International Telephone and Telegraph and special representative for Eastern Europe; he had been charged with espionage and held incommunicado despite daily official American protests. Noel Field of the Unitarian Service Committee had been detained even earlier. A pattern was emerging, and it seemed as if Jacobson and Vogeler had become victims of the deepening East-West "Cold War."

Nevertheless, Jacobson was handled gently, as far as arrests by Communist secret police go. He was prevented from communicating with the American legation, but he wasn't confined to a cell. He was placed in an office that had a desk, a chair, a divan on which he slept, and he had the use of a toilet next door. Physically, he wasn't touched, but on some days he was interrogated by security officials for eighteen to twenty hours at a stretch. The interrogators insisted on knowing everything he had done during his two years in Hungary. They accused him of spying, threatened him with prison and even death. Lieutenant General Gábor Peter, the dreaded chief of security services, whom Jacobson remembered as a "quiet, small man," attended some of the sessions, but he asked very few questions.

One question Peter did ask was why Jacobson did not confess to espionage. After all, Jacobson's interpreter and assistant, a young Hungarian named Thomas Farago, who spoke excellent English, had done so. Jacobson remembered that the night he was arrested, Farago was brought to him with black-and-blue marks on his face. "Mr. Jacobson," Farago said, "you are an American agent. Your work was to undermine the People's Democracy of Hungary, and I know because I helped you do it." "I blurted out, 'Tommy, why do you lie like this?' "

Farago was released from prison in 1956, and when he came to the United States he admitted to Jacobson that he had accused him falsely because the police "had taken him past a cell where blood was coming under the door and a woman was shrieking." They told him that it was his mother, who had operated one of the Joint's soup kitchens, and that they "would kill her that evening if I didn't do this." As it turned out, Farago's mother had not even been arrested, but Jacobson believed Farago's story.

The Hungarians didn't have much of a case against Jacobson—or they chose not to construct one. His hours of interrogation were shortened and he was even allowed to read two books of his own choosing: the Bible and a volume of the works of Shakespeare. "I became overtly more religious than ever," he recalled. "I read the Bible. I started silently praying, hoping there was a God and He would listen, and then reading Shakespeare's plays and sonnets. It was terrifically heartening . . . I tried to joke with the interrogators about *Much Ado about Nothing*."

On December 27, after twelve and a half days in police detention, Jacobson was set free without any explanation, though he had to sign documents in Hungarian. There had been a great public outcry and intense U.S. government pressure on Jacobson's behalf. Former Treasury Secretary Henry Morgenthau, Jr., and New York's Governor Herbert Lehman had contacted Secretary of State Dean Acheson about Jacobson's fate, and President Truman himself took a special interest in his case. But Jacobson's theory was that

Rákosi, who was visiting Moscow at the time, raised the matter with Stalin, who in turn sent orders to release the American prisoner. That was also the version Jacobson was given by Dr. László Benedek, head of the Budapest Jewish Hospital and the Joint's medical director. Benedek was also a well-connected member of the Communist Party, and Jacobson never heard another explanation.

Jacobson's car and his other possessions, including the case containing his Hungarian decorations, were returned to him as he left the secret police headquarters. But they kept his police dog, Prince. Jacobson drove to the Austrian frontier with a police escort and, after prolonged complications with the Soviet authorities, reached Vienna.

Jacobson's arrest and deportation marked the conclusion of the Joint's independent operations in Eastern Europe. No American representative was allowed to replace him in Budapest. Three weeks after Jacobson's release from jail, Henry Levy, the Joint's director in Prague, was ordered to leave the country and to liquidate all of the organization's operations by the end of January 1950.

It was the end of an era. The Joint had helped rescue more than 700,000 Jews in Eastern Europe and played a humanitarian role—in size and daring—beyond that of any other private American organization. In financial terms, between 1945 and 1950 the Joint spent over $300 million (approximately $3 billion in 1991 dollars). Over 700,000 Jews in Eastern Europe were kept alive by the Joint during that period. Without the Joint, there would have been mass starvation.

The decision to finance the Mossad, the result of Joe Schwartz's efforts to link the Joint to illegal immigration, enabled 115,000 European Jewish refugees to reach Palestine between 1943 and independence in 1948. It made it possible to transfer the 40,000 Jewish detainees from Cyprus to Israel, and afterward to organize, in cooperation with the Jewish Agency, the immigration of most of the 239,576 Jews who traveled to Israel in 1949. Between 1948 and 1950, nearly 440,000 Jews—270,000 refugees from Europe and 167,000 from Moslem countries—arrived in Israel with the cooperation of the Joint.

All in all, 684,201 Jews from seventy countries emigrated to Israel between independence in 1948 and the end of 1951—doubling the Jewish population of what until recently had been Palestine.

For the Aliyah Bet, this was the great triumph of a struggle that had lasted over a decade. What the British called the "Mossad Machine" had carried the day.

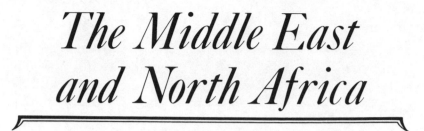

The Middle East and North Africa

XXV

On the Wings of Aliyah

With Israel's independence, Jewish immigration was unfettered, and the DP camps began to disgorge huge numbers on their way to Palestine. To Joe Schwartz, however, the Joint's responsibilities to Jewry abroad were simply entering a new phase.

On May 23 Schwartz addressed an emergency conference of the United Jewish Appeal in New York. New achievements brought new obligations, he remarked. "This year, 1948, will mark the beginnings of the large-scale exodus of the Jews from Germany and other DP areas." But, he warned, "the Joint cannot let down the people who stay in Europe—and, under the most favorable circumstances, 1.3 million of the present 1.5 million Jews will still be there at the end of 1948."

Schwartz then raised the issue of Jews in Moslem countries. Approximately 800,000 Jews lived "under Moslem rule from Morocco to Yemen," and while their problems had been relatively simple until now, they were exacerbated by the creation of a separate Jewish state. Already the Joint had had to make emergency grants to Jews who were victims of pogroms in Aden, riots in Yemen, outbreaks in Aleppo, Syria, and Tripoli in Libya. These Jewish communities, Schwartz concluded, "are living on a volcano."

Even as Schwartz spoke, the Joint was secretly underwriting and helping organize Jewish emigration from Yemen, Aden and Iraq. In late 1946, the Mossad launched Operations Ezra and Nehemiah (known together as Operation Babylon) to save Jews from successive regimes in Iraq. This was really the second phase of an operation that dated back to March 1942, when Avigur smuggled himself into Iraq.

Ephraim Krasner Dekel, the head of the Shai, had introduced Avigur to a Jewish sergeant in a British Army transport company which ran regular routes between Tel Aviv and Baghdad. Avigur disguised himself as the assistant driver of a military truck—it was the only time in his life he ever wore *any* military uniform—and went to survey the situation of the Iraqi Jewish community of some 150,000, one of the oldest Jewish communities in the world. After crossing the Syrian desert in unbearable heat, Avigur wasted no time in Baghdad contacting Jewish community leaders. He was told that young Iraqi Jews were preparing themselves to resist new Arab attacks, but he saw the fear in their eyes. Under the rule of a pro-Nazi minister, Rashid Ali al-Hailani, at least 120 Jews had been killed and 700 injured during a pogrom in June of the previous year. Returning to Tel Aviv, he reported to Ben-Gurion that there was "an urgent need to help the Jews in Baghdad."

Avigur was convinced that there was no future for the Jews in Iraq. The Mossad then began planning what ultimately became—between early 1947 and 1951—the huge

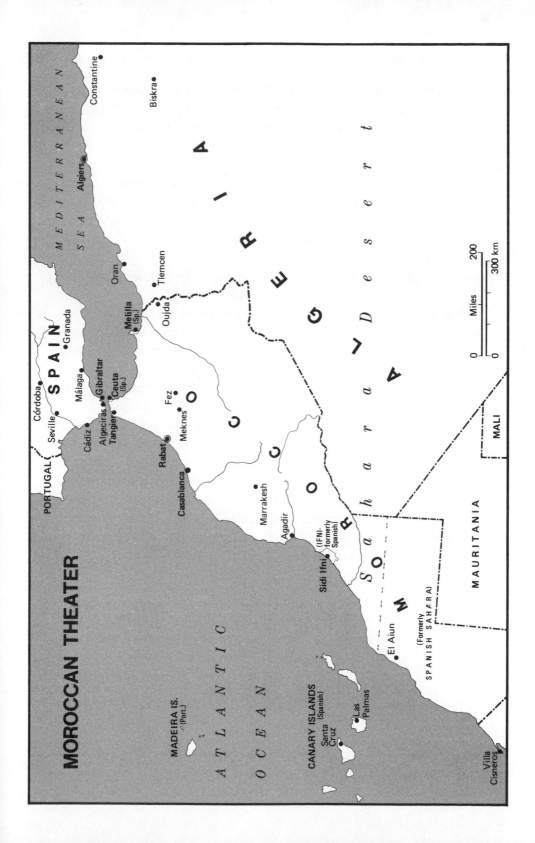

exodus of the Iraqi Jewry. During 1942 and 1943, Avigur made four more secret trips to Baghdad to set up the Mossad machinery, including the installation of a clandestine radio transmitter that broadcast daily to Tel Aviv headquarters for eight years. But Jewish departures, legal and illegal, did not start from Iraq until 1947, when enough pressures and bribery finally moved the royal government to let the Jews go, albeit gradually. The Iraqis would not allow direct flights to Tel Aviv, so the Jews were flown to Cyprus, then moved by air and sea to Israel.

Operation Magic Carpet, launched in December 1948 and continuing over a twenty-one month period, resulted in the ferrying of 49,000 white-robed Jews from Yemen (including 7,000 Yemenite Jews stranded in Aden by pogroms) to Israel aboard planes chartered from U.S. (including Alaskan) and Cuban airlines—rickety DC-4s and C-46s.

Avigur kept Schwartz informed of this enterprise and the Joint was able to finance the lion's share of the airlift—$4 million—which in the end brought 120,000 Jews from Iraq to Israel. It was the Joint's largest—but not the last— immigration operation after Israel's independence, and it marked Schwartz's personal farewell to the world of Mossad and Aliyah Bet. American Jewish organizations would subsequently mount great intelligence enterprises with the new Mossad to rescue hundreds of thousands of Jews from Morocco and much of the Middle East.

XXVI

Another Handshake

History seemed to repeat itself on a steamy day in August 1961 when an emissary from Jerusalem and the head of the principal private American Jewish immigration agency shook hands in New York on a secret agreement to cooperate in negotiating and organizing departures of Jews from Morocco to Israel, both legally and illegally, in the largest postwar enterprise of its kind. The handshake was between Jewish Agency representative Baruch Duvdvani, a sixty-five-year-old veteran of Palestinian illegal immigration operations, and Murray I. Gurfein, a fifty-four-year-old noted American jurist and president of the United HIAS Service.

The essence of their agreement, an oral one, as was customary in such cases, was that HIAS would provide an American cover for the activities of underground Israeli agents in Morocco, which included organizing Jewish emigration from the North African kingdom, the arming of Jewish Moroccan communities for self-defense and a variety of other clandestine programs, in addition to highly discreet negotiations with the Moroccan government to facilitate the Jewish exodus. American HIAS officials would be directly involved in the orchestration of sea and air departures, often under cover of darkness, and HIAS would finance the majority of the operational costs—including covert payments to the Moroccan government for each emigrant. The scope of the accord between a foreign government—the Jewish Agency was de facto part of the Israeli government—and a private United States organization was without precedent. But it was a replay, fifteen years later, of the equally secret deal in Paris between Shaul Avigur and Joe Schwartz.

Under the 1961 arrangement between HIAS and the Jewish Agency, over 100,000 Moroccan Jews, including entire villages in the Atlas Mountains, were directly helped by the Americans in emigrating to Israel; thousands more were later indirectly assisted by HIAS in leaving the country. The cost to HIAS, which relied on contributions from American Jewry, was close to $50 million.

However, the activities of HIAS in North Africa and the Middle East have never been disclosed, except in the barest fashion. One reason was that while HIAS's agreement was formally with the Jewish Agency, the quasi-governmental organization in Israel in charge of all immigration and resettlement of Jews from around the world, the Israeli operatives in Morocco and Europe connected with this project were handpicked members of the Mossad. Only HIAS's top officials in New York and abroad were aware of it, and they were as cautious and secretive about it as the Israelis.

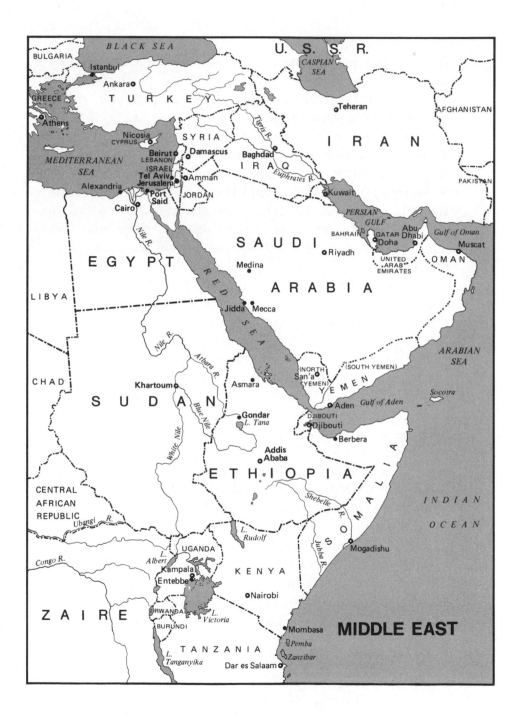

BULGARIA

BLACK SEA

Istanbul

Ankara○

U. S. S. R.

CASPIAN SEA

GREECE

Athens○

T U R K E Y

Teheran○

AFGHANISTAN

Nicosia○
CYPRUS

MEDITERRANEAN SEA

SYRIA

Beirut○
LEBANON
Damascus

Baghdad

I R A Q

Tigris R.

I R A N

PAKISTAN

Tel Aviv○
ISRAEL
Jerusalem○

○Amman
JORDAN

Euphrates R.

Alexandria

Cairo○

Port
Said

PERSIAN GULF

Kuwait○

BAHRAIN○
QATAR○
Doha

Abu
Dhabi

Gulf of Oman

Muscat○

Nile R.

S A U D I

Medina○

Riyadh○

UNITED
ARAB
EMIRATES

O M A N

LIBYA

E G Y P T

A R A B I A

RED SEA

Jidda○ ○Mecca

ARABIAN SEA

CHAD

Nile R.

Athara R.

Khartoum○

S U D A N

Asmara○

(NORTH
YEMEN)
San'a○

(SOUTH YEMEN)

Y E M E N

Aden○ *Gulf of Aden*

Socotra

Blue Nile

Gondar○
L. Tana

DJIBOUTI
Djibouti○

Berbera○

White Nile

**Addis
Ababa**

E T H I O P I A

Shebelle R.

S
O
M
A
L
I
A

INDIAN OCEAN

CENTRAL
AFRICAN
REPUBLIC

Ubangi R.

*L.
Rudolf*

Congo R.

*L.
Albert*

UGANDA

Kampala○
Entebbe○

K E N Y A

Jubba R.

Mogadishu○

Z A I R E

RWANDA
BURUNDI

*L.
Victoria*

○Nairobi

T A N Z A N I A

*L.
Tanganyika*

Mombasa○

Pemba

MIDDLE EAST

Dar es Salaam○ ○Zanzibar

Immigration and intelligence structures in the United States and Israel had changed completely since the days of the collaboration between the Palestinians and the Joint. But a few key people remained.

Within a month of Israel's independence Prime Minister Ben-Gurion ordered the organization of the new nation's intelligence services. Separate military intelligence, a domestic secret service (which would later be known as the Shin Bet) and a foreign intelligence service under the auspices of the Foreign Ministry were created to replace the Shai, the intelligence branch of the Haganah, which in turn became the regular Israeli Army.

Ha-Mossad le-Aliyah Bet (Institute for Illegal Immigration) was maintained under Shaul Avigur and absorbed into the new intelligence community. But since Jews could now freely enter the country, Avigur's department had less to do with illegal immigration: the post-independence problem was how to help Jews *leave* their homelands. Avigur devoted most of his time to the acquisition of weapons for the armed forces and served briefly as Deputy Minister of Defense. But his personal influence diminished due to numerous disagreements with Ben-Gurion. Avigur was kept at arm's length from the illegal immigration operations in North Africa; his involvement with refugees was confined to Eastern Europe and the Soviet Union, then a limited sphere of activity. But the clandestine program to encourage Soviet Jews to try to immigrate to Israel, launched by Avigur almost forty years earlier, was the cornerstone of the massive Soviet Aliyah in the early 1990s, when 400,000 Jews went to Israel during a two-year period. Shaike Dan, the Balkan expert and ex-parachutist from the old days, worked with Avigur on these problems.

On April 1, 1951, the Israeli intelligence community was reorganized again. The most significant change was that foreign intelligence operations were placed under a new and powerful unit, the ha-Mossad le-Modiin ule-Tafkidim Me-yuhadim, translated as the Institute for Intelligence and Special Tasks. The new intelligence agency became known simply as the Mossad, and Ben-Gurion appointed Reuven Shiloah, who was the Shai's co-founder with Avigur, as its director. Avigur was excluded from the new Mossad altogether, and his old Mossad was formally abolished a year later. Thereafter, whatever underground or illegal immigration operations were required came under the jurisdiction of the new Mossad. Late in 1951 the Jewish Agency and the Mossad signed an agreement which gave the latter the job of "underground activities . . . to make contacts with Jews" in Arab countries and to bring them to Israel.

In the United States the approach to immigration by private agencies also underwent a postwar transformation. The Joint and HIAS frequently overlapped in their immigration functions, and this resulted in an unnecessary duplication of effort and expenditure. In 1954, a merger proposal was approved by both organizations. HIAS (incorporating the United Service for New Americans, Inc.) assumed the Joint's immigration functions and became the unified American Jewish migration agency under the name of United HIAS Service, Inc. (later shortened to HIAS, Inc.). Henceforth, the Joint concentrated on relief, education and other tasks in support of Jewish communities abroad—including preparation for emigration to Israel or elsewhere.

HIAS was the perfect vehicle for the Mossad's emmigration activities in Morocco. Not only was it respected internationally, but it had had an office in Casablanca since 1955 to assist the legal emigration of individual Jews. Moreover, Murray Gurfein, a prestigious lawyer who had been an assistant district attorney under Thomas E. Dewey in New York and who was elected president of HIAS in 1956, was well known to top Israeli leaders.

During the 1948 independence war, Gurfein had assisted in the acquisition of arms in the United States for the Haganah. The Mossad also had an old ally on the HIAS board: Joe Schwartz. Schwartz had left the Joint to run the Israeli Bonds campaign in the United States, and he had always advocated a major emigration effort in North Africa. Although HIAS had been informally helping the Jewish Agency in Morocco since the mid-1950s, the Israelis now felt the need for a comprehensive arrangement with the Americans.

The Israeli partner was Baruch Duvdvani, the operational head of the Immigration Department of the Jewish Agency. He worked with Moshe Sharett, the former Prime Minister and current chairman of the Jewish Agency, and Shlomo-Zalman Shragai, a writer and scholar who had served as mayor of Jerusalem from 1950 to 1952 and then became the director of the Jewish Agency's Immigration Department. In that post, Shragai was directly in charge of the Morocco project, working hand in hand with the Mossad.

Shortly after his meeting with Duvdvani, Gurfein visited Jerusalem, where he gained new insight into Israeli policy-making. He conferred with Prime Minister Ben-Gurion, Sharett and Golda Meir, then Foreign Minister. Gurfein, a former lieutenant colonel in the U.S. Army, understood perfectly what the Mossad faced in its latest endeavor. On September 14 he reported to the HIAS executive committee and was given full support in the co-venture to protect and rescue the ancient Jewish community in Morocco.

Approximately 270,000 Jews lived in Morocco in the early 1950s. It was the largest Jewish community in North Africa and the Middle East, but a small minority among Morocco's 8 million Moslems. It may also have been the second-oldest Jewish community in the world outside of Judea, dating back to the first century of the Christian era.

In A.D. 70 the Roman armies under Titus destroyed Jerusalem and the Second Temple, and thousands of Jewish captives were sent west to settle the reign that today constitutes Morocco. The oldest Jewish community after biblical Judea was in Iraq, believed to have been established in Babylonia by Jews fleeing their lands following the burning of the First Temple—the Temple of Solomon—by Nebuchadnezzar in 586 B.C. The black Jews of Ethiopia, known as the Falashas, may descend from the Lost Tribe of Dan, as alleged by some Sephardic scholars, or from the times of King Solomon in the ninth century B.C. According to yet another theory, they derive from the very same Jews who fled after the destruction of the First Temple.

Descendants of the Jewish captives from Judea are said to have converted to Judaism a number of Berber nomadic tribes in what today is Morocco. The Jewish community in Morocco also expanded with exiles from Spain and Portugal when Jews fled there to escape persecution by the Visigoths in the sixth century and the Inquisition in the fifteenth century.

But from the onset of Islam in North Africa, Jews (as well as some Christians) were treated as second-class citizens, supposedly "protected" but decidedly inferior. For example, under the so-called Pact of Omar (the second caliph, ruling in the seventh century), Jews paid heavier taxes than Moslems, could ride only mules and donkeys—not horses—and were forbidden to carry swords. Moreover, they were restricted from holding public office and from numerous professions. But they were allowed to become goldsmiths and silversmiths, grain merchants, and even financiers and diplomats.

Under King Idris II, who ruled in Fez at the end of the eighth century, the concept of "protection" grew even more restrictive. Supposedly to safeguard Jews, Idris built a walled Jewish quarter called the *mellah*. But in time the *mellahs* in Moroccan cities became ghettos and slums, to which the Jews were confined. Little had changed by the early twentieth century. In 1912, when Morocco was split into French and Spanish protectorates, the bulk of Moroccan Jews were still bottled up in rural and urban *mellahs*. Only a small fraction were allowed to participate in economic and social development or to devote themselves to Jewish scholarship and religion.

But the ancient concept of protection actually did save a great many Jews when Morocco was under pro-Nazi French rule emanating from Vichy during World War II. Sultan Sidi Mohammed V, who governed Morocco under the protectorate, refused to obey Vichy orders for the deportation of Moroccan Jews to France (and presumably to their deaths at German hands). He declared that the Jews too were his "children" and that all of his subjects would have to be deported before he allowed Jewish families to leave. Vichy dropped the matter. Yet the Jews were never granted Moroccan citizenship by the sultan, and they lived under his "protection" without a defined nationality.

The wave of nationalism that rolled across the Middle East and North Africa in the 1950s filled Moroccan Jews—and the Israelis concerned for their fate—with grave forebodings. The protectorates in Morocco, Tunisia and Algeria were regarded by France as part of the French Republic, although all three North African entities demanded independence. But Paris was not yet ready to grant sovereignty to Morocco and Tunisia. Indeed, independence for "Algérie Française" was not even a subject for discussion among most French leaders. Algeria was designated as a *département* of metropolitan France.

In Tunisia, the nationalist leader Habib Bourguiba had been in prison since 1952 for agitating for freedom. In August 1953, French authorities deposed Morocco's Sultan Sidi Mohammed and exiled him to an island in the Indian Ocean because he sided with the nationalists. The sultan was very popular with Moroccans, including the Jews, and this act only heightened pro-independence fervor. Finally, on November 1, 1954, a full-fledged revolt against France exploded in Algeria.

Prime Minister Pierre Mendès-France's attempts to defuse the North African crises were frustrated by French nationalists, and he was forced to resign in February 1955 after only eight months in office. Mendès-France was the first Jew to serve as France's Prime Minister since Léon Blum in 1936 (both were moderate French socialists), but even during his brief tenure the Jews in Morocco grew more and more worried. Moroccan independence leaders and activists filled the prisons of the protectorate, which led to rising tensions and more frequent clashes. There were deaths almost daily in the struggle between nationalists and "counterterrorists." As part of Morocco's transition to independence, France had planned on restoring the sultan to his throne.

Anticipating a crisis certain to affect the Jewish population, HIAS executive director Arthur Greenleigh considered opening an office in Morocco. In October 1954 he made a discreet visit to Casablanca, and his confidential report to the board of directors painted a bleak picture:

> The situation for all non-Moslems in Morocco is extremely tense. The Moslems are determined to drive out the French and achieve independence . . . In the meanwhile, the economic and political situations have rapidly deteriorated. Jews who have lived for centuries in the interior have found it necessary to move into the bigger cities to save their lives. Jewish businessmen have been threatened with death by the terrorists unless they make substantial financial contributions to the terrorist cause. . . . Morocco is now an armed camp—no non-Moslem is safe on the streets at night and every day . . . someone is killed by the terrorists.

For the first time in 2,000 years, Moroccan Jews were convinced they would have to leave the country. The only question was when. As a result of Greenleigh's report, the HIAS board of directors approved a $400,000 "contingency fund" for North Africa for the following year and requested an evaluation to determine "the needs and possibilities for [the] emigration program . . . which had already been requested by Jewish leaders in Casablanca and Tangier (in Spanish Morocco)." But the board cautioned that "in view of the delicate political situation," HIAS could not "widely publicize the initiation of this emigration program." Although this was six years before Israel secretly requested HIAS's full-fledged collaboration in taking Jews out of

Morocco, the New York organization was already advancing on its own into the new field.

Among HIAS senior officials involved in the initial stages of the Moroccan situation was Gaynor Jacobson, an old hand at this type of operation. After his release from jail in Budapest in December 1947, Jacobson had decided that he had had his share of risky foreign assignments and he returned to the United States.

In 1950–51, Jacobson served as executive director of the Association for Jewish Children in Philadelphia, a child placement agency. But after Eastern Europe, Philadelphia wasn't much of a challenge for the thirty-nine-year-old activist, and he gladly accepted the post of executive director of the American Technion Society of New York, which supported Israel's Institute of Technology in Haifa with money and educational expertise. When the post in Paris of HIAS director for Europe and North Africa became vacant in early 1953, Schwartz persuaded Jacobson to take it—not that it took much persuading. This was just when the Joint and HIAS were preparing to merge.

Jacobson arrived in Paris in May 1953 with the title of Director of Operations, a somewhat lesser position than he had expected. He renewed the contacts and friendships with Israeli immigration and intelligence officials he had developed in Eastern Europe in the 1940s. And HIAS's responsibilities in the region, ranging from the closing of the last DP camp in Germany to the preliminary planning for Morocco, kept him busy day and night.

So long as France controlled Morocco, Jews were free to leave at will. In November 1954, Raphael Spanien, the HIAS deputy director for Europe, had written his friend André Pelabon, Prime Minister Mendès-France's Cabinet chief, that his organization was contemplating opening an office in Morocco. The Joint already had a Moroccan office, but it dealt only with relief and education, not emigration. The Jewish Agency also maintained an office in Casablanca and a nearby camp specifically to handle emigration to Israel. France, moreover, was extremely generous in granting transit visas to Jews.

In a report to HIAS officials, Greenleigh estimated that the Jewish Agency was dispatching between 2,000 and 2,500 Jews monthly to Israel and that by the end of 1954 more than 10,000 would have been evacuated. In the next fifteen months, they planned to "emigrate" more than 30,000. Actually, the Jewish Agency did even better: Israeli statistics show that Moroccan Jewish immigration to the Holy Land soared from 8,171 in 1954 to 24,994 in 1955. Then the entire situation changed.

The Jewish fear, of course, was that once Moroccan independence was achieved—and this was considered inevitable before long—the whole Jewish community might be endangered and emigration halted. Spanien undertook a survey of Morocco during February 1955, pretending that he was "on vacation" to avoid arousing unnecessary curiosity in local political quarters. Because he had worked in Casablanca during the war and had returned to Morocco many times afterward, Spanien had unparalleled access.

The most interesting items in Spanien's survey were his observations on the social, economic and cultural conditions of Moroccan Jewry and how these conditions affected the conduct of potential large-scale emigration programs. Spanien found a Jewish community that was backward in every sense, especially in the isolated villages where roughly half of the Moroccan Jews lived in an almost medieval state. Greenleigh had noted that out of 250,000 Moroccan Jews (the figure was closer to 270,000 at the time), only 25,000 to 50,000 were "Westernized." Spanien was more specific: "There are very few Moroccan Jewish doctors or lawyers . . . Among the 50,000 Jews who emigrated to Israel since the war, there is not even one doctor. The two lawyers who left for Israel were old men and went there to retire from business and not to take up the practice of their profession . . . We are faced with a Jewry without an elite," Spanien concluded. The elite were Jewish foreigners—French, Algerians, Spanish and even Tunisians—who, when confronted with imminent danger, could readily reach safety outside Morocco. Even the leaders in Moroccan Jewish communities, he added, were "themselves inclined to follow instructions issued by the alien Jews of Morocco."

Concerning the prospects for emigration, Spanien reported that "when dealing with Jews who have had, up to the present, little contact with Western civilization, dressed in the native fashion with djellabahs and black skullcaps, no other country outside of Israel is in a position to absorb them as they are." But he also noted that many other Moroccan Jews tended to dress as Europeans, "which is the main condition for their assimilation and immediate possibility of integration in new countries." Moroccan Jews, Spanien felt, should be able to choose between emigration to Israel and emigration to South America or Canada, where a certain number could be admitted. At that point, HIAS had no commitment to direct all Moroccan Jews to Israel; in fact, it did not wish to appear to be competing with the Jewish Agency, although the latter thought that the Americans were trying to take Jews away from it.

Despite immensely primitive conditions in the villages,

Spanien observed cultural improvements in the cities. "Jewish girl servants who, formerly, were serving barefoot and dressed like natives, working for low salaries, are now dressed as Europeans, wearing nylon stockings and shoes . . . Their wages are now almost equivalent to those of European servants. They used to work them from dawn until late in the night; they are now employed for a reasonable number of hours . . . In large cities, young Jewish boys and girls are properly dressed in the European fashion, even with a certain elegance, and do not look different from the French or the Spanish. Some wear eyeglasses, which proves that the fight against eye diseases—the curse of the country—has been fruitful."

An excess of births over deaths, nearly 25,000 annually, Spanien cited, kept increasing the Jewish population at a time when "there is an undeniable desire to emigrate on the part of Moroccan Jews." With a crisis seemingly around the corner, this trend threatened to complicate the possibilities of emigration.

In July 1955, the HIAS board voted to open an office in Casablanca. Sigisbert Plasterek, a French citizen, was appointed to run it, and Hélène Cazès Benatar, a leading local attorney, would provide legal support. A Tangier office was set up three weeks later. HIAS was now equipped to assist the emigration of individual Moroccan Jewish families and promoted South America as the most promising destination.

Jacobson was named director for Latin America, and he left Paris early in 1955, going first to Buenos Aires and then to Rio de Janeiro, where he installed his headquarters. He persuaded Brazil's newly elected President, Juscelino Kubitschek, to allow the immigration of thousands of Moroccan and Egyptian Jews—the first time the Brazilians accepted Jewish refugees from Africa—and later to open the doors to Hungarian Jews fleeing after the 1956 anti-Communist revolt. At one point, Jacobson recalled, the Joint and HIAS agreed to pay a Brazilian consul general in Frankfurt $25 per visa for Jewish DPs stranded in Germany. "We got a few thousand people out of Germany with Brazilian visas at this price," he claimed.

The foundations had thus been laid for future activities that would prove to be far greater than the HIAS directors could visualize at this juncture.

Events moved rapidly in Morocco. On November 6, 1955, the French government brought Sultan Sidi Mohammed back to Rabat, the capital, and restored him to the throne as a constitutional monarch with limited national autonomy. As independence approached, the Jewish community grew more alarmed. Despite the many restrictions it suffered, it was happier under the protection of the sultan—and France. But the community leaders had to avoid antagonizing the nationalists, who were certain to wield much power before too long.

An internal HIAS report warned that the situation in Morocco was "urgent" because the Jews were not French citizens and they were not given any status under the new regime. The report added that Moslem nationalist movements in North Africa were motivated in part by the desire of the Arabs to replace the French and Jewish middle and lower middle classes in the economic life of the region and that this drive "continued regardless of the political framework . . . and regardless of the political guarantees which may be obtained for the protection of the rights of the Jewish population." On an ominous note it concluded: "There can be no guarantees against the boycotts and economic pressures which have already uprooted the Jewish population in these countries . . . This situation is reminiscent of the economic upheaval which took place in the Eastern European countries between the two world wars and served to uproot the Jews there from their relatively secure economic positions, and which preceded their physical persecution and annihilation under the Hitler regime."

The HIAS board accepted the report's findings and recommendations and set up a $1 million "contingency item" in the 1956 budget. Then France resolved to cut Morocco loose. Independence was declared on March 3, 1956, under Sidi Mohammed V, and many of the dire predictions came true. The Jewish Agency was ordered by the new government to close down its operations and its embarkation camp near Casablanca. This put a halt to legal immigration to Israel and stranded 2,000 Jews from remote villages waiting to leave Morocco. Upon his return the sultan reaffirmed his commitment to the Jews, and Léon Benzaquen, a Jew, was named to the new Cabinet as Minister of Posts and Telegraph. But an internal HIAS report in July informed the board of directors that "there appears to be clear evidence that the Istiqlal [Nationalist] Party or the government or both have initiated a policy of disrupting Jewish community life in the country."

At that point, the Jewish Agency opened the first secret talks with HIAS on the subject of covert cooperation for extricating Jews from Morocco and for protecting them there. In even greater secrecy, Israel had already put in place a clandestine Mossad structure that exceeded anything the young intelligence service had accomplished since its birth in 1951.

XXVII

Operation Framework

The secret Israeli structure erected in North Africa in 1955 was Framework—Misgeret in Hebrew—and it was based upon the concept of self-defense which some Jewish communities had developed as protection from the Arabs and other foes. In time, Framework grew into a superbly integrated organization in Morocco, Tunisia and Algeria, and conducted a most imaginative illegal emigration program for nearly six years. In all three countries, the Mossad created clandestine but well-armed home units, educational systems and even a postal link with Israel when regular service was suspended by the Arab governments.

The idea of Jewish self-defense was not new, of course. The Haganah had been established in Palestine under Britain's rule to protect the kibbutzim and other Jewish communities from the Arabs, as well as from the British. With the memory of the Holocaust and of pogroms in Eastern

Europe and in Middle Eastern and Arab countries—Kielce, Aden and Yemen in particular—painfully fresh in their minds, the Israeli leadership had to assume that the security of some, if not all, of the 860,000 Jews living in Moslem nations at the time of Israeli independence was in jeopardy. In British-ruled Aden and in the towns of Yemen, Arab crowds frequently attacked Jews, their homes and businesses in the postwar years. Executions of Jews in Iraq had occurred more than once.

The Mossad and the Jewish Agency spoke of the Arab lands as "countries of distress" for Jews; if the Arab governments were disposed to launch a war against the new Israeli state in the aftermath of its independence, the Jewish populations under their control would naturally be regarded as the enemy and therefore were not safe. The foundation for the Israelis' concern was the history of anti-Semitism in the Middle East, which, it was believed, would be further aggravated by the new wave of Arab nationalism.

But there was another factor which influenced Israeli leaders, and that was a sense of historical shame for having allowed themselves to be led, virtually without protest, to the Nazi death camps. The Warsaw and Vilnius ghetto uprisings and the formation of the first Jewish partisan units to fight the Germans were, of course, instances of active resistance, but they were the exceptions. With their own state and their victory in the 1948 independence war, the Jews of Israel affirmed that "never again" would they be persecuted, "never again" would they face the horror of another Holocaust. The protection of Jews everywhere was paramount, and it became the cornerstone of Israeli policy. In fact, the first attempt to create a Jewish self-defense force had been made in Egypt three years before the 1948 war, when Avigur dispatched a small team to Cairo to train young Egyptian Jews in the use of weapons.

Framework was the brainchild of Isser Harel, a slim, diminutive Russian-born intelligence and security genius who replaced Reuven Shiloah as the Mossad's director in September 1952. A personal friend of Prime Minister Ben-Gurion, Harel first ran Israel's internal security organ, the Shin Bet.

The Shin Bet had been set up, Harel explained, because "we had dissidents, we had Jewish terrorist groups." In Harel's eyes, most of the Labor Party's opposition right-wing groups were suspected of subversion and even terrorism. Harel's principal target was Menachem Begin, who had led the anti-British Irgun terrorist underground in the 1930s and the 1940s and now headed the Herut Party; later he served as Prime Minister.

According to the Israeli intelligence historian Shmuel Segev, Harel kept Begin under surveillance and reported to Ben-Gurion that Begin's Herut Party planned to establish a "mini-underground" in the Army (a charge for which there appears to be no foundation). Harel also pursued members of the Stern Gang, another pre-independence terrorist group (whose chief, Yitzhak Shamir, would become Israel's Prime Minister in the 1980s), on the grounds that they were planning political assassinations. And Harel's Shin Bet smashed several tiny rightist organizations connected with Jewish religious zealots. It was a dark period in the history of Israeli intelligence, but Ben-Gurion kept Harel on as overall intelligence chief—the *memuneh*—until 1963.*

With regard to the Jewish community in Morocco, Harel explained, "I had to consider what would happen at the

---

* Harel's fame came with his capture of Adolf Eichmann in Argentina in May 1960, which he personally coordinated in Buenos Aires while still the Mossad's chief. His accomplishments with the Framework, by contrast, were little known publicly.

moment the Arabs took power there." Israeli fears were based in part on the creation in 1945 of the Arab League. Now, Egypt's Gamal Abdel Nasser was a leading influence in the League, and Nasser's radicalism, recalled Harel, had become "very violent and very strong." Although it was still a French protectorate, "there was much terrorism" in Morocco. Harel concluded that "with this very big Jewish community in Morocco, the Arabs might do as they did in Iraq during the war, when they perpetrated that terrible pogrom in Baghdad."

Harel assigned Shlomo Havillio, a senior Israeli Army officer who came from one of the very oldest Palestinian families, to assess the Arab threat to Moroccan Jewry and determine whether the young Zionists among them could be relied on to establish their own self-defense. The Israelis "would do everything to help them, to guide them, to supply self-defense knowledge, and it will be a clandestine operation," Harel made clear. "But they will have to do it themselves."

In 1943, Havillio had been named commander of Haganah combat units in Jerusalem. Two years later, Shaul Avigur requested that he go to Cairo to organize a Jewish self-defense force for the Egyptian community. Havillio, who was fluent in Arabic (as well as English, French, Spanish and Hebrew), went to Egypt in the British uniform of a Jewish Brigade soldier. He then used the cover of a businessman acquiring British war surplus equipment there. After more than two years in Egypt, Havillio established a self-defense force of 500 men—300 in Cairo and 200 in Alexandria—and a six-week course for officers who were smuggled into Palestine for training. This was perfect preparation for Framework in Morocco.

Havillio left for North Africa in January 1955 and went first to Morocco, where there was considerable fighting between the French and the Moroccan nationalists. Next door in Algeria, the National Liberation Front (FLN) had launched the war against French domination two months earlier. Havillio traveled with an Israeli passport and posed as an inspector for the Jewish Agency; its Casablanca office supervised Jewish immigration to Israel, which was entirely legal at the time. "I saw everything in Morocco," he recalled. "I talked to everybody."

Framework was born the moment Havillio submitted his report to Harel. Havillio advised the intelligence chief: "When the Moroccans arrive at independence, they will become an Arab country like the other Arab countries, and we must start to organize not only self-defense but also illegal emigration." There was danger, but there were courageous, well-organized young Jews who could be depended upon, in addition to the traditional Zionist movements.

Havillio told the Mossad chief that he needed two years and $250,000, which was provided by the Joint, to set up this structure. Framework became yet another secret Jewish intelligence operation financed from New York.

Harel named Havillio to direct Framework for the Mossad. His first step was to assemble a "core support" group of about twenty army officers—"all with a fighting background and all of them with at least one language, French or Arabic." In Israel the team underwent six months of specialized training in covert operations.

They left for Morocco during the summer of 1955 and began to organize small groups for the Jewish self-defense force. Under the secret cell system, the members of each group knew only one another—and their Mossad commander. Recruits first had to swear allegiance on a Bible and a revolver; then they were trained in the use of sidearms and grenades, clandestine activities, underground organization and physical conditioning. The weapons they used had been shipped secretly from Marseilles, where Mossad agents had packed them in ten cases marked as tools—the first of many such shipments. Everything was organized at the Moroccan end, from the lookouts to the commanders. Even local chiefs of police were on the Mossad's payroll.

If the French authorities suspected any unusual activity, it did not seem to trouble them. Several months later, when Havillio dispatched 35 to 40 leading self-defense trainees aboard Air France airliners for advanced courses in France to assemble "a special force," there were no questions asked. There had also been no interference with the installation of eight illegal wireless stations linking Casablanca and Tangier with Oran in Algeria, Paris and Israel. These same Moroccan self-defense leaders were later sent to Israel for still more training, and Harel even brought Ben-Gurion to watch their military progress.

Framework's security was maintained so well because "we could trust every Jew" in Morocco, Harel claimed. At one point, Harel flew to Morocco to inspect the operation with several Mossad aides; he carried an Austrian passport, and his companions had American and British passports. He was warned by Jewish friends at a synagogue in Casablanca that the police were after him. "My people told me, 'Get out of there quickly because we have to escape from them.'" But when he saw the faces of the worshippers, he replied, "Nobody will interrupt the prayer." In fact, the police were following them, but "they managed to come after us every time a day late," even at the isolated Jewish villages Harel visited in the Atlas Mountains.

Because Framework covered Algeria and Tunisia as well as Morocco, Havillio moved his headquarters to Paris at the end of 1955. Israeli commanders from the Mossad were now in charge of self-defense and secret operations in each country. In Morocco, the self-defense force grew to 700 men, all armed, mainly with revolvers and German Schmeisser and British Sten submachine guns. The self-defense force in Algeria had 600 fighters and the Tunisian force approximately 500.

Only in Algeria, however, did the Jewish self-defense force engage in combat. Algeria was still under French jurisdiction, so there was no emigration problem and there were no travel restrictions for Jews. But the Israelis feared that the Jewish community might become a target of the FLN rebels in the uprising against the French that had exploded with such violence in November 1954. Indeed, in May 1956, about eight months after the Mossad began organizing the Algerian self-defense force, the FLN initiated attacks on Jews in Constantine, the major city in eastern Algeria. Bombs exploded in the Jewish quarter and Havillio rushed to Constantine aboard a French military aircraft to see what he could do to help protect the local community.

He found a dusk-to-dawn curfew in effect and self-defense force leaders who "very courteously said to me, 'We must also throw bombs at the Moslem quarter . . . What do we have to do?' " Havillio told them, "You have a list of the main FLN activists here. Send them a message saying that the Jews in Constantine have nothing to do with the war between the French and the FLN, and we warn you that we will not tolerate our blood being spilled." Havillio then organized armed self-defense patrols around the Jewish quarter.

One Saturday the FLN threw a bomb at the entrance to the Jewish quarter, and as Havillio described it: "When they went away, two patrols of our people came from two sides and they asked the Algerian FLN people, 'Why did you do it?' They answered, 'It is none of your business.' So our people opened fire and killed them, and threw bombs all around . . . There were about fifteen Moslems killed there

. . . And with this action we stopped the attacks of the FLN on the Jews. It never happened again."

Decades later Jewish Agency and Mossad leaders take the view that the use of force against the FLN was absolutely essential in protecting the Jewish communities in Algeria. Shlomo-Zalman Shragai, who was the first director of immigration of the Jewish Agency and represented it in dealings with the Mossad in North Africa, said that the violence in Constantine happened at about the time of the abduction and execution by the FLN of two Israeli "emissaries" in a village near the Moroccan border. The two Mossad men had gone there, according to Shragai, "to organize local Jews for their departure to Israel," but "they were grabbed and disappeared." Despite discreet discussions with representatives of the FLN at the United Nations in New York—who had promised that "you will see your men tomorrow, but you will have to pay a certain amount of money"—the Algerians "finally confirmed that they lost their lives . . . that they were killed by the FLN."*

* Harel was inspired by the North African experience to set up a self-defense force in Argentina after the ouster of the dictator Juan Perón in the military coup of September 1955. Perón's followers included an ultranationalist organization, and after his fall they began physically attacking Jews in Buenos Aires. "It was a very dangerous mob," Harel said, and the Israeli embassy alerted the government in Jerusalem to the need for defending Argentine Jews. Israel advised them to start organizing their own self-defense, but they couldn't decide who would actually lead it. Harel then flew to Buenos Aires, stayed for ten days and organized the force for them. "They thought it was a miracle that Israel came to help, and all of them accepted my leadership. We did wonders. We found weapons, and they were prepared to withstand any attack."

Actually, Harel exaggerated the threat to the 200,000 Jewish citizens of Argentina, where no systematic anti-Semitic activities were recorded. Perón had tolerated limited anti-Semitic harassment by the Alianza Libertadora, an extreme nationalist but quite small splinter organization headed by a political thug named Guillermo Kelly which supported his regime, but Perón forbade violence. The Alianza was destroyed by the Argentine Army in the aftermath of Perón's ouster by the military and never resurfaced. However, right-wing military regimes in Argentina in the 1970s practiced selective anti-Semitism, sometimes arresting and torturing its critics, some of whom were Jewish, such as the newspaper publisher Jacobo Timerman.

XXVIII

Conspiracy in Morocco

With the proclamation of independence in Morocco on March 3, 1956, Mossad's Framework faced the challenge of assuring the Jews that they would be able to continue to emigrate to Israel. The new royal regime, in an attempt to appease left-wing nationalists of the Istiqlal Party, instituted an immediate ban; henceforth all departures to Israel would be illegal. But the Mossad had anticipated the edict, and Framework provided the mechanism to start illegal emigration operations almost immediately. By that time, Framework had expanded into an organization that specialized in many spheres—all of them clandestine.

Harel believed that King Sidi Mohammed V, who decided to freeze Jewish emigration to Israel at the moment of independence, was pressured by the powerful Istiqlal, which was "very much under the influence of Nasser, who had boasted that he would destroy all of us."

The Moroccan ban on Jewish emigration applied only to those bound for Israel. But this in effect halted most departures by Jews until the Mossad launched its illegal programs. As Raphael Spanien had pointed out in his report, the majority were primitive Jews from the villages whom no nation other than Israel would accept.

The first Moroccan target was the Jewish Agency's emigration operation in Casablanca, the principal port of embarkation for the Jews. General Mohammed Laghzaoui, chief of national security, had ordered all departures halted. Over 2,000 Jews, mostly families from remote mountain enclaves who had sold their homes to emigrate to Israel, were stranded at the Agency's camp near the harbor. Laghzaoui threatened to close down the camp altogether and he gave the Jewish Agency's Israeli personnel eight days to leave Morocco. He ordered the border police to prevent any Moroccan with an Israeli visa from departing.

Moroccan authorities tried to force the Jews in the camp to return to their villages, but when they refused, the government agreed to issue a collective visa for their departure. Gradually they began to leave, but the camp was becoming bigger rather than smaller, and soon held close to 7,000 people.

What was happening was the result of the Jewish community's ingenuity—aided by the Mossad—in trying to beat the odds. They were simply replacing the emigrants who had left with new ones so that they too would be covered by the collective exit visa. When General Laghzaoui asked the Jewish Agency officials still in Casablanca to post guards to prevent additional people from entering the camp, he was told to send his own policemen. According to an internal

HIAS report: "For a short time, there were police outside the camp; nevertheless the people were able to get in . . . Then the police were withdrawn, apparently on the theory that Laghzaoui feared that if he posted police at the camp, the Western world might consider that it was a concentration camp and that people were being held there against their will." It took thirty shiploads to transport the camp's population to Marseilles.

But Laghzaoui then went a step further and ordered the seizure of passports already held by Jews, preventing *all* Jewish travel abroad. Under powerful pressure by foreign governments, who had been alerted by the Israelis, he rescinded the order. It was nonetheless an example of the new political climate.

With the expulsion of the Jewish Agency and the end of legal immigration to Israel, the Mossad stepped into the breach. Ben-Gurion and his top associates had resolved that "special measures" might be required to bring Jews out of Morocco after Moroccan independence, and the Jewish Agency—responsible for all immigration—turned to the Mossad. Shlomo-Zalman Shragai, who was then the head of the Agency's immigration department, approached Harel, and they decided to inaugurate illegal emigration from Morocco. But, Harel advised, the Jewish Agency and the government—not the Mossad—had to determine which communities would leave first. "And we shouldn't interfere with each other," Harel added.

Harel's point touched on the serious problems he knew would arise over selections and priorities in illegal emigration: whether only young and healthy Jews should be taken out, leaving behind the old and the infirm in the villages; or whether everyone wishing to go should be helped in emigrating. Harel believed that the Mossad should not have the power to make what was essentially a policy decision; he suspected—and correctly—that his associates would favor young men of military age. Harel insisted that the Jewish Agency's immigration department approve the priorities set.

Avigur had "also submitted an offer" to the Jewish Agency to run the Moroccan illegal emigration with his Aliyah Bet veterans, but he was turned down. To Harel, Avigur had become "the old-timer who didn't want to know old people," implying that he would have concentrated on bringing only the young from Morocco. Avigur's role in security affairs was by now over, and this represented his last attempt to have at least a bit part. But, he noted ruefully in his memoirs, "it didn't work. One has to know when to go, when to leave the chair, before the chair leaves him." For more than a decade, however, Avigur continued to run his secret "Soviet Jewry" project from a special foreign ministry office code-named "Lishka."

The clandestine North African operation was composed of five branches. The first one was self-defense, and from this force Havillio chose commanders for the other branches. The second branch was information and intelligence in support of Framework's own operations: it had to know everything it could about the Jewish communities, Moroccan government decision-making and the activities of Moroccan police and security organs. The third branch was illegal immigration. In the fourth branch, young Moroccan Zionists "worked in the underground with the Mossad." Their main function, Havillio explained, was to establish the first contact with Jewish families "to ask them if they [were] ready and willing to go." The fifth branch was public relations aimed at obtaining secret support from key members of the Jewish community. This branch, which included an underground medical organization and maintained contacts with foreign diplomats and the press, would approach community members and say, for example, "You have industries, you can help us organize a secret stock of arms."

In mounting the illegal emigration from Morocco, Harel recalled, "we started with passports. But we couldn't adjust them to everyone, except young people or young couples, so we started our own production of different passports, including American passports. And believe me, they were much better than the originals."

At first, the Mossad tried to manufacture the fake passports in France, but it was too complicated because lists of names and photographs had to be smuggled out of Morocco. Harel therefore decided to add an artist to the Moroccan operation, Shalom Weiss, known as "Danny." Danny was so good that Harel took him four years later to Argentina—to prepare identity documents for the Harel team—on the mission to capture Eichmann.

The Mossad manufactured Moroccan as well as foreign passports (there were different requirements for city dwellers and for the villagers) and the Mossad artist soon acquired local helpers. The real problem was that each province issued passports directly, signed by local officials, and the forgers had to match signatures from Casablanca, Fez or Rabat on travel documents supposedly issued in those cities. It required considerable research to obtain the names of regional governors and officials—and their signatures. But "we were very well ·organized," Havillio matter-of-factly explained. Havillio himself had so many passports for his own use that "it was a question of knowing which passport to use at which airport, and what passport to show in which hotel," as he traveled continually between Paris and North Africa.

On one occasion, when the Mossad's commander in Tangier was returning to his post from Paris with two suitcases containing 300 false Moroccan passports, Spanish border guards arrested him as he tried to cross into Gibraltar, from where he planned to take a boat home. At the jail in the Spanish frontier town of Algeciras, he demanded to see the local chief of police and told him, "I am an Israeli . . . The passports I have are Moroccan passports to help get the Jews out." Aware of the hostility between Spain and Morocco, he continued: "I think that your interests and our interests are the same, so why don't we operate together?" This was an offer to provide the Spanish authorities with intelligence about Tangier, and the chief of police took him over to confer with the military governor of the Spanish province. The deal was struck, and the fake passports were safely in Tangier the next day.

The basic plan for the "Moroccan Exodus," as Havillio called it, was to extricate Jews aboard small boats from unguarded ports on both the Atlantic and Mediterranean coasts. Linked by the Strait of Gibraltar, they included the Spanish enclaves of Ceuta and Melilla on Morocco's Mediterranean coast in the north; Ifni in the south on the Atlantic coast bordering the Spanish Sahara; and Tangier, an international zone. To reach these ports the Jews often had to be driven hundreds of miles across the desert by bus, truck or taxi. They were exhausting journeys for families with elderly members and children. And there was always the risk of being stopped or captured by Moroccan security agents. Sailing was even more perilous because the open water off both coasts was frequently stormy and turbulent. All in all, it was infinitely more difficult and dangerous than the Jewish flight from Europe in the 1940s and the famous saga of *Exodus '47*.

But, once out, the Moroccan Jews would have no trouble going across the borders of the countries through which they had to pass in order to ultimately reach Israel. They freely entered Spain and France, and were then flown or shipped from Marseilles to Tel Aviv or Haifa.

Indeed, a large measure of the Mossad's success in illegal immigration was due to the extraordinary—and mostly discreet—cooperation of French, Spanish and British authorities in the region. There were Mossad representatives stationed permanently in Ceuta, Melilla, Ifni, Algeciras, Gibraltar and Madrid to receive and guide the arriving Jewish emigrants and channel them on their way to Israel. To assure the safe passage of Jews, Mossad officers dealt directly with the respective Spanish governors. But no money ever changed hands, Havillio pointed out, "only cooperation ... Yes, they were *señores*, gentlemen." As payment, however, the Israelis increasingly provided the Spaniards with intelligence about Morocco. Both Havillio and Harel were convinced that the orders to cooperate with the Mossad came from the very top in Madrid: Generalissimo Francisco Franco.

In the beginning, the mainstream was through Tangier, though the Mossad later sent people directly from Morocco to Gibraltar and Algeciras on the Spanish coast. Harel believed that Spain cooperated with the Israelis out of resentment of Moroccan policies. "Then I came to the conclusion that even though Franco cooperated with the Fascists and the Nazis during the war, he didn't like their attitude toward the Jews," Harel said. "I was told that Franco helped to save many Jews during the war. And he remembered well what happened five hundred years ago, when the Spaniards expelled the Jews. . . . I think Franco was rather genuine. I can't believe the Spaniards did so much without his blessings. . . . It *was* a dictatorship."

In fact, Franco made transit relatively easy for Jewish refugees streaming south after the fall of France in 1940 (though some of them were temporarily placed in detention camps). It had long been believed in Spain that Franco himself descended from Sephardic Jews who converted to Christianity during the Inquisition—his matronymic was Bahamonde, a Sephardic-sounding name—and this, it was supposed, was a reason for his quiet aid to Jewish communities in distress. Many Spanish scholars feel Spaniards have a sense of guilt over Queen Isabella's 1492 edict forcing Jews to convert or be expelled. Moreover, Spain had adopted a law early in the twentieth century extending Spanish citizenship—and passports—to Jews anywhere in the world who could plausibly claim Sephardic identity and descent.

The Mossad's Spanish connection was so strong that when Havillio needed to fly to Ifni, Spanish authorities placed a military aircraft at his disposal. The British also proved to be accommodating. "It was rather unbelievable," Harel pointed out, "that the British agreed to be so very helpful to us after their terrible attitude toward the survivors of the Holocaust after the war. I'm sure it was with the consent of the English government. They gave us bases in Gibraltar and they let us smuggle our people there without passports and let them stay until we were prepared to take them to Marseilles . . . I think the British wanted to make good." The Moroccan government complained to Britain and Spain, who promised they would try to uncover the illegal immigration operation. "But they continued to help us instead," Harel maintained.

Framework had other important allies in unexpected places. One of them was Max Braude, an American who was the director general of the Organization for Rehabilitation and Training (ORT), an American Jewish organization that specialized in setting up vocational schooling around the world. Braude, whom Havillio had met in Geneva, had excellent contacts in Morocco because the ORT operated a technical school in Casablanca, and he agreed to cooperate with the Mossad in its operations. At Havillio's request, he approached Jewish instructors at the school to recruit them for the self-defense force and other activities. On another occasion, Braude, who had been a major in the U.S. Army during the war, brought Framework a shipment of weapons from France aboard a private aircraft that landed in Rabat. "If you have a private plane and you have connections at airports and in the Air Force, you can accomplish a lot," Havillio remarked. "No problem."

Framework also ran an overland escape route from Morocco to Algeria in the late 1950s. Normally, the French let Moroccan Jews enter freely through a gate at the border town of Oujda—a barbed-wire fence ran the length of the frontier—but sometime in 1959 they closed the gate, preventing thousands of emigrants from crossing. This route led the Jews to Oran, a major Algerian port, and then on to Marseilles and Israel. Fortuitously, the Israeli military attaché in Paris, Uzi Narkiss, had graduated from France's War College and maintained close friendships throughout the French armed forces.

On one occasion Narkiss took Harel to a cabaret in Paris, where Harel posed a question: "You're always boasting that you have such good relations with the French. Why don't you open the gate at Oujda for us?" Narkiss replied, "Okay, I'm ready to try." The French commander in the area turned out to be a friend of Narkiss from the French War College.

"I wrote him a letter and gave the letter to one of our people, which said: 'My Dear Friend: Please open the gate. It's not fair that you don't let our people go' . . . He opened the gate."*

Another venture of the Mossad was Operation Mural, which was cleverly designed to send Moroccan children on summer vacations to a full-fledged recreation camp in Switzerland. Naftali "Nat" Bar-Giori, a German-born, Arabic-speaking specialist on legal and illegal immigration, who was "lent" by the Jewish Agency to the Mossad in 1959, came up with the idea of a Swiss vacation program which would be open to all children—with the understanding that Moslem children would return home and Jewish children would be sent on to Israel. He set up an office in Casablanca as part of Framework, and its Moroccan Jewish activists visited Jewish families, urging them to register their children for Swiss summer vacations. The parents of the Jewish children registered for the Swiss camp "were perfectly aware that the children would not come back," said Bar-Giori, who operated in Morocco under the cover of a German businessman. "We took an enormous risk. Sometimes a mother would get hysterical and ask, 'What have you done to my child?' But the trust between the Moroccan Jews and us was unbelievable."

All of the children traveled on collective passports, which concealed the Jews among them, and over 800 Moroccan Jewish children made it safely to Israel during the two years of the Swiss operation. The Moroccan authorities never suspected that this was a Mossad enterprise—or that much

* Eight years later, Narkiss, then a general, commanded the Israeli troops who captured the Old City of Jerusalem on the third day of the Six-Day War in 1967.

of it was financed by HIAS. The real heroes, Bar-Giori reflected, were the Moroccan Jewish mothers. In Israel, sadly, rival religious parties battled publicly for control of the arriving Moroccan children.

Framework was so successful in conducting illegal emigration to Israel that in early 1959, after the flight of some 30,000 Jews over a two-year period, General Laghzaoui recommended in a confidential report to King Sidi Mohammed that Moroccans be forbidden to maintain relations with Jewish organizations. Scores of Moroccan Jews were arrested—presumably to smash the illegal operations—and, according to Harel, they were often tortured. But no Mossad operative was ever caught. Havillio believed that it took the authorities at least five years to realize that they were dealing with the Israeli intelligence service.

The Moroccans were also unaware that a silent and vicious battle raged among Jewish groups around the world over the strategy to be pursued in making the emigration of Moroccan Jews to Israel possible. American Jewish groups and even HIAS found themselves caught up in this debate.

While all parties agreed that an ideal solution would be for King Sidi Mohammed to authorize a new Moroccan Jewish emigration to Israel, the dispute centered on whether this was attainable. The World Jewish Congress, headed by the American Nachum Goldman, took the view that it was entirely possible; indeed, the Congress maintained friendly relations with the king and his government even after emigration to Israel was halted. It advocated negotiating with the royal government for an agreement that would permit the legal emigration to Israel of 1,000 to 2,000 Jews a month, with a ceiling of 40,000 or 50,000 people. Senior

HIAS officials who participated in these discussions during the late 1950s were prepared in principle to let the Congress inform the king that HIAS, as an independent non-Israeli organization, might be willing to take on such a program. But in the end, HIAS went in the opposite direction, siding with those—Harel, in particular—who believed that the king wouldn't make the slightest concession.

Harel's view was, to a large extent, shared by his Jewish Agency partners, and he sought a confrontation with the Moroccan government. "As they increased their oppression, we increased our activity." Harel thought that the Moroccans would ultimately be forced into a deal over Jewish emigration to Israel once they realized they could not stop it. The Mossad's defiance of the Moroccan government might embolden other groups opposed to the new regime. Harel was furious with Goldman's efforts to placate the king, which ran counter to his plan for bringing things to "a point of crisis." Harel convinced Ben-Gurion that battling the Moroccans was the only viable path for rescuing Morocco's Jewry. The result, of course, was greater power for Framework in the field and the decision to enlist HIAS secretly—but completely—in Israel's Moroccan policy.

In a way, Harel's position had been vindicated in 1957 when Nasser authorized all Egyptian Jews to emigrate to Israel in the aftermath of the Sinai war. Harel believed all along that Arabs must be challenged to let Jews emigrate. The Sinai war was stopped, in effect, by the United States; President Dwight Eisenhower and Secretary of State John Foster Dulles thought it was a dangerous and unnecessary adventure. This saved Nasser as the leader of Egypt and, to a much lesser extent, of the Arab world. Ironically, Nasser's decision to let his Jews go, apparently a goodwill gesture toward the West, rendered virtually irrelevant an attempt by Israel during the short Sinai campaign to assist some 70,000 Egyptian Jews to flee to the Holy Land.

This operation was code-named Tushia (Cunning), and it was devised by Shaul Avigur shortly after Ben-Gurion and Harel froze him out of the Framework enterprise in Morocco. Tushia was manned only by Lieutenant Colonel Lova Eliav, an outstanding Aliyah Bet naval commander who had served under Avigur during the European exodus, and one other officer and a radio operator. All three were attached to the French forces in the assault on the Suez Canal area, which spearheaded the abortive war. When it became evident that, as Lova Eliav put it, "we weren't going to Cairo and we weren't going to Alexandria," the three men concentrated on the town of Port Said, where there was a small Jewish community. After ten days in Port Said, the three Israelis managed to assemble about a hundred Jews who were inclined to follow them—without knowing exactly to what purpose. The Jews were taken out aboard two fishing vessels and transported to Haifa, where they finally realized that they were being brought to the Promised Land.

In terms of size, this was a most disappointing effort. But it did make the fundamental point that Israel would miss no opportunity anywhere in the world to rescue Jews from danger or, at least, give them the opportunity of coming to the Jewish state. This had been Avigur's own magnificent obsession since the 1930s, and he was faithful to it until his death at the age of seventy-eight in 1978.

Even if he was excluded from it, the Framework operation in Morocco was, as much as anything else, a tribute to the ideas and imagination of Shaul Avigur, the invisible man of Israeli history.

XXIX

Stalemate

By 1961, after roughly five years of Framework's illegal emigration operations, the Mossad had taken more than 60,000 Jews out of Morocco under exceedingly difficult conditions. It was the largest single covert operation conducted by Israeli intelligence since the country's independence. In numbers, it added up to more than Aliyah Bet's clandestine immigration to Palestine in the 1940s. But there still remained nearly 200,000 Jews in Morocco, and it was quite obvious to all concerned that a compromise solution had to be found reasonably soon. The running battle between Framework and the Moroccan government simply could not go on forever.

In 1960 the organization of Framework had been reshuffled. Harel recalled Shlomo Havillio from Paris because of his policy differences with the Jewish Agency, and replaced him as the overall North African commander with forty-six-year-old Efraim Ronel, a veteran of the Haganah, the Jewish Brigade and Brichah operations in Europe.

Harel and the Vienna-born Ronel were close friends. When Harel became director of the Shin Bet, the internal security agency, he brought Ronel over as his deputy. Ronel remained with the Shin Bet as deputy director until 1960, when Harel asked him to go to Paris and assume responsibility for Framework.

The problem leading to Havillio's removal was the "selection" issue. Havillio felt that Israel could not afford to bring in nonproductive people, and thus advocated leaving the old and sick behind. But at a high-level conference in late 1959, as Ronel recalled, Ben-Gurion had made his position on the issue clear: "If you take out a whole village, you can't leave behind sick, old and blind people . . . you have to bring all of them."

The reorganization of Framework also led to the appointment of a new station chief in Casablanca: Alexander ("Alex") Gattmon, perhaps the most remarkable and most accomplished of all the Israeli figures involved in the Moroccan project. He arrived there with his wife, Carmit, in late 1960.

Two wholly unrelated events occurred at the outset of 1961 to break the Moroccan stalemate on Jewish emigration to Israel. The combination of these events resulted, in turn, in the emergence of HIAS as a full-fledged private American partner of the Israelis—albeit a secret one—in the final phase of the emigration of the Moroccan Jewry.

King Sidi Mohammed V died in February and was succeeded by his son, Hassan II. Notwithstanding his wartime protection of Moroccan Jews from deportation to Nazi Europe and his protestations that they were his "children," the king had remained inflexible on the question of their emigration to Israel after Morocco's independence. Shortly before his death he announced that Jews were free to leave Morocco—but not for Israel.

Hassan, on the other hand, was more sophisticated and more willing to entertain new ideas than his father, including the question of emigration to Israel. In fact, various intermediaries had discussed it with him informally even before he ascended the throne on March 3, 1961—the fifth anniversary of Moroccan independence.

Hassan's ascension came in the wake of tragedy. On January 11, the *Egoz* (earlier known as the *Pisces*), a small vessel carrying illegal Jewish emigrants from a little port on Morocco's Atlantic coast to Gibraltar, sank in heavy seas. Forty-two refugees and an Israeli escort perished. The sinking of the *Egoz*, which flew the Honduran flag and had made thirteen safe crossings, turned into an explosive issue for both sides.

The Israeli and Jewish public learned for the first time that perilous immigration activities were being conducted. As a result, there was an outcry demanding alternative ways of bringing Jews to Israel. Ben-Gurion was moved to instruct the Jewish Agency and the Mossad to seek other solutions.

In Rabat, Information Minister Moulay Ahmed Alaoui charged that "Zionist criminals" were responsible for the loss of the ship, remarking that Jewish emigration was a "betrayal and desertion" of Morocco. "It is unjust," he declared, "that Moroccans should take the place of Palestinian Arabs in Israel, and this is why we stop the Jews from leaving." The atmosphere seemed conducive to a resurgence of anti-Semitism. The press reported in March that in two Casablanca cinemas where the film *Mein Kampf* was being shown, the audience applauded and cheered when an actor exclaimed, "We must exterminate the Jews."

The convergence of these developments led to Operation Yakhin (Yakhin being one of the two main pillars that supported King Solomon's Temple in Jerusalem). While continuing all Framework activities, Ben-Gurion hoped to negotiate in secret a compromise solution on Jewish emigration with King Hassan. The Israelis sought nothing less than a deal with the king that would allow for totally free Jewish emigration.

Meanwhile, Framework became the central mechanism of Yakhin. In Tel Aviv, Shmuel Toledano, a top Mossad officer and leading specialist in Arab affairs, took over policymaking for Yakhin, and shared his responsibilities with Ronel in Paris. With Yakhin launched, Israel entered into quiet but urgent talks with HIAS in New York, hoping to make it one of the new operation's principal pillars by providing an intelligence cover, key professional advisers and substantial financing.

The deal ironed out in New York in August 1961 between HIAS president Murray Gurfein and the Jewish Agency's Baruch Duvdvani was, indeed, unprecedented in scope. According to Jacobson, who was sent back to Paris as director of European and North African operations for HIAS because of his familiarity with Israeli problems and personalities, the agreement "provided for the fact that HIAS would legally be responsible for all the emigration of Moroccan Jews and that whatever staff was working in Morocco . . . would become HIAS staff."

Once the Rabat government accepted the compromise on

Jewish emigration, the entire operation would be legal from the Moroccan point of view. In the meantime, the Israelis working in Morocco for Framework and in connection with Yakhin—as well as Moroccan Jews involved in the operation—were put on the official HIAS payroll. Offices in Morocco would be used under the HIAS name "and expanded as necessary."

Only Alex Gattmon would be without a HIAS identity, operating instead under his own cover as a British businessman. This, too, was spelled out in the verbal HIAS–Jewish Agency accord, which named Gattmon as the "top person responsible for the operation in Morocco." But Gattmon had no visible link with the HIAS Casablanca office at 16, Rue de Foucaulte, where many of his subordinates worked undercover.

A similar arrangement was set up in Paris, where Mossad officers worked in the HIAS office on the Rue de Lota, near the Champs-Elysées, as HIAS employees. When Jacobson decided in early 1962 to move his headquarters to Geneva —given France's problems in North Africa and the escalation of the Algerian war—the entire office with its telephone system was turned over to the Mossad. The office still functioned under the name of HIAS, though the Mossad, which assigned five operatives to the Rue de Lota, expanded it.

Under this system of collaboration, Jacobson went to Paris almost every week for strategy sessions at Ronel's apartment. Gattmon flew from Casablanca about once a month to attend meetings that sometimes lasted all night. Paris was the only place where Jacobson had personal contact with Gattmon. When he visited Morocco in his official capacity as HIAS European director, he naturally stayed away from the Framework commander in order not to put him at risk.

Jacobson also made frequent trips to Israel as a normal part of his HIAS functions to touch base with Jewish Agency executives. To assist him in the delicate aspects of the operation, he relied heavily on his deputy, Raphael Spanien, the gregarious, 300-pound Frenchman who had extensive official and private contacts in France and North Africa. The thickly mustachioed Spanien spent much of his time in Morocco, where he had been a key player in the complex negotiations that began to develop during the latter part of 1961. Spanien attended many of the Paris strategy sessions with Jacobson, Ronel, Gattmon and Mossad and HIAS officials involved in Operation Yakhin.

But Jacobson insisted on an ostensible American presence in Morocco. He assigned Irving Haber, a former Joint executive who spoke fluent French and who was in U.S. Army intelligence during the war, to act as the HIAS director in Casablanca. Haber played, in effect, a double role: he directed HIAS's official programs for Jewish emigration from Morocco to countries other than Israel (HIAS had never before handled emigration to Israel from Morocco), and he acted as a secret negotiator with top Moroccan officials as the compromise deal was being concluded.

It was at that time that Jacobson, on the advice of Mossad and Moroccan friends and with the concurrence of the State Department, officially changed his name from Israel Gaynor Jacobson to Gaynor I. Jacobson. Jacobson may have been exaggerating this concern, but he felt that it might be awkward for a man named Israel to be dealing with anti-Israel Moroccan officials. His concern, nonetheless, reflected the delicate environment in which HIAS functioned as part of Yakhin. He immediately obtained another U.S. passport with his new first name. The State Department, according to Jacobson, was kept fully informed by top HIAS leaders about the Moroccan undertaking, but it chose to express no official reaction to it—which was tantamount to endorsement.

Alex Gattmon was the "lifeblood," to use Irving Haber's phrase, of the Moroccan campaign. He was involved in all of its aspects—political, diplomatic, intelligence, military and illegal immigration operations. A tall, handsome man with Old World charm, a brilliantly analytical mind and a talent for languages (he spoke eight), Gattmon was responsible for coordinating the entire negotiation process in Morocco aimed at lifting the emigration ban through formulas that would be acceptable to all sides. He supervised the intricate web of discussions involving Moroccans in power and Moroccan intermediaries, as well as HIAS, which bore the brunt of the actual day-to-day negotiations, and his own Mossad and Jewish Agency superiors living in Paris and Israel.

But in Casablanca, Gattmon remained completely in the shadows, impeccably protecting his cover personality. Those Americans, Israelis and Moroccans who worked with him in the secrecy of Yakhin felt that without Gattmon the whole enterprise might have foundered. Indeed, Gattmon's extraordinary background seems to have prepared him—from an early age—for his role as leader of the Yakhin operation.

A Jewish partisan during the war at the age of fourteen, Gattmon (born Guttman in Poland in 1926) was caught with his partners in the Hungarian underground and sentenced to death at the age of eighteen by the Gestapo. At a prison east of Budapest, the Germans placed him on the gallows and put a rope around his neck to force him to talk. But Alex remained silent, and for no apparent reason he was taken back to his cell. His real execution was scheduled for 10 a.m. on November 29, 1944. At eight o'clock he looked through his barred window and suddenly saw a Soviet tank coming down the street, its gun turret turning back and forth. He later told his wife, Carmit, "I was praying for him to keep moving forward because my life depended on it." Two hours later, Soviet troops captured the prison and liberated the inmates. For Alex, it was a miraculous escape. Gattmon already suffered from angina, which was improperly treated during the war, and he was left with a severe heart condition for the rest of his life. "He treated his heart," Carmit remarked, "as if it belonged to somebody else." Gattmon wasn't one to be passive.

After the war Gattmon studied criminal law in Vienna and worked to track down Nazi war criminals. He signed up with a Zionist terrorist group, and during the struggle for Palestine helped to blow up a hotel where British military resided. In 1948 he emigrated to Israel and promptly joined the new Israeli Air Force. Because of his heart condition he could not train as a pilot, and for a time he held administrative jobs. He decided, nonetheless, "to do something really active," and got himself reassigned to the Air Force's Eagle Unit, a special paratroop unit designed to capture airfields behind enemy lines. But this didn't satisfy his thirst for adventure either, and in 1954 he volunteered for the Mossad. It was in 1956, on a mission to Brussels, that he met his wife, Carmit, and together they formed one of the most elegant and unusual teams working under cover after the war.

Born Christine Lenz in Hong Kong in 1935, Carmit (her Hebrew name) was the blond, blue-eyed daughter of a German father and a Belgian mother, both Roman Catholics. Her father, an engineer, belonged to a liberal German family and he left Europe "on principle because he saw the Nazi problem rising." The family moved to Shanghai and spent the war years in the French Concession there. After the war, Carmit and her mother went to Belgium; her father, because of his profession, was detained by the Chinese Communist authorities for four years. Carmit finished high school in Belgium and graduated from Brussels University with a degree in political science in 1955. Alex happened to be the cousin of her best friend on the faculty of the university. She never suspected that he was a Mossad operative.

Gattmon was recalled to active duty in the 1956 Sinai war, but he kept in touch with Carmit. He didn't propose for another year, when he finally announced that "there is no place for a wife in my life, but if you are ready to marry me on this basis, it's okay." Gattmon also had to overcome his uneasiness about her father being German, even though he had been an anti-Nazi.

Carmit went to Israel at the end of 1957, converted to Judaism in January 1958, and she and Alex were married the following month. The first place he took her in Jerusalem was the Yad Vashem shrine to the victims of the Holocaust. "Look at these people," he said before photographs of concentration camp inmates. "These people belong to my nation. So if you can't identify with them, you must understand them because they are part of the scenery here." Carmit quickly learned Hebrew and gradually adapted herself to the new cultural environment. Her background couldn't have been more different from Gattmon's, but their marriage was both romantic and lasting.

Officially an Air Force officer, Gattmon kept his Mossad link in absolute secrecy. His international experience, fluency in languages and organizational talents made him an ideal candidate for commander of Operation Yakhin.

Carmit started her own undercover training immediately, learning how to use weapons and communication procedures, "what to do with a dog that bites you, how to check whether you're being followed, what to do to shake a tail." Before leaving for Morocco, she informed her parents that they were going abroad, but she could not reveal the true destination. "We decided that Alex was named ambassador to Togo. My memory of political science courses was still fresh and I knew who the ministers and the president were there." Her letters to her parents about "life in Togo" had to be sent from Morocco to the Foreign Ministry in Israel for delivery.

The cover the Mossad devised for Gattmon was that of a British businessman; the name on his British passport was "George Sellers." Carmit went as his mistress. Her British passport, to which she was entitled as a native of Hong Kong, bore the name of "Christine Blake." As one Mossad expert explained:

> We made it a policy and a practice of using real passports instead of forging passports, whenever possible. This was particularly true in Europe. We would take the passport of a deceased person or a disappeared person, or a passport obtained in some other way, and with calligraphy we would adjust the name of the bearer for the covert mission operator and insert his picture. On some occasions slightly different ink must be used if it is necessary to alter the name slightly. The psychological theory is that chances are that customs and immigration police at the airports would probably not look up to the light to see whether ink was different on the name page of a passport and on other pages—if the passport appeared to be absolutely genuine.

Their cover story was that "George Sellers" was a wealthy businessman with a wife back in England who didn't want to grant him a divorce. "Moroccans have an understanding for love stories, they are very romantic people, they like that sort of thing," explained Carmit, "and that made it easier for us to meet people, to establish contacts."

On their way to Casablanca, the Gattmons stopped off in Hamburg to be introduced to the co-owner of the Kupferberger Company, a successful import-export firm, which Alex was to "represent" in Morocco. The co-owner, a Polish Jew, was a friend of the Mossad official in charge of the Gattmon cover story, and without asking any questions he explained to Gattmon how the company functioned. Gattmon was then given the necessary credentials and materials to act on behalf of the Kupferberger Company in Casablanca. The Mossad even took a photograph of the Gattmons with the co-owner, a Mr. Kudler. From Hamburg, they flew to Paris, where Alex conferred with Ronel, the new Framework commander in chief, and from Paris it was a direct flight to Casablanca.

As Carmit saw it: "Alex and I were noticed right away because he was very tall and aristocratic . . . We weren't like people who are easily forgotten." Alex stood six feet four and had eyes that were a "beautiful amber, brown, green. He was a very striking man." Carmit, then twenty-six, was a beautiful woman.

The Gattmons functioned smoothly in Casablanca. They rented an apartment on Rachal Meskini Street in the prosperous part of the city, and then they rented an office for the Kupferberger Company on the Avenue de la Grande Armée. Alex's room had a separate entrance because he used it as the Mossad headquarters and as a meeting place for his undercover associates. To legitimize the Kupferberger firm in Morocco, he wrote a stream of letters to officials in the copper industry, the Ministry of Commerce and Industry and the Chamber of Commerce making general inquiries and proposing various deals. In the end, the Gattmons helped construct a small plywood plant and almost set up a factory for manufacturing shoes in partnership with a Swedish company. They even joined a Casablanca golf club to make themselves socially visible.

During the Gattmons' first year in Casablanca—late 1960 —all emigration to Israel was still illegal; Framework considered it a top operational priority. Alex personally supervised the clandestine departures, often seeing off departing Jewish families from beaches in the middle of the night. Every once in a while, the two of them accompanied convoys coming from Jewish villages in the south to Tangier in the north, over 600 miles away and over rugged terrain.

But Gattmon managed to devote more and more of his time to the secret negotiations for an emigration deal conducted by HIAS with the Moroccans, all the while running the Kupferberger business and maintaining an active social life as "George Sellers," companion to "Christine Blake."

Carmit, for her part, maintained contact with Framework radio operators and with the alleged HIAS employees who were checking on the readiness of Jewish families to leave on a moment's notice. She regularly telephoned the yacht club, sometimes twice or three times a day, to check on the level of the sea to determine whether it was safe to sail. (Though the Gattmons did not belong to the yacht club, Carmit had contacts there who were willing to keep her informed.) If the waves were no higher than three feet, the boats could sail from Casablanca; if they were six feet, the boats were beached and families had to camp out on the sand until the sea was calm. Sailings were easier on the

Mediterranean coast. Sometimes the weather seemed to threaten the entire Framework effort.

The big danger, of course, was interception and arrest by the Moroccan authorities; those caught attempting to leave illegally were often jailed. The Gattmons also had to handle Israeli agents who arrived clandestinely to train the self-defense force and to organize Jewish Boy Scouts for departures to Israel.

Security was a major problem. The Gattmons never received Arab visitors at home, and they made sure not to keep regular visiting hours, so the concierge wouldn't suspect a pattern of activity. At least two Mossad agents lived in the building where HIAS had its offices, and this made unobserved contact easier. Occasionally, Alex went out at night to meet his contacts at preassigned locations. But they became accustomed to life under strict security. "It becomes like a glove, like second nature," recalled Carmit, who took advantage of the Casablanca female gossip network, a valuable source of intelligence—at the hairdresser, the golf club and the best Casablanca cafés.

After the sinking of the *Egoz* in January 1961, Gattmon decided to precipitate a crisis. He felt that given the degree of risk, illegal emigration could not continue much longer. An agreement with the Moroccans was vital, but he also knew that the Moroccans had to be pushed, and the Jews had to be reassured that the *Egoz* tragedy did not mean the end of all departures for Israel. Consequently, he arranged for the clandestine printing of 10,000 copies of a pamphlet declaring that no Jew and no Zionist who wanted to leave Morocco for Israel would be kept against his will in the kingdom; despite the sinking of the *Egoz*, illegal emigration would continue. It was also intended to convince the king that he should not keep people against their volition in order to foster the belief that Morocco was a tolerant country.

The pamphlet, supposedly printed by an underground Zionist organization, was circulated throughout Morocco, and the government hit the roof. The Moroccan ambassador to the United States, Mehdi Ben Aboud, said in a speech before an American Jewish audience in Washington that the wreck of the *Egoz* had "brought to light [the] clandestine immigration operation . . . which has been exploited in a premeditated press campaign of distortion intended to serve Zionist purposes . . . We have had no Jewish problem in Morocco in the past, and we do not have a Jewish problem in Morocco today." *Al-Istiqlal* magazine, speaking for the nationalist opposition party, wrote that the pamphlets "were distributed by adventurers, hired by the Zionist state."

Gattmon's pamphlet corresponded to Harel's scenario— that a wedge had to be forced between the royal government and the Moroccan Jewish community and that anti-Hassan nationalists had to be used as leverage as well if a compromise over emigration to Israel was ever to be attained.

Illegal emigration was an embarrassment to the regime because it was unable to halt it; it also provided ammunition to the nationalists. King Hassan dreaded another sinking of an emigrant ship for reasons of international prestige, as much as the Jews feared it out of humanitarian concerns. The Moroccan government, keen on continuing to obtain U.S. support for its economic development projects as well as military aid, certainly could not afford to antagonize American public opinion.

For that matter, the Eisenhower administration also faced a quandary: it supported the king against his radical Algerian foes—the two countries would fight a desert war in 1962—

and it wanted air bases in Morocco so that its B-52 bombers would be closer to the Soviet Union in the event of an East-West conflict. In general, Americans were unaware of the Moroccan Jewish issue, while the U.S. government was not yet concerned with the protection of human rights abroad. But Washington naturally shared Rabat's hope that nothing dramatic would happen again involving Moroccan Jews to inflame U.S. opinion.

Pressures were rising on all sides. A truckload of Jews with forged passports was stopped by the Moroccan police as it was about to cross into the Spanish enclave of Melilla in October 1961, while the Istiqlal's newspaper, *Al-Alam*, affirmed that "any Jew attempting to emigrate to Israel deserves the death penalty." Increasingly, Framework and the Moroccan government had a common interest in rationally resolving the emigration conflict. What had to be devised was a mutually acceptable agreement, and that is where HIAS and its helpers entered the picture.

XXX

Operation Yakhin

"The negotiations really took place on two levels," said Irving Haber, resident director of HIAS in Casablanca, "below-board and above-board."

The "below-board" talks were handled by Gattmon in Casablanca and in furtive meetings in Paris. The "above-board" negotiations, essentially classical diplomacy with a dash of the unconventional, were in the hands of Raphael Spanien, the Frenchman who was HIAS's deputy director for Europe and North Africa. Spanien was, unquestionably, the ideal negotiator in the Moroccan situation. In Casablanca, he worked with Haber and Morris Laub, another American HIAS official on temporary assignment in Morocco. In the HIAS chain of command, Spanien was under only Jacobson and James P. Rice, the executive director in New York.

On the "below-board" level, quiet initiatives had begun in mid-May 1961, when Gattmon established close contacts with three immensely powerful and influential Moroccan Jews. The most important of this trio, as it developed, was Sam Ben-Asraf, an old-line Moroccan Jew who inherited a sugar-business fortune from his father, Rafael. Ben-Asraf had a number of government ministers as friends, including Mohammed Ben-Jelloun, the Minister of Education, who in turn had a personal relationship with King Hassan. The second was Dr. Léon Benzaquen, who had served as Minister of Posts and Telegraph in King Sidi Mohammed's first post-independence Cabinet and was now King Hassan's personal physician. The third was Alfred "Jacques" Cohen, a wealthy Casablanca merchant.

It was chiefly in conversations with Ben-Asraf that Gattmon devised the face-saving concept that became the "compromise" agreement: the government would agree to unrestricted departures of Moroccan Jews on collective passports—for example, one hundred names on a single passport for people from one or more villages or urban *mellahs*—with the proviso that the passports would be valid for "all countries other than Israel."

The proviso, of course, was the key element in Gattmon's formula. The government could insist that it remained faithful to its anti-Zionist stance and it need not take cognizance of the fact that most of these Jews "changed their minds" upon arriving in Marseilles and proceeded, instead, to Israel. Finally, Gattmon, along with Jewish Agency executives in Jerusalem, was convinced that an American partner was required to give an aura of neutrality to the enterprise and that HIAS was the only logical organization for the role. While HIAS had wide experience in organizing emigration movements, it had never handled immigration to Israel and therefore was not identified with Zionism. HIAS also seemed to have unlimited funds. From the outset, Gattmon understood that hefty payments in one form or another to various Moroccans would be involved if the proposed arrangements were accepted in Rabat.

Gattmon let Ben-Asraf know that he was an Israeli citizen living in Casablanca, though he certainly didn't mention the Mossad or his other Jewish friends there. Telling Ben-Asraf that he was an Israeli was a calculated risk, but it had to be done if anything at all was to develop: it was simply a matter of trust. He authorized Ben-Asraf to tell his government friends that he had met "someone representing Jewish organizations, the Jewish Agency and the Jewish Moroccan underground." In the meantime, the Gattmons enjoyed a social relationship with Ben-Asraf and his wife, a Spanish countess from the Basque country, though apparently she was never told that "George Sellers" and his mistress were really the Gattmons and that they were Israelis.

Ben-Asraf took Gattmon's message to Ben-Jelloun and reported back that the minister was interested in pursuing the subject. Alex felt this was the right moment to comment that Israel had always compensated countries for economic losses resulting from departures of Jews—their education, for instance, was a lost asset—and that surely this principle would apply to Morocco. No elaboration was required, and Ben-Asraf advised him that Ben-Jelloun would like to meet him in Paris. The minister had not been told the name of the person "representing" the Jewish Agency; Ben-Asraf and Alex agreed that this would be too risky.

When he arrived in Paris, Gattmon briefed Ronel and then asked Spanien to accompany him to the meeting with Ben-Jelloun. HIAS and the Jewish Agency had already held preliminary discussions about a "partnership," and Spanien was authorized to go with Gattmon in order to become directly engaged in the operation.

Gattmon went to the meeting in disguise. He had a thick mustache and dark glasses, and he introduced himself as "Aleksander Ben-David." Spanien had no reason to conceal his identity. The three men spent hours discussing the project and agreed to meet again as soon as possible; Ben-Jelloun indicated that he needed the king's approval before they could move further ahead in the negotiations. But he also made it clear immediately that the Moroccan side considered HIAS's participation a basic condition of any agreement.

It was on the strength of this conversation that the Jewish Agency's Baruch Duvdvani flew to New York in August to finalize the deal with HIAS president Gurfein. In Rabat, wasting no time, Spanien requested a conference with the Moroccan Interior Minister and Deputy Prime Minister, Reda Guedira, who was also a close friend of the king. He was received by him at the ministry in Rabat on August 28. This was the opening move on the "above-board" level of negotiations, and Spanien chose to start out by concentrating on a technicality.

Because HIAS offices in Casablanca and Tangier had not been granted "official recognition" when they were permitted to function in 1955, the government ordered them closed four years later. HIAS naturally complied, to the extent of not being open for normal emigration business, but both offices had gone on operating discreetly since July 1959, the date of the order. Haber and Laub remained in Casablanca and continued to provide Gattmon and the Mossad operatives with a cover.

In requesting "official recognition" from the Interior Minister, Spanien reminded him that HIAS was a nonpolitical American emigration organization with a tradition of pre-independence work in Morocco. The number of Moroccan Jews who wished to emigrate was growing considerably, and it would be most helpful, Spanien suggested, if HIAS could process them in Morocco rather than in Paris, as had been the case since 1959. Spanien also emphasized HIAS's traditions of efficiency and discretion.

Spanien summed up his request in a formal letter to the minister a few days later. He expressed his gratitude for being received and informed of "the especially liberal attitude of His Majesty King Hassan II concerning the free circulation and movement of Moroccan emigrants, for which we owe *Him* infinite thanks." In his courtly French, Spanien added that HIAS was ready to cooperate with the ministry in preparing "collective travel documents" for Jewish travelers to avoid the "additional costs that could result from individual applications, burdening your services unnecessarily."

The negotiations on both levels were proceeding apace.

Gattmon and Education Minister Ben-Jelloun met five more times in Paris and Geneva during the summer and early fall of 1961 in the most conspirational fashion. Spanien was present at some of these sessions; one was attended in Geneva by the Israeli ambassador to France, Walter Eytan.

At a meeting in late July, Ben-Jelloun spelled out his notion of "compensation," referring to the not so veiled suggestion Gattmon had made during their first encounter. Official permission for Jews to depart freely on collective passports for countries "other than Israel" would require a down payment of $500,000. Ben-Jelloun also informed Gattmon that a $250 payment would have to be made for each Jewish emigrant leaving on such a document, to cover, he claimed, some of the related travel expenses. Gattmon was instructed to deliver the funds in cash to a Moroccan envoy in Geneva.

Early in September, Spanien was granted an audience with King Hassan in Rabat, an unusual gesture of goodwill. It had been arranged by Ben-Jelloun, whom Spanien had met with Gattmon. The conversation with the king was confined to pleasant generalities on the subject of free migrations, but Hassan used the opportunity to tell Spanien that HIAS was being granted official status and therefore its offices in Morocco could again function openly. Spanien concluded that the audience was intended to convey Hassan's consent to the "compromise" as well as the acceptance of HIAS as the channel through which the Moroccan government wished to conduct all of the official business.

Spanien was well aware that illegal emigration had been mounting steadily since midsummer. In a report to HIAS headquarters in New York, he estimated that at least 1,000 emigrants each month would leave directly for Spain from Morocco through a new route opened "by our friends of the Aliyah," in addition to 700 Jews who were being taken out every month through Gibraltar and escorted through France to Israel. Spanien suspected that this was one of the reasons Hassan was ready to make a deal.

Gradually, the outlines of such an agreement began to emerge. Spanien took advantage of his visit to Rabat to meet a number of top Moroccan officials, the most important of them Colonel Mohammed Oufkir, chief of the national security service. Oufkir was one of the most powerful advisers to the king, and Spanien had met him on several occasions in the past. Up until then, the colonel had not been involved in the negotiations for Jewish emigration, but Spanien expected that he would play a central role in supervising it once the agreement was reached, and it was useful to renew the acquaintance. Interior Minister Guedira, whom Spanien saw again, was now a firm advocate of an agreement.

Spanien recalled also that following the royal audience one of the palace advisers had referred him to a Casablanca travel agent who was described as the best man to handle the Jewish emigration arrangements. Remembering that one of Ben-Asraf's good friends in Casablanca was a travel agent and that Ben-Asraf had introduced Gattmon to Ben-Jelloun, he did not take this as an idle remark. The travel agent was to be part of the arrangement. Everything seemed to be falling into place.

But late in September, the governor of Casablanca, Colonel Driss Ben Aomar, startled Gattmon and Spanien by announcing that all Casablanca Jews, half of the country's Jewish population, which then stood at 180,000, were free to depart with individual passports. There was no mention of any prohibition on travel to Israel, and HIAS frantically searched for ships and planes to take out the Jews. But the order was rescinded a few days later.

In Jerusalem, the Jewish Agency and the Mossad received the request for the secret payments with great equanimity. "To take Jews out of countries where you have obstacles, you pay to overcome them," said Shlomo-Zalman Shragai, the head of the Jewish Agency's immigration department. Isser Harel, the Mossad chief, recalled that when the Moroccans asked for the $500,000 down payment, they "told us, 'We want to know if you are serious about it.' They wanted to stop illegal emigration until they reorganized themselves, and we were afraid that it was a trap for us." Harel decided it was worth the risk and he went to Prime Minister Ben-Gurion with his request. "How do you know they will deliver?" Ben-Gurion questioned. "I don't know," Harel replied, "but I know another thing for sure: If we don't pay, there will not be any great Aliyah." Levi Eshkol, Israel's Finance Minister, opposed the payment, saying that

Israel could not afford it. Harel claimed later that without his relationship with Ben-Gurion "nobody would have gotten the half million dollars."

Morocco put two conditions on the agreement, according to Harel: "First of all, officially it wouldn't be Aliyah to Israel, just normal emigration, and second, they didn't want to deal officially with us, but only with HIAS." The Moroccans also demanded that illegal emigration be stopped at once, but this triggered considerable opposition among Mossad officers. Ronel and Gattmon, for example, were loath to interrupt the flow of emigrants until they were absolutely certain that the Rabat government would keep its word—and could control its independent-minded regional governors. In the end, the issue was sidestepped with the tacit understanding that the problem would, in effect, take care of itself if the basic accord held. Harel delivered the down payment, and the government began to release Jews.

The actual method of payment was extremely complex. Gattmon flew to Paris to work out the details with Ronel, and together they went to Geneva. Eran Laor, the Jewish Agency's representative in Switzerland, collected $500,000 in cash at a bank, put the money in a suitcase, which he gave to Gattmon, who handed it over to Ben-Jelloun at a Geneva hotel. Like most other Mossad and HIAS officials, Ronel never believed that the money paid for the Jewish departures went personally to King Hassan, nor did he particularly care where it went, as long as Jews were being freed.

Funds for the rescue of the Moroccan Jews came primarily from the United States through Israel. According to Jacobson, money from fund-raising campaigns of the United Jewish Appeal was normally channeled to the United Israel Appeal for a variety of programs in Israel, and a percentage of it went to the Jewish Agency for legal and illegal immigration projects. HIAS also received a share of UJA fund-raising, and HIAS money went to the Jewish Agency for Moroccan emigration as well. Because of the secrecy of these operations, these funds did not appear in the regular HIAS annual budget; they were part of a special fund, and only top HIAS executives were aware of its existence. A relatively small percentage of the money spent for the Moroccans came from Canadian, British and South African Jewish communities.

Funds to pay HIAS's Mossad employees in Morocco and related expenses went directly from HIAS to Morocco via Switzerland. Haim Halachmi, a Tunisian-born Israeli who headed the HIAS Morocco office in Paris after Jacobson moved the European headquarters to Geneva, was in charge of paying for the actual Jewish departures based on the $250-per-head formula. "The travel agent of the king came to Paris every three months to collect" for emigrants, and Halachmi paid him from HIAS funds transferred from New York via Geneva to Paris. HIAS funds also paid travel expenses to enable the Jewish emigrants in Morocco to get from their homes to ports of embarkation.

It is difficult to determine precisely how much money under the compromise agreement flowed through HIAS— or was paid from HIAS's special fund—for the Jewish emigration from Morocco to Israel. But between 1961 and 1966 approximately 100,000 Jews left Morocco as part of this enterprise, which, at $250 per person, would come to $25 million. The Geneva down payment and the direct expenses in Morocco probably added another $5 million, bringing the total close to $30 million.

In an internal HIAS memorandum in 1963, I. M. Dijour, who worked for the organization in Europe in the postwar years, wrote of the Moroccan operation that even the "highly restricted group" of top HIAS officials aware of the secret operations "does not realize the extent of our role in present-day immigration to Israel. . . . This is a case without precedent in Jewish history, when a Jewish organization is doing a job so honestly, so selflessly, with such an amount of self-effacing, having replaced an illegal movement [in Morocco] full of hazards and dangers to the people involved, as well as to the entire foreign policy of the State of Israel, by a migratory movement perfectly legal, smoothly organized, taking place without a shadow of publicity and sensationalism."

Only James Rice and Gaynor Jacobson, who served as HIAS executive directors from 1966 to 1981, as well as three HIAS presidents during that period—Gurfein, Carlos Israels and Harold Friedman—knew the truth.

The break for this "perfectly legal" emigration movement came on Saturday, November 25, 1961, when Haber was urgently summoned to Rabat to meet with Colonel Oufkir, chief of the national security service. Haber and Spanien had been alerted that the compromise agreement would be finalized that week. They immediately began to prepare ships for the transport of emigrants. But as Haber related in a letter to HIAS headquarters, "by a strange quirk of fate, Spanien, who was waiting for this moment like an expectant father, departed for Paris on the morning of the 25th." Haber was left alone for the historic moment, and caught the first plane for Rabat.

Oufkir received Haber in his apartment that afternoon, "arrayed in the traditional Arab garb, displaying very cordial hospitality" and serving tea. After a discussion of "the essentially humanitarian role of HIAS and the benevolence of His Majesty, including the dangers and sacrifices involved," Oufkir announced that he was prepared to sign the collective passports allowing Jews to go anywhere "except Israel." There was no need to sign a formal agreement: it was a discreet, verbal arrangement under which all concerned simply had to keep their word so that it could be implemented. Money had changed hands, the Mossad had grudgingly stopped illegal emigration in mid-October, and with the collective passports about to be signed, Jews could be readied for departure.

At 10 a.m. on Tuesday, November 28, 105 Moroccan Jews sailed from Casablanca aboard the SS *Lyautey* for Nice, a voyage organized by HIAS. It was, Haber wrote, "the fruition of months of efforts, punctuated by periods of exuberance and depression . . . it was really a sight to see the cabs full of prospective beneficiaries of the new generous (but discreet) emigration policy pour out . . . and move on to pass the 'very much simplified' departure formalities." He confessed that "it put a lump in my throat to see these very simple people prepare to leave this country in broad daylight," but added that "one also could not help notice the look of satisfaction tinged with amazement on the faces of some of those who have been engaged in this work for some time over the demonstration of goodwill and helpfulness."

That afternoon, Gattmon's Framework headquarters in Casablanca received this radio message over the clandestine network from the Jewish Agency in Jerusalem: "We congratulate all those involved in the effort who labor day and night in the work of support and rescue." Operation Yakhin was officially born. On December 4, the Jewish Agency's Shragai wrote Gurfein, the HIAS president, congratulating him "on the threshold of the implementation of our plan . . . when so many difficulties presented themselves in the way of its fulfillment." He singled out for special praise

Haber, Jacobson and Raphael Spanien, "who has conducted negotiations so wisely."

But during the first year or so, it was not all smooth sailing for Operation Yakhin. In a sense, the "compromise" was a charade inasmuch as the Moroccan government knew perfectly well that the overwhelming majority of the "legal" Jewish emigrants were going to Israel—and it chose to ignore it. HIAS took the official position that it was responsible for transporting Moroccan Jews to France, but it had to respect afterward their "freedom of choice" if they wished to go elsewhere. The government never remonstrated with HIAS over this issue—it was all part of the game—yet it could not ignore domestic public opinion.

Much as HIAS operatives tried to keep the departures as quiet as possible, they could not be hidden altogether, and the nationalist press erupted in savage attacks against the "Zionist" emigration to Israel. Consequently, the king halted all departures on December 14, 1961, a little more than two weeks after they had begun. In a report to New York, Haber wrote that the Moroccan authorities "were caught completely by surprise by the flood-like or 'exodus' proportions taken by our program . . . the image of officially sanctioned yet relatively uncontrolled departures of vast numbers precipitated the decision for a stoppage." The ban was lifted on February 8, when the king concluded that he had appeased the opposition for the time being in the chaos of Moroccan politics.

But the HIAS and Mossad crews had to be extremely careful about the movement of Jews. Travel from villages to the ports and airports had to be undertaken at night to attract as little attention as possible. Ships and airplanes left in darkness. At one point the Casablanca governor, General Driss Ben Aomar, decided on his own to halt departures from his city, the main gateway of emigration. HIAS and Framework decided to shift some of the load to Tangier. There Haim Halachmi, the former HIAS director in Paris and now head of the northern region (bearing a fake passport under the name "Julien Labiche"), and Haber persuaded the Tangier governor to allow at least one ship to sail. But it had to be done in such secrecy that the emigrants went in a silent motorcade under police escort at night. HIAS personnel replaced stevedores in loading the baggage, because the governor did not trust the port workers. Even Jacobson, who happened to be visiting Morocco from his Geneva base, was drafted to help carry luggage.

Subsequently, the Arabic-speaking Halachmi became a central figure in the process of clearing the Jews for emigration. Having learned that Colonel Oufkir had authorized one of his top aides to sign Oufkir's name on the collective passports and to place the Interior Ministry stamp on them, Halachmi befriended the official. Soon he was able to invite him to come for weekends from Rabat to Casablanca (with a girlfriend) as a guest, and bring along the Interior Ministry stamp with him. At the Casablanca hotel, the aide signed and stamped the passports, but finally told Halachmi, "Do me a favor. Take the stamp to your office, stamp the passports yourself and then return the stamp to me when you're finished." Halachmi happily agreed, and though he would not confirm it, there are sound reasons to believe that he and his HIAS-Mossad friends did all the actual signing and stamping of the documents themselves at their Casablanca office. This obviated weekly trips to the Interior Ministry in Rabat and all the official red tape.

But in June 1962 the king again stopped the departures and closed down the HIAS offices. He had just returned from an Arab summit meeting in Cairo, which may have influenced him in taking a firm anti-Zionist stance. The real reason, however, was that Orthodox Jewish organizations undertook to smuggle young Jews to yeshivas in the United States and France, bribing officials for illegal passports. Gattmon and Haber, working through Moroccan government contacts, succeeded in having the ban lifted, but now the authorities restricted departures to Saturdays and to groups not exceeding 120 people daily. Emigration was suspended once more after an El Al airliner was forced by bad weather to land at Nice just after the arrival of an Air Maroc plane from Casablanca with a load of Jewish emigrants. The Moroccans concluded that HIAS was violating the understanding by trying to transfer the passengers to an Israeli aircraft in plain view, and it took some time to convince the nervous regime in Rabat that it was an accidental situation. Normally, HIAS officials assured maximum discretion in such transfers.

Human problems compounded the difficulties of deracinating tens of thousands of people from villages and *mellahs* where families had dwelled for generations and transporting them on short notice to harbors and airports for voyages to a world they hardly knew existed beyond the confines of their ancient homes. Most of them were illiterate. Many were so attached to their village religious values and traditions that they resisted leaving. Others were simply confused. Because HIAS had been dispatching Moroccan Jews to Canada under separate legal programs, the emigrants en route to Israel were instructed to say that they too were going to Canada. In one instance that became famous among HIAS and Mossad workers, an emigrant was told to remember the name "Canada Dry" when border police inquired about his destination. "Oh," the man said earnestly, "I'm going to Coca-Cola."

By mid-1963 Operation Yakhin had become virtually routine. Colonel Oufkir, the new Interior Minister in Morocco, and Meir Amit, the new chief of the Mossad, concluded a secret pact that year providing for the training of Moroccan security services by the Israelis and limited covert military assistance in exchange for a flow of intelligence on Arab affairs and continued free departures of Jews.

In 1965, the Mossad rendered Oufkir the shocking and sinister service of tracking down Mehdi Ben-Barka, the leader of the leftist opposition in Morocco, whom both the king and his Interior Minister wished dead. Amit agreed to locate Ben-Barka, and Mossad agents persuaded him to come to Paris from Geneva under false pretenses. Near a restaurant, French plainclothesmen arrested Ben-Barka and handed him over to Oufkir's agents. They then took him to the countryside, killed him and buried him in a garden. Investigations by the French government uncovered the truth, and the Ben-Barka affair became a political scandal in France, Morocco and Israel. In 1979, Oufkir mounted a coup against King Hassan and was captured and executed.

The hidden collaboration between the Mossad and Moroccan security services demonstrated once more that in the world of intelligence organizations there are no real ideological allegiances and certainly no great concern for ethics. Israel and Morocco regarded each other as enemies in the Arab-Israeli confrontation, but their intelligence agencies, guided by tactical self-interest, had no trouble working together in secrecy, when required. For Amit to betray Ben-Barka was simply an operational decision, just as it was for Oufkir to accept it. This shows how one covert operation, even a well-intentioned one such as the rescue of Moroccan Jews by the

Mossad, can easily lead to a sinister alliance and precipitate deadly covert operations.

The Mossad, for instance, later developed an intimate working relationship with the SAVAK, the murderous secret police of the Shah of Iran. Israeli advisers also trained and supplied the armies of the right-wing dictatorship in Zaire and the Marxist dictatorship in Ethiopia—because this suited the national interest of Israel in Africa and helped to rescue Jews there.

Of course, it is impossible to know in most cases of this kind as well—and this is true for U.S. and Soviet intelligence agencies—whether such actions are actually authorized by top government leaders in their countries or represent "rogue" enterprises by the agencies themselves. While the Mossad has a reputation for "rogue" operations, its deal with Oufkir had nothing to do with HIAS's financing of Jewish rescues in Morocco: the HIAS money went to pay for Jewish exit permits and the running of the cover for the Mossad— no more. The Mossad interest was in penetrating an Arab's secret service.

By 1990, the ancient Jewish community in Morocco numbered only 10,000 out of a population of 25 million. Some 262,000 Jews had departed for Israel and tens of thousands more for Canada and Latin America, mostly after 1956. They are the remnants of a saga that was as extraordinary as it was secret.

XXXI

Waltzing with a Dictator

At the same time as its Moroccan activities, HIAS was deeply involved with the secret operations by Mossad agents to "buy" Jews out of Romania. These were conducted by Shaike Dan, who by then had worked in the Balkans for over twenty years to rescue Jews. Nicolae Ceauşescu, the Romanian Communist dictator, charged the Jewish Agency between $800 and $1,200 for individual Jewish exit permits, supposedly to compensate Romania for the loss of educated citizens; after his execution in 1989, it turned out that much of that money—perhaps $100 million or $200 million—had gone into Ceauşescu secret family bank accounts in Switzerland, according to the new revolutionary regime.

Over 300,000 Romanian Jews emigrated to Israel in the postwar years, at a cost, due to the secrecy of the arrangements, that is ultimately impossible to determine. According to Jacobson, in the 1960s HIAS reimbursed the Jewish Agency for payments to Romanian Jews who emigrated to the United States after leaving their country with Israeli visas. Jacobson estimated that these reimbursements averaged $1 million per year for several years.

Most of the money for the Romanian Jews going to Israel came from the United States. Funds collected by the United Jewish Appeal and the United Israeli Appeal were forwarded routinely to the Jewish Agency. Then Shaike Dan hand-carried millions of dollars in cash in suitcases to Bucharest for delivery to Ceaușescu's representatives. Jacobson alleges that the State Department was kept fully informed by HIAS of all these transactions—and that it did not choose to object.

This, of course, raises a serious ethical issue with regard to U.S. policies. Because Romania allowed the free emigration of Jews, the Nixon, Ford, Carter and Reagan administrations successively rewarded it with the grant of the Most Favored Nation (MFN) clause in trade with the United States, giving Romanians preferential access to the American market in terms of lower customs tariffs. The Soviet Union, on the other hand, was denied MFN status because in those years it forbade Jewish emigration. What the U.S. government did not disclose, however, was that these dealings with Romania were a sham because of the secret payments to Ceaușescu for Jews, financed by American Jews who were kept in the dark. The leadership of the Romanian Jewish community was fully cognizant of these clandestine arrangements, and fully cooperative in facilitating them. From its viewpoint, freedom for Jews to emigrate loomed as the top priority, and, like Israeli officials, Romanian Jewish leaders did not think in terms of the ethics of cash-for-Jews; nor did they protest against the ruthless practices of the Ceaușescu dictatorship. In fact, Romania was the only Communist country to maintain diplomatic relations with Israel after the Six-Day War in 1967; both governments remained coolly pragmatic about the situation.

As for the United States, the respective administrations were so enchanted with Ceauşescu's occasional gestures of independence from the Soviet Union (Nixon went to Bucharest in 1969 as the first American President to visit a Communist country) that the extreme brutality of his regime was deliberately ignored up until Ceauşescu's execution in December 1989.

XXXII

Business with Nasser and Saddam

The commitment of American Jewish organizations to the rescue of Jews in "countries of distress" did not end with the Moroccan and Romanian enterprises. Over the years, they engaged in a dozen or more other operations, some open and some covert, often in close cooperation with Israel. These were run in Ethiopia, Yemen, Iraq, Iran, Syria, Libya, Albania, most of Eastern Europe before the collapse of Communism in 1989 and the Soviet Union. Two outstanding rescues involved Spain and the Egyptian Jews and the Kurds and the Iraqi Jews.

In 1967, at the start of the Arab-Israeli Six-Day War, the Egyptian government imprisoned approximately 500 Egyptian Jewish males between the ages of eighteen and fifty-three. They belonged to a Jewish enclave of some 2,500 people who were the remnants of what had been an ancient community of 80,000, dating back to the exodus from Spain at the time of the Inquisition in the late fifteenth century. The majority of Egyptian Jews had emigrated in 1957, when Nasser suddenly decided to let Jews leave. But with the war, he ordered all the remaining Jewish males of military age to be put in two high-security prisons.

How to free them became an immediate and urgent concern of HIAS, the only organization in a position to at least make an attempt. Because Egypt broke diplomatic relations with the United States at the time of the war, Washington was unable to intervene on human rights grounds. Few other governments (except France) were prepared to become involved with the fate of Egyptian Jews. Israel, of course, was the enemy, and the Mossad had no structure in Egypt enabling it to play a covert diplomatic or clandestine operational role to release the prisoners. That left only HIAS and *its* secret diplomacy. Accordingly, Jacobson, the executive director, arrived in Madrid in the autumn of 1967 to explore the possibilities of discreet Spanish assistance.

While Spain maintained close ties with the Arab world, it had a history, in the twentieth century, of assisting Jews, as its cooperation during Operation Framework attested. Through American and Spanish friends in Madrid Jacobson sought to establish a low-profile contact with the Foreign Ministry to ask for help for the Egyptian Jews, most of whom were of Sephardic origin. He was received almost immediately by Gabriel Manueco de Leceq, the Deputy Foreign Minister in charge of the Middle East. To Jacobson's astonishment he discovered that, indeed, the Spaniards were prepared to assist—on the condition that their role in this situation would be absolutely secret. Jacobson was just as keen on keeping HIAS out of the limelight.

Spain's ambassador in Cairo was Angel Sagaz, an experienced diplomat and a man of great charm, who had served earlier as head of the North American department in the Foreign Ministry. When Egypt broke relations with the United States during the Six-Day War, Spain represented American interests in Cairo and the Spanish flag flew over the U.S. embassy. But even more promising was the fact that during the war, as Jacobson learned, Sagaz was the Spanish consul in Bucharest, where he acquired a reputation for granting Spanish visas to virtually every Romanian Jew requesting one and Spanish passports to the few there who claimed Sephardic heritage. Sagaz was the perfect man for the situation, Jacobson thought, and Sagaz was instructed by the Foreign Ministry in Madrid to intervene with the Egyptian government for the release of the Jews.

By December 1967, Sagaz had obtained the release of 200 Jewish prisoners and permission for them to leave Egypt. HIAS then chartered planes to fly the new emigrants to Italy. Sagaz made a point of personally escorting the men from prison to the airport. On at least one occasion, he retrieved from the Egyptian authorities jewelry and valuables taken away from the prisoners and hand-delivered them at the door of the airplane.

But the Egyptians were slow in releasing all of the Jews, and by mid-1969, there were still 82 Jews left in Tourah prison. The Cairo representative of the UN High Commissioner for Refugees advised HIAS officials, according to an internal memorandum, that he was "very pessimistic about the future release of prisoners from Tourah as . . . the bitterness toward Israel and the frustration of Egyptian officials make it extremely difficult to get a sympathetic hearing for any demarche." In the end, Sagaz obtained freedom for all of the prisoners. And in less than nine months from the start of the war, he had issued 118 Spanish passports to Egyptian Jews who had not been arrested.

Spanish ambassadors in all of the Arab countries were instructed to help the Jews as Sagaz was doing in Egypt. The ambassador in Syria reported, however, that the situation of the 4,500 Jews in that country was "bad" (as was the situation of Catholics in that Moslem nation). Jews in Syria were under severe restrictions concerning freedom of movement, and the Spanish ambassador did not believe that he would have much success in getting them out. Unlike Egypt, which accepted the Sephardic origin of the Jews as a reason for their release, "there is no possibility from the ethnic composition of the Jews in Syria to claim any real tie with Sephardism," he observed.

In Iraq, rather unexpectedly, the Spanish embassy reported that the situation of the Jews "is relatively stable . . . no persecutions, schools and synagogues are open and professionals work normally." But there were only 5,000 Jews in Iraq left at that point and their future would be resolved in a different fashion before too long.

Just as HIAS was negotiating on behalf of the imprisoned Egyptian Jews, its services were also demanded by the situation in Libya. In the aftermath of the Six-Day War, King Idris had become concerned over the safety of the kingdom's 1,500 Jews; others had emigrated earlier in light of the rising political and religious radicalism in the Arab arc sweeping from Mauretania in the west to Iraq in the east. Fearful of attacks, King Idris convinced the community leaders that the time had come for the Jews to go elsewhere. The king paid for their air transportation to Italy, but HIAS still had to organize this sad little exodus. A year later, Idris was overthrown by the military revolution led by Colonel Muammar al-Qaddafi, Zionism's sworn enemy.

In Iraq, the situation of the 5,000 Jews who remained from what once was a community of 130,000 had changed catastrophically after the takeover led by military revolutionaries Colonel Ahmad Hassan al-Bakr and Colonel Saddam Hussein in 1968. An internal HIAS report in 1968 described the Jews in Iraq as "virtual prisoners, cut off from communication and contact with the outside world . . . Jewish houses are under surveillance by the security police . . . Jews are forbidden to travel within the country. No Jew is permitted to emigrate or to travel abroad." There were public hangings of eleven Jews in Baghdad on false espionage charges "and torture of at least eighteen more to death." HIAS and the Israelis feared that "what had taken place with this public hanging could happen to many more," according to Jacobson, "so we redoubled our efforts, each of us, to do something, to see what could be done to rescue the Iraqi Jews."

Help came first from the Kurds. These fierce mountain tribesmen who had been fighting Iraqi central governments for decades to achieve autonomy had begun a far-reaching clandestine alliance with the Mossad in the mid-1960s. Israel, which viewed Iraq as one of its chief adversaries since independence, had considerable self-interest in supporting the Kurds in their struggle. The Mossad's military experts provided training to the guerrillas of Mustapha Barzani, the principal Kurdish chieftain, along with weapons and even a field hospital. Now that the Jews needed aid, the Kurds were ready to provide it. Working with Mossad officers, the Kurds led approximately 1,500 Jews to safety across the border with Iran, where Iranian Kurds took over. The Shah's security police, the SAVAK, which, as noted, had close ties to the Mossad, provided added protection. At that stage the

Kurds in Iran were at peace with the Shah. From Teheran, HIAS flew the refugees to Israel.

But over 3,000 endangered Jews still remained in Iraq, and the Israelis and HIAS had to find ways to free them. That was when Jacobson came up with a fresh approach, engaging HIAS in an amazing diplomatic adventure. It involved not the chairman of the Revolutionary Party, but the man with real power in Iraq, deputy chairman of the Revolutionary Command Council (RCC): Saddam Hussein.

To gain access, Jacobson persuaded Prince Saddrudin Aga Khan, the UN High Commissioner for Refugees, to visit Baghdad in a personal capacity to take up the question of allowing the Jews to emigrate. As head of the Moslem Ismaili sect, the prince enjoyed great prestige in the Islamic world, and therefore he had no trouble in conferring with the most important figures in the Iraqi regime, including Saddam Hussein, when he arrived in Baghdad in March 1969. Saddrudin reported to his HIAS friends on his Baghdad conversations, and his description of the state of Iraqi Jewry was contained in a closely guarded internal HIAS memorandum:

> The prince argued that the public image of Iraq has been terribly tarnished by the hangings and that in order to recoup, a gesture such as allowing free emigration of the Jews would "rehabilitate" the Iraq government. He was told that the government would think about his suggestion and would eventually let him know.
>
> The prince said he had met with a few Iraqi Jews and their condition was most pathetic. He used the words "terrible" and "pathetic" to describe their impoverishment, with property continuing to be sequestered, the schools closing down because of lack of funds, and

he even went so far as to say that if the Jews were not allowed out within a year they might all perish because of lack of food. The prince said that if no reply had come from Iraq by the time he returned from the U.S. in the second half of April, he would go back there. He was satisfied that finally a dialogue had begun and that at least he could speak about the problem officially, something he had never been able to do before.

According to the HIAS document, Saddrudin was warned that Iraq would not let the Jews go if they intended to go to Israel, but he assured the Iraqis that "most would not go to Israel." At about the same time, HIAS was privately informed by the State Department's Near East Bureau that "certain large expenses" might be incurred in connection with the Jewish emigration from Iraq and that Prince Saddrudin might be asked in Baghdad to make such a commitment. The HIAS board of directors sent word that it would come up with funds to back it.

It is unclear precisely what happened during the balance of 1969 and in 1970; there was only silence from Baghdad. But the matter was reopened in early 1971, when Jacobson persuaded a Toronto-based Arab-Canadian real estate millionaire named Carl Rahey to fly to Baghdad to use his special contacts to push at the highest levels for Jewish emigration. Rahey, who owned a Rolls-Royce and a lavish home, told Jacobson that he was not interested in being paid for the mission; all he wanted was reimbursement of travel expenses to the Middle East for himself and a friend. Rahey went to Baghdad in early May 1971, and in a confidential report to HIAS he described his meetings with Saddam Hussein, General Saadoun Ghaidan and Nasim Haddad.

The Iraqis "agreed to carry out the project," which provided for delivery of passports to Iraqi Jews to leave as "tourists" for Beirut or Europe "as long as guaranteed payments are made." The payments would be "about $1,200 per person" or "one million dollars for 1,000 persons." But the departures "could not be a mass movement," Rahey reported; they would have to be staggered.

A Syrian career diplomat, Ghassan Arnaout, also met with Saddam Hussein at Jacobson's behest, and evidently a deal was struck immediately, for HIAS was able to announce in its 1971 annual public report, but without elaboration, that 1,247 Jews left Iraq during 1971, 1,100 of them without passports. Jacobson paid about $1 million for the 1,100 Jews in the course of that year, and he is convinced that these arrangements were made possible by Prince Saddrudin, Carl Rahey and Ghassan Arnaout. During the operation, aircraft chartered by HIAS brought the Jews in groups from Baghdad to Beirut, then to Amsterdam and Zurich. Finally, they flew to Israel, winding up one of the most secret HIAS rescue enterprises.

According to Jacobson, the Iraqi regime issued passports and exit permits to the Jews; the UN High Commissioner's office supplied him with copies of these documents. Jacobson then instructed Harry Friedman, the HIAS vice president for finance, to deposit payment funds for Iraq in designated bank accounts in Switzerland, and groups of Jews were permitted to leave. This procedure was repeated with each batch of exit permits. The High Commissioner's office remained fully active in this operation until the end—naturally in secret. The State Department in Washington was kept posted on the Iraqi enterprise by Jacobson, and remained entirely supportive.*

---

* Prince Saddrudin was back in Baghdad in the spring of 1991, this time as a private citizen on a special UN mission, to negotiate with President Saddam Hussein the fate of Kurdish and other Iraqi refugees in the aftermath of the Persian Gulf war.

In its 1973 annual report, HIAS announced (without explaining the methods employed) that "in 1972, HIAS, working in concert with friendly governments and other Jewish agencies, was able to help 583 Iraqi Jews to leave that country." It said that before the Arab-Israeli war erupted in October 1973 "passports and exit permits had been secured for 100 Iraqi Jews." In his own report as executive director, Jacobson stated that "in 1972–73, 23 Jews were murdered in Iraq, the highest total ever."

In spite of their dire situation, Jacobson noted, some 300 to 400 Jews refused to leave Iraq because their ancestors were buried there since Babylonian times "and that's where they wanted to be buried."

In 1973, HIAS set up another underground railway, this time to smuggle Syrian Jews into Lebanon. There were only 4,500 Jews in Syria, but they lived under considerable oppression, and time was running out. Those who were able to cross the border successfully were taken into the homes of Lebanese Jews and, when the opportunity arose, emigrated out of Lebanon. But this grew increasingly risky; the Syrians carefully surveyed the activities of their neighbors in Lebanon. To evacuate Syrian Jews from Lebanon, HIAS officials talked Beirut authorities into allowing a foreign airliner to transport them if it could land after midnight and take off before 5 a.m., to avoid being noticed. In spite of police help, this air route was closed after the first flight because the refugees told the story to Israeli newspapers upon their arrival in Tel Aviv, and Pan Am, the only airline willing to undertake such an operation, refused to do it again.

In 1980, HIAS arranged for over twenty young Jewish

Syrian women to emigrate legally to the United States to get married. No Jewish males of marriageable age were left in Syria. There are only a few thousand Jews, mostly elderly, now there.

Prior to the Ayatollah Khomeini's Islamic revolution in 1979, the 80,000 Jews in Iran comprised one of the oldest Jewish communities. They were free to leave, and some 40,000 of them did so immediately after the fall of the Shah. But departures became increasingly difficult when the war with Iraq erupted and the regime tried to draft young Jews into the Army. Since Iraqi as well as Iranian Kurds were old friends of the Mossad, "small but significant numbers," according to a HIAS report, were able to leave Iran "by walking through the mountains to Turkey with the help of Kurdish guides . . . but this route is extremely dangerous and costly."

HIAS set up a human-smuggling network to bring young Jews out of Iran that included paths into Pakistan and Turkey. Jacobson assumed that Pakistani security people were aware of this clandestine traffic, but, according to "the secret rule of payoffs," it wasn't publicized. HIAS estimated that approximately 3,000 Iranian Jews emigrated through the illegal Turkish and Pakistani routes.

XXXIII

The Black Jews

For more than thirty years the Falashas in Ethiopia—the black Jews—were a concern of Israel as well as HIAS and the Joint. Although they numbered no more than 30,000 out of a population of 32 million in the early 1970s, the Falashas were the beneficiaries of countless secret operations to bring them to Israel and they have attracted international attention to an astonishing degree.

The word "Falasha" means "stranger" in Amharic. The unknown origins of the Falashas and the fact that they are the only black people in the world who have observed the Jewish faith for centuries—if not millennia—under the most difficult conditions imaginable have combined to create myths and legends—even romance.

Hanan Bar-On, a senior diplomat who was the first to represent Israel in Ethiopia after independence and is a leading authority on the subject, believes that the black Jews crossed the Red Sea from southern Yemen along with Amharic invaders three or four centuries B.C. Today's Falashas speak the Ge'ez language, derived from Amharic, and they say their prayers in Amharic, a Semitic language. The Amharic people settled in what is now central Ethiopia's Gondar province—where the Falashas lived until the exodus to Israel beginning in the mid-1970s—but how they became Jewish in the first place remains a mystery. One legend has it that the Falashas are a "lost tribe" of Israel. Another posits that they descend from a night of love in Jerusalem between King Solomon and the black Queen of Sheba, who came to visit him from the south of Arabia. Indeed, the Bible recounts that "King Solomon gave unto the Queen of Sheba all her desire" and "she turned and went to her own country" (1 Kings 10:13). According to that story, the Queen converted to Judaism as she returned to Gondar, which marked the birth of the black Jews. Ethiopian emperors, including Haile Selassie, were referred to as "Lion of Judah" among their other titles.

Israeli authorities believed from the outset that the black Jews should also come to the Promised Land, knowing through decades of contacts between Ethiopia and Palestine that the Falashas, for the most part primitive peasants, were immensely conscious of Judaism. Ethiopia had been liberated from Italian occupation in 1942 by British forces led by none other than Brigadier Wingate, the great guerrilla leader who secretly helped to train the Haganah when he served in Palestine. Indeed, Wingate's aide-de-camp was a Palestinian officer named Abraham Akavia.

But by the late 1950s, Israel and Ethiopia had still not

established full diplomatic relations. In 1958, when Hanan Bar-On was leaving for Ethiopia as consul-general, Israeli President Yitzhak Ben-Zvi ordered him: "Get me the Falashas."

Bar-On found that "the idea of Jerusalem had become a Messianic obsession" with the Falashas. Another reason the Israelis pressed for the Falashas' emigration was that, in Bar-On's words, they suffered "relentless discrimination," although there were no actual persecutions. "They were not allowed to possess land although they were allowed to work it, and they were driven into more marginal professions."

Though he met repeatedly with Haile Selassie during his three years in Ethiopia, Bar-On was unable to convince the emperor to allow the Falashas to emigrate. He said that Haile Selassie's main concern was to preserve the "Amharic supremacy" in Ethiopia, which is today the supremacy of the Christian Coptic Church. He feared Moslem intervention if he showed favor to Israel.

At the same time, however, Haile Selassie allowed a Jewish ORT vocational school to be established in Addis Ababa. "He didn't inhibit the Falasha leadership from *visiting* Israel," said Bar-On, and he encouraged non-Jewish Ethiopians to study in Israel, especially in the fields of agriculture and education." Moreover, the emperor gladly accepted the training of his army by Israeli military advisers as well as arms from Israel. The military relationship, much of it covert, sustained Ethiopian-Israeli ties into the 1980s.

Unable to win freedom of emigration for the Falashas during the 1950s and 1960s, Israel held back from launching special rescue operations until the mid-1970s. Between 1972 and 1974, devastating droughts afflicted Ethiopia, and famine affected the Falashas as it did the rest of the population. In November 1974, the emperor was overthrown in a leftist military coup led by Lieutenant Colonel Mengistu Haile Mariam and his colleagues, and soon thereafter Ethiopia was at war with neighboring Moslem Somalia, facing pro-independence rebellions in the provinces of Eritrea and Tigre. Under the circumstances, "the Falasha problem became more and more urgent and more and more important," as Bar-On put it.

The time had come to act. Prime Minister Yitzhak Rabin, the Mossad's director, Major General Yitzhak (Haka) Hofi, and the leadership of the Jewish Agency, now responsible for organizing the emigration of Jews, agreed to turn to the old bag of Aliyah tricks—principally the strategy of negotiations used in Morocco. Earlier attempts in 1975 and 1976 to transport the Falashas illegally through the border of Kenya failed and culminated, sadly, with the arrest and torture of twenty-eight refugees. The Israelis knew well that the Americans could be of help.

Late in 1976, Yehuda Dominitz, then the Jewish Agency's director of immigration, approached Haim Halachmi, who now headed the HIAS office in Israel, to ask him whether he was "ready to write another page of glory." Halachmi was one of the key HIAS-Mossad operatives during the Moroccan operation fifteen years earlier, and Dominitz proposed that he go to Ethiopia to work with Mossad officers "to save the Jews there." Halachmi, who said he had never before even heard of the Falashas, agreed on the condition that he would operate as a HIAS official—and if HIAS in New York authorized it. Dominitz asked Jacobson, HIAS executive director, for permission for Halachmi to travel to Ethiopia in the name of HIAS "to bring some Jews under the program of families' reunion." Jacobson quickly agreed.

Halachmi and the Mossad decided to seek out the 150 Falashas who already lived in Israel and ask them to provide the names and addresses of all of their relatives in Ethiopia. This produced approximately 1,200 names. Halachmi then flew openly to Addis Ababa in April 1977 to negotiate with the Ethiopian government on behalf of HIAS seeking permission for these Falashas to join their families in Israel. Mossad officers based in Ethiopia had excellent government contacts, and they immediately introduced Halachmi to the Interior Minister, Colonel Tesfay. Halachmi gave the minister the list of relatives he had brought with him from Israel; about 80 percent of them lived in the Gondar region and the balance in Tigre.

The colonel was surprisingly accommodating, but he pointed out that a civil war was in progress in Tigre and, in general, overland communications between the capital and the rest of the country were in a deplorable state. As it happened, Halachmi's presence in Ethiopia coincided with the elevation of Menachem Begin to the post of Israeli Prime Minister and Mengistu's secret request to him to obtain weapons in Israel for his embattled army. The United States had refused to sell weapons to the pro-Soviet Mengistu regime, but Begin felt so strongly about rescuing Jews that he agreed to give Ethiopians arms as a quid pro quo for the Falashas. The deal was struck, but it was exceedingly difficult to implement because of Ethiopian bureaucracy and the state of chaos throughout the country. The Interior Minister, for example, asked Halachmi to locate a Falasha leader in the Gondar to serve as contact between Gondar authorities and the central government. Remembering his problems in Tangier in 1962, Halachmi thought, "This is Morocco all over again."

But he had with him the names of four Gondar teachers who had studied in Israel and now taught at the ORT vocational school in the area. Having arranged to bring them to the capital, Halachmi went back with his list to the Interior Minister, who agreed to start processing the exit permits for Falashas in the Gondar first, leaving the Jews in Tigre for later. But the minister said, "I am prepared to give you six families." It was a great disappointment for Halachmi.

Resourceful as he was, Halachmi convinced his Mossad associates that they had to find the largest possible families, with ten members each. The ministry was soon sent a list of 60 persons seeking authorization to leave the country. Delays developed and Halachmi went home for a month.

On his return, he discovered that most of his ministry contacts had been purged and probably executed, but he was unexpectedly handed departure permits for 60 Falashas. More time was wasted when the *kess*, the Falasha high priest (there were no Falasha rabbis), in one of the villages refused to leave unless Halachmi came down to invite him personally; if the *kess* did not go, the villagers would not either. Finally, the old priest agreed to travel to the capital, and Halachmi thought he had resolved the departure of the first group of black Jews. The Foreign Ministry was in charge of issuing passports, and, as in Morocco, Halachmi proposed a shortcut to the officer in charge: he would personally help to fill out the passports and stamp them. He recalled that "the guy gave me his chair, his desk . . . and that same day we prepared all 60 passports." Next he telephoned Yehuda Dominitz in Jerusalem to ask for an aircraft to transport the Falashas.

The Boeing 707 belonged to an Israeli company with links to the Defense Ministry, and was flown to Addis Ababa by a military crew on an August evening. It landed without any problems even though Israel and Ethiopia had had no diplomatic relations since the 1973 Arab-Israeli war and there was no normal air traffic between them. Halachmi took the crew to dinner at a Chinese restaurant, informing them that the government would provide Army command cars to take the Jews to the airport in the most discreet manner; the Ethiopians wanted to keep the whole affair secret. The nightly curfew expired at 5 a.m., and the Army cars were at Halachmi's hotel at exactly that time. Five minutes later, the Falashas were picked up in front of the central police station, where they had been told to assemble. They had no baggage because they owned nothing except the white tribal clothes on their backs. The motorcade entered the airport through a back gate and came alongside the Israeli plane, its engines revving up. Israeli security guards checked every Falasha boarding the aircraft, and just as the 707 was set to go, the Ethiopian colonel in charge shouted, "Mr. Halachmi, you cannot take off because you have one more person on the plane." Halachmi asked a Mossad officer standing next to him for two fifty-dollar bills, then proposed to the Ethiopian colonel that they bet a hundred dollars on whether there were 60 or 61 passengers on the plane. When the colonel announced that there were 61, Halachmi said, "Great! You win the bet!" He thrust the money into his hands and pushed him down the plane's ramp. "We closed the doors," he said, "and we took off." Only then did Halachmi tell the Mossad man, "I have news for you. We have 62 persons aboard—one is hiding in the bathroom." On Friday, August 5, 1977, they landed in Tel Aviv. Halachmi sent a cable to Jacobson in New York stating that, thanks to HIAS, the Israelis were able to bring the first 62 Falashas out of Ethiopia. Jacobson cabled back: "Congratulations. At this rate it will take you fifty years to bring out all of them."

Halachmi went back to Ethiopia in November 1977 and brought out 60 more Falashas in the same fashion, though this time a commercial charter airliner was used. But when Halachmi returned to Addis Ababa in February 1978 to keep the departures going, he was told that the whole deal was off; Moshe Dayan, the Israeli Foreign Minister, had stated publicly in Zurich that Israel was supplying Ethiopia with military equipment. Embarrassed, the Ethiopians put an end to the HIAS-Mossad program, which had transported 122 Falashas to Israel.

Five years later, an American Jewish organization was back in Ethiopia undertaking relief work. Following lengthy negotiations, the Ethiopian regime authorized the Joint in 1983 to launch humanitarian projects among the black Jews in the Gondar. Working with the government, the Joint set out to build medical clinics, train health workers, dig wells, plant nurseries, sponsor electrification projects and establish cottage industries. Prior to the Joint's arrival, there was one doctor per 56,000 people in the Gondar; six years later the ratio was seven doctors per 20,000. As in Eastern Europe decades earlier, the Joint's policy was to look after non-Jews as well.

The actual emigration of the Falashas was resumed only in 1984, when Israel devised its secret Operation Moses to rescue black Jewish refugees from camps in the southern Sudan, where they were arriving in huge numbers fleeing hunger and war. Prior to Operation Moses, HIAS and the Mossad were able to extricate 1,500 Jews from these camps —they were flown to Europe, and then to Israel—through a mechanism devised by the UN High Commissioner for Refugees, but this was hardly sufficient. The camps were overcrowded, disease was rampant and people were dying. Some of the refugees had lived in the camps for two years.

The operation itself was a clandestine arrangement between the Israeli and Sudanese governments; the Moslem

Sudan could not acknowledge it was helping Jews. The Falashas were brought to Khartoum, the capital, by Sudanese authorities and then flown to Brussels aboard a Boeing 707 belonging to TEA, a charter airline operated by a Belgian of the Jewish faith. This escape route was closed, however, in March 1985 when an Israeli official inadvertently mentioned Operation Moses to the local press—and the secret was out. But about 13,000 black Jews were rescued through Operation Moses. Approximately 600 remained in the Sudanese camps at that point, but the U.S. government had them flown out quickly—and without secrecy—aboard Air Force C-130 transport planes.

Roughly 20,000 Falashas remained in Ethiopia (their numbers had grown considerably since Bar-On first went there in 1958), and for over four years there seemed to be no hope for them to emigrate to Israel. Nevertheless, many more continued to make their way to Addis Ababa and Sudanese border camps, creating new pressures.

In November 1989, Israel and Ethiopia once more resumed diplomatic relations, and the regime allowed black Jews to go to Israel at a meager rate of fifty per month. Nonetheless, this was an opening, and the Joint, true to its tradition of ingenuity and improvisation, jumped at the opportunity. Once again, Americans participated in a secret international alliance to save Jews halfway across the world.

In early 1990, with the Mengistu Marxist military regime threatened by rebel armies advancing on the capital, thousands of Falashas began streaming into Addis Ababa. There was a sense of urgency about the safety of the black Jews. The Joint, and of course, the Israeli government, feared that a major battle could erupt in the capital or pro-Mengistu gangs would engage in assaults on the Falashas in an outburst of vengeance against Jews who were "protected by Zionist imperialists," as the official propaganda often described them. In response, the Joint's New York headquarters and its Jerusalem office—JDC/Israel—secretly created a separate organization to oversee new attempts to rescue the Falashas, picking up where HIAS and the Jewish Agency left off in 1977 after the failure of Haim Halachmi's last mission.

The Joint's new organization was named Almaya, which means "The World" in Aramaic. Eli Eliezri, a tough, wiry official of the JDC/Israel office and a veteran of earlier secret enterprises, was appointed its chairman. Almaya was to operate closely with the Jewish Agency in Jerusalem and with the Joint's office in Jerusalem and its New York head-quarters.

In the autumn of 1990, Prime Minister Yitzhak Shamir selected Uri Lubrani, the Israeli government's coordinator for Lebanon and one of the country's top negotiators and political operatives, to be in overall charge of the operations. Lubrani flew to Addis Ababa, where he met with President Mengistu in direct secret negotiations that would stretch over eight months. Lubrani also met quietly with Jacob ("Kobi") Friedman, the JDC/Almaya representative, who had been dispatched to Addis Ababa in June to supervise the preparations for the large-scale rescue planned by the Americans and the Israelis. Friedman, a specialist in covert operations, had been given the cover of vice-consul at the Israeli Embassy. His task, which kept him busy around the clock, was to ready the Falashas for emigration, as soon as Lubrani's negotiations were completed and Mengistu gave the green light for departures. This process, however, would be long, tedious, and nerve-racking, lasting a full year.

Eliezri, the Almaya chairman, and Ami Bergman, the deputy chairman, opened a $150,000 operational account at the National Bank of Ethiopia in May 1990. The money came from an initial $250,000 transfer from the Joint's New York office to the Almaya team in Ethiopia, sent via banking channels in Basel, Switzerland. The Joint's time-tested international banking operation proved again to be highly efficient.

Initially, the Almaya group acted openly, using Joint funds for housing and medical aid to the Falashas. The regime welcomed their presence, presumably not aware that preparations for a mass flight of Jews were underway. The Joint was drawing on seven years of goodwill earned with its humanitarian efforts on behalf of the Falashas and non-Jewish Ethiopians. It spent about $7 million annually in Ethiopia, operated a clinic, and provided food assistance to keep healthy 4,000 Falasha families in compounds in the vicinity of the Israeli Embassy in Addis Ababa. Between July 1990 and February 1991, these medical programs brought the Falasha mortality rate down from 39 per 1,000 to 7 per 1,000. JDC/Almaya also ran an elementary school for 4,500 Falasha children (Kobi Friedman said it was "the biggest school in the world"), and provided daily cash payments for food for the Falashas in the capital and for the additional 3,000 who were still in their remote Gondar villages.

By the end of 1990, Falashas were moving into Addis Ababa in growing numbers. Friedman and his deputy Doron Tashtit had established a veritable Falasha town in the Ethiopian capital, complete with all facilities—including a synagogue. Over 21,000 black Jews lived there, and JDC/Almaya had some 2,000 people on its local payroll—security guards, schoolteachers, health personnel, social workers, and construction crews who built housing for the new arrivals. Simultaneously, representatives of the American Association for Ethiopian Jews, a relatively small organization, helped other Falashas make the 300-mile journey between their villages and Addis Ababa. The Association, which had been criticized earlier (even by the Israeli government) for encouraging the flight of the Falashas from the mountains, provided food and housing for many Jews until JDC/Almaya took over all of the support functions.

None of these preparations would have been possible, however, without the pioneering work of Haim Halachmi in the 1970s. Though he could no longer take Falashas out of Ethiopia after 1977, Halachmi had patiently assembled a list of 28,126 black Jews in the country, the bulk of them from 530 Gondar villages. Halachmi's compilation was derived from a 1976 census financed by the Joint and conducted by ORT schools in the region, and from interviews with most of the 15,000 Falashas who had come to Israel in Operation Moses. The list included names and addresses—essential for planning what would be Operation Solomon (Shlomo, as it was known in Hebrew among civilian and military organizers).

Halachmi turned his information over to JDC/Almaya's Ami Bergman—the Jewish Agency naturally had access to it, too—and the Joint's Amos Avgar established a computerized data base for it. Only with these data in hand could the Israelis and JDC/Almaya deal in an orderly fashion with the Ethiopian regime, knowing exactly how many people needed to be extricated. It turned out that Halachmi's lists were 98 percent accurate, and they became known, collectively, as "the Bible."

As Israel's foremost expert on Ethiopian emigration, Halachmi himself, of course, was involved from the outset in Operation Solomon. He worked closely with the Jewish Agency on rescue planning—again with the blessing of HIAS—as he continued to serve as HIAS director for Israel in his Tel Aviv office.

While the negotiations between Mengistu and Lubrani dragged on from late 1990 to early 1991, the regime restricted Falasha departures. Only 5,500 were allowed to emigrate during 1990—and the Ethiopians interrupted the flights several times. These pressures were part of their negotiating tactics in the talks with Lubrani—to press Israel to make a deal on Mengistu's terms. But during the Persian Gulf war the Israeli airline El Al was able to maintain more or less regular flights from Addis Ababa to Tel Aviv—at the same time that flights brought Soviet Jews (who began emigrating in huge numbers in 1990) from transit points in Eastern Europe. It was at this stage that the Israelis stopped using the word "Falasha" and began calling the Ethiopians black Jews, which the Ethiopians vastly preferred.

The deadlock in these secret negotiations stemmed from Mengistu's determination to obtain weapons from Israel in exchange for the black Jews—he desperately needed arms to fight the rebels—and Israel's refusal (firmly supported by the United States government) to provide them. As Lubrani remarked later, Mengistu truly expected Israel to replace the Soviet Union, which had abandoned him, as Ethiopia's main arms supplier.

In the course of their fourth consecutive meeting, held in November 1990, Lubrani offered Mengistu two small Israeli water-desalination plants as payment for the Jews, but the Ethiopian turned him down. The Joint and Israel turned for help to the Bush administration in Washington. With the Mengistu regime crumbling, the plight of the black Jews seemed dire.

On March 13, 1991, Uri Lubrani and Eli Eliezri, the Almaya chairman, flew to New York for discreet consultations with the Joint's Executive Vice President, Michael Schneider. There they agreed that a committee of top

American Jewish leaders should be formed to press President Bush to appoint a personal emissary to persuade Mengistu to free the Jews. The following week Lubrani and Eliezri went to Palm Beach, Florida, where they met with Max Fisher, a Detroit industrialist who had been advising the Nixon, Reagan and Bush administrations on Jewish affairs for the past twenty years. Fisher passed the emissary's request on to the White House, but on April 1 the envoys from Israel were informed that President Bush had turned down the proposal to send a personal representative to Addis Ababa.

Thereupon, leaders of the American Jewish community formed a special committee, with Michael Schneider acting as coordinator, to urge the administration to act before it was too late. Herman J. Cohen, the Assistant Secretary of State for African Affairs, attempted to negotiate a ceasefire between Mengistu's forces and the rebels to bring about a bloodless transfer of power. He had visited Addis Ababa during the winter, and finally helped persuade Bush that the White House should become directly involved in saving the Falashas. Bush then picked Rudy Boschwitz, a former Republican senator from Minnesota (and a Jew), to undertake a secret mission to Ethiopia to convince both Mengistu and the rebel chiefs to allow the Falashas to emigrate to Israel before the civil war reached its critical moment. Boschwitz reached Addis Ababa early in May, and made it clear that the U.S. attached the greatest importance to the departure of the "black Jews."

This was the turning point in the Falasha saga. Mengistu agreed to resume negotiations with the Israelis—and the Joint—and instructed his close friend Kasa Kabede, the former ambassador to Switzerland, to conduct the talks. Kabede was the perfect choice. He had studied at the Hebrew

University, spoke Hebrew, and was Ethiopia's top expert on Israel.

On Monday, May 20, Lubrani and a three-man JDC/ Almaya team arrived in Addis Ababa to try to iron out a deal with Kasa Kabede to authorize the immediate departure of the black Jews. But Mengistu had fled to Zimbabwe the night before. Hoping that it was still possible, the Israeli Air Force and El Al stood ready to begin the airlift. That same day, Bush sent a personal letter to the Acting President, Lieutenant General Tesfaye Gebre-Kidan, urging him to authorize the airlift. Based on a draft sent by Eliezri in Addis Ababa to the Joint's offices in New York, Bush's letter made it clear that the Ethiopians could expect a "persuasion" payment.

On Tuesday, Lubrani opened negotiations with Kasa Kabede, who initially asked for $100 million for the black Jews (earlier the Mengistu regime had requested a $120 million loan from Israel). Lubrani refused what he called "bazaar dealings," and told Kabede the amount was out of the question. Kabede went down to $85 million, then to $57.5 million, finally accepting Lubrani's offer of $35 million. The rebels were now on the capital's outskirts.

The deal—the exchange of money for Jews—was struck on Thursday, May 23, and Lubrani rushed to London the next morning to plead with Herman Cohen to delay the planned U.S.-sponsored ceasefire conference with Acting President Gebre-Kidan. He needed enough time to let the Falasha evacuation take place, and Lubrani feared the airport in Addis Ababa might be closed down if the rebels took the city. Cohen obliged Lubrani and effected a postponement over the weekend.

At 10 a.m. on Friday, May 24, the first Israeli aircraft— two Air Force C-130 Hercules transports and two El Al Boeing 707 airliners—took off from Tel Aviv for Addis

Ababa. Haim Halachmi was aboard the first plane with a group of Hebrew-speaking Ethiopians to help the ground operations. In the capital, however, the new finance minister could not find the number of the Ethiopian account at the Federal Reserve Bank in New York, and therefore Eliezri could not instruct the Joint to make the transfer. (He was erroneously given the number of the bonds account instead of the cash account.) Meanwhile, the airlift planes were denied permission to land, and had to circle over the airport until the confusion in Addis Ababa (of which the pilots knew nothing) was resolved. Finally, the minister produced the account number an hour later, and at 1 p.m., Ethiopian time (6 a.m. in New York), a $35 million payment was transferred to the New York account of the National Bank of Ethiopia by the Federal Reserve Bank. The money, in keeping with the Joint's history, came mainly from American Jewish organizations.

Over a thirty-three-hour period between Friday and Saturday, May 25, thirty-two Israeli and one Ethiopian aircraft flew 14,420 black Jews from Addis Ababa to Israeli airports in one of history's most intensive and daring airlifts. A Boeing 747 airliner, built to transport 400 passengers, brought out a record 1,180 Falashas on one of the first flights. And Haim Halachmi flew back on the last plane of the airlift. "It took me fifteen years to complete my mission," he observed.

The next day, Sunday, the rebels entered Addis Ababa and the airport was closed. Kabede fled aboard one of the last Israeli Air Force planes, and then requested and received political asylum in Israel. It is unclear who got their hands on the $35 million in New York (it worked out to $2,427 per Falasha, roughly what Ceaușescu charged in Romania for an exit permit for a Jew).

Israel announced Operation Solomon on Saturday, May

25, after the first plane landed back in Tel Aviv. Until then, it had been veiled in secrecy, although hundreds of bus drivers, medical personnel, and social workers had been mobilized and hotels emptied to make room for the arriving black Jews. Israelis estimate that the 1,700 Falashas who remain in Ethiopia, because they could not make the flights in time, and the Ethiopian Jews who converted to Christianity—perhaps as many as 100,000—may also be brought to Israel someday.

In New York, Michael Schneider of the Joint informed top American Jewish leaders that Operation Solomon "was made possible by a combination of outstanding operators in the field, the leadership of the organized American Jewish community, the support of the U.S. government, and the efforts of the Israeli government, and the Jewish Agency in Israel." As Ralph Goldman, the former head of the JDC, cabled a friend: "The role of the Joint in the 40's in Europe was repeated in the 90's in Ethiopia." It was the final act of a secret saga played out over nearly fifty years.

Epilogue

Between 1943 and 1991, American Jewish organizations played a vital role in helping rescue nearly two million Jews from Eastern and Western Europe, the Middle East and North Africa. In this decade, they are continuing to play a significant role in the mass migration of Soviet Jews to Israel. The majority of all these Jews settled in Israel and became part of the new nation. The contribution by the American Jewish Joint Distribution Committee and HIAS over this period of nearly a half century was first and foremost in leadership, ideas, imagination, courage and dedication. Hundreds of Americans engaged in scores of open and covert rescue and relief operations on three continents. Hundreds of millions of dollars were expended, but American Jewish donors never begrudged the money.

From the outset, the secret alliance between American Jews and Palestinians (later the Israelis) raised a host of practical and ethical problems.

One may question whether it was proper for private American citizens representing the Joint and HIAS to engage in covert operations to rescue Jews when the U.S. government itself was reluctant to take action. Undeniably, the initiatives of American Jewry had a powerful impact on international events and U.S. foreign policy. When Joe Schwartz of the Joint and Shaul Avigur of the Mossad carried out their strategy of filling up DP camps with Jews from Eastern Europe, for example, they succeeded in creating irresistible pressures that led to the creation of the State of Israel. But private covert intelligence operations carried out by private American citizens also set a dangerous precedent.

The issue, naturally, is complicated by the history of the Jews. Indeed, it seems impossible to suggest that American Jews should have looked the other way and ignored the fate of the victims of the Holocaust—or of other Jews in "countries of distress"—to comply with formal foreign policy procedures. It is important to stress that at no time was any U.S. law broken by American Jewish organizations, as far as is known. And for that matter, the U.S. government, fully informed at all times of the various rescue activities, never attempted to interfere with them, directly or indirectly, with the exception of State Department officials spying on the Joint in Italy in 1947. In fact, as has been noted, the Joint and later HIAS had considerable discreet logistical support from Washington.

To be sure, Jewish and Palestinian causes had enemies in the American government, notably in the State Department and, to a lesser extent, in the military departments. But there were also friends and advocates just as highly placed in the executive branch. This point was made when President Truman overruled Secretary of State Marshall on the questions of Palestine's partition and U.S. recognition of the Israeli state. In the end, one must acknowledge the risks involved when a private, nongovernmental organization takes U.S. foreign policy into its own hands. But what counts most, nearly a half century later, is that hundreds of thousands of lives were saved as a result of Joint and HIAS activities.

Debates have been waged for years now over the issue of "money for blood" or "cash for Jews," from the deals cut with Adolf Eichmann and other Nazi commanders to secret arrangements made with dictators such as Ceauşescu in Romania and Saddam Hussein in Iraq and rulers like King Hassan of Morocco. But moral and ethical qualms were put aside in those situations where the rescue of the Jews was paramount. In retrospect, the survival of Jews, whether of a few or thousands of them, seems to have warranted the "trades," and perhaps there should have been more of them.

The Mossad, for its part, has been severely criticized for its secret cooperation with Moroccan security services, the late Shah's SAVAK political police and various unsavory rulers in Africa. The Israelis tend to take the view that saving Jews justifies anything and everything, an attitude that only they can resolve in their own society.

For some Americans, however, criticism of Israeli "dirty tricks" operations undertaken for humanitarian reasons amounts to the application of a double standard. Our Central Intelligence Agency, the British MI6 and other intelligence services in Western "democratic" nations have embarked on equally questionable associations, often for less noble reasons. The CIA, for example, was even closer to the Iranian SAVAK than the Mossad was. Yet each case must be judged on its merits. When it comes to saving human lives, there can be no absolute standards.

Saving Jewish lives has cost lives too. On August 20, 1967, the body of fifty-nine-year-old Charles H. Jordan, executive vice chairman of the Joint, was found floating in the Vltava River in Prague. Czechoslovak Communist authorities claimed at the time that Jordan had committed suicide, but much evidence emerged subsequently to suggest that he was murdered, possibly by Arab terrorists. The Joint had reactivated its program in parts of Eastern Europe in the 1960s, and Jordan arrived in Prague from Bucharest, where he discussed projects with Jewish community leaders and government officials. He may have been suspected of being involved in Jewish emigration to Israel. A quarter of a century later, Jordan's death remains a mystery. Indeed, throughout Eastern Europe and the Middle East many local agents for the Joint and HIAS have disappeared over the years, their names unrecorded.

And now most of those who devised and conducted the great Jewish rescue causes are gone, too. Joseph J. Schwartz, who preceded Jordan in the Joint post, died in 1975 from a heart attack at the age of seventy-six, after a life devoted to Jewish causes worldwide.

Shaul Avigur died embittered and largely forgotten at his kibbutz at the age of seventy-eight in 1978.

Alex Gattmon resigned from the Mossad after the Moroccan operation (though he undertook a top secret mission in Iran just prior to retirement) and went back to Tel Aviv in August 1963 to start a business and a family. He became the chairman of the board of an iron rolling mill company, and he also involved himself deeply in anti-drug programs for young people. He and Carmit had a son and a daughter, but Alex's weak heart betrayed him. He died, at the age of fifty-five, in 1981. Carmit still lives in Tel Aviv.

Angel Sagaz, the Spanish ambassador in Cairo who rescued Jews from Egyptian prisons in 1967, died of cancer while serving as envoy to the United States ten years later. Israel honored him by awarding him the title of "Righteous Gentile," and his name is inscribed at the Yad Vashem shrine of the Holocaust in Jerusalem.

Epilogue

———

But the saga of Jewish rescues did not run its course with their deaths, and in 1991 a handful of survivors of the glorious years could watch the new operations—and even participate in them.

Gaynor Jacobson now divides his time between Arizona and New York, and at seventy-nine remains a deeply involved adviser to HIAS. Ralph Goldman, who helped the Brichah as a U.S. soldier in Italy and then rose to become the Joint's executive vice president, is now honorary executive vice president. He virtually commutes between New York, Moscow and Jerusalem, supervising the Joint's programs linked to the emigration of Soviet Jewry to Israel. Shaike Dan at the age of eighty-one continues to travel to the Soviet Union and the Balkans on missions that he likes to keep under wraps. Zoltán Toman is also eighty-one and maintains regal residences in Santa Barbara, California, and Caracas, Venezuela, having donated millions of dollars to Ben-Gurion University in the Negev and continued his devotion to Jewish causes.

In the Soviet Union, the Joint now runs extensive programs in support of the Jewish community. This effort includes the establishment of 150 libraries in Jewish communities throughout the country—in Russian and in Hebrew—to teach Soviet Jews about Israel and Jewish history, religion and affairs. Some 185,000 Jews were allowed to emigrate from the U.S.S.R. to Israel in 1990, and tens of thousands arrived during 1991, even as Iraqi Scuds fell on Tel Aviv and Haifa during the Persian Gulf war.

But the rescue of Jews never seems to be complete. In June 1991, more than 14,000 black Jews were flown to safety from Ethiopia to Israel in the course of a thirty-three-hour

(3 1 1)

airlift, the culmination of secret negotiations, supported by the U.S.*

In Syria, the regime of President Asad remains steadfast in refusing to allow the emigration of its 5,000 Syrian Jews. In May 1991, just as the Falashas were flying out of Ethiopia, two Syrian Jews were arrested and imprisoned for trying to cross the border into Turkey. Yemen still holds several thousand Jews. Nevertheless, Israel and its American friends are determined to gain freedom for all.

In the finest Schwartz-Avigur tradition, the Joint also played a covert role in establishing contact with the tiny Jewish community in Albania—until 1990 the most hermetically sealed country in the world—and acting as intermediary in their emigration to Israel between December 1990 and April 1991. The Albanian operation was among the best-kept secrets until the last of the 400 Albanian Jews had departed, most of them for Israel. The Joint had begun its quiet activities in Albania in the 1960s by arranging to send Passover matzoh and wine to Albanian Jewish families through relatives living in Greece. The rest of the story was described in an internal Joint memorandum:

> In 1983, when a Jew from Greece was at long last permitted to visit a sibling in Albania, a report on the state of the Jewish population enabled the JDC to design a most discreet system of relief transfers to needy

---

* After Operation Solomon, the Israeli government began to consider whether black Jewish converts to Christianity, pejoratively referred to as the "Feres Mora," may be allowed to come to Israel. This was based on the assumption that some of the Feres Mora had converted against their will—in order to survive—as Marrano Jews did in Spain after the 1492 expulsion order issued by the Spanish crown. The converts remained a separate group, compounding the difficulty of determining who is a Jew under Jewish law. A commission of Israeli rabbis was formed to go to Ethiopia to try to rule on the matter.

individuals. All transfers were addressed from a family member outside Albania to a relative inside Albania, and were carefully staggered as to time and destination. Over the course of the next several years, sporadic visits by others took place, enabling the JDC to refine and augment the relief rolls. Through these indirect means of communication, word reached the outside Jewish world that the Jews wanted to leave. When the doors of Albania opened, the JDC's list functioned as a guide and reference to agencies in a position to assist. . . . The JDC notified the Jewish Agency, which handled the operation after the Albanian and Israeli governments made the arrangements. . . . No Jewish religious service has been held in Albania since World War II. There are no synagogues in the entire country, and the Albanian [Jewish] citizens often were unable to find out when religious holidays fall, much less celebrate them. . . . The exodus was completed on April 11, 1991.

The rescue of millions of Jews from dozens of nations spanning three continents over the course of a half century was a remarkable adventure. It was shared by men and women of different nationalities, religions, beliefs and political affiliations. Those who saved them, through the Brichah, Operations Babylon, Magic Carpet, Yakhin, Moses and Solomon and the enterprises in Iran, Iraq, Ethiopia, and Albania, have a unique place in an extraordinary historical chapter distinguished by vision and generosity, courage and ingenuity. With hundreds of thousands of Soviet Jews immigrating to Israel in the early 1990s, it is a universal story whose end is yet to come.

Bibliography

Books

Avigur, Shaul. *With the Generation of the Haganah*. Tel Aviv: Israeli Ministry of Defense, 1962. (In Hebrew)

Avriel, Ehud. *Open the Gates*. New York: Atheneum, 1975.

Bauer, Yehuda. *Flight and Rescue: Brichah*. New York: Random House, 1970.

———. *Out of the Ashes*. Oxford: Pergamon Press, 1989.

Ben-Gurion, David. *The War of Independence: Ben-Gurion's Diary*. Edited by Gershon Rivlin and Dr. Elhanan Orren. Tel Aviv: Ministry of Defense, 1983. (In Hebrew)

Dekel, Ephraim. *B'riha: Flight to the Homeland*. New York: Herzl Press, 1972.

———. *Shai: The Exploits of Hagana Intelligence*. New York: T. Yoseloff, 1959.

Elfenbein, E. *Grauel: An Autobiography*. Freehold, N.J.: Ivory House, 1982.

Gruber, Ruth. *Destination Palestine: The Story of the Haganah Ship* Exodus 1947. New York: Atheneum, 1948.

———. *Rescue: The Exodus of the Ethiopian Jews*. New York: Atheneum, 1987.

Habas, Bracha. *The Gate Breakers*. New York: Herzl Press, 1963.

Handlin, Oscar. *A Continuing Task*. New York: Random House, 1964.

Hillel, Schlomo. *Operation Babylon*. London: Collins, 1988.

Hochstein, Jerry, and M. Greenfield. *The Jews' Secret Fleet*. New York: Geffen Press, 1988.

Katz, Samuel. *Days of Fire*. Tel Aviv: Steimatzky's Agency, 1980.

Kimche, Jon and David. *The Secret Roads*. London: Secker & Warburg, 1954.

Klieger, Ruth, with Peggy Mann. *The Last Escape*. Garden City, N.Y.: Doubleday, 1973.

Lacouture, Jean. *Mendès-France*. Paris: Editions du Seuil, 1981.

Laub, Morris. *The Last Barrier to Freedom: Internment of Jewish Holocaust Survivors on Cyprus*. Berkeley, Calif.: Judah L. Magnes Memorial Museum, 1985.

Lendvai, Paul. *Anti-Semitism Without Jews*. Garden City, N.Y.: Doubleday, 1971.

Mardor, Munya. *Haganah*. Edited by J. R. Elston. New York: New American Library, 1964.

Meir, Golda. *My Life*. New York: Putnam, 1975.

Melman, Yossi, and Dan Raviv. *The Imperfect Spies*. London: Sidgwick & Jackson, 1989.

Morse, Arthur D. *While Six Million Died*. New York: Random House, 1968.

Perl, William R. *Operation Action*. New York: Ungar, 1978.

Pogue, Forrest C. *George Marshall: Statesman, 1945–1950*. New York: Viking, 1987.

Porat, Dina. *The Blue and the Yellow Stars of David*. Cambridge, Mass.: Harvard University Press, 1990.

Sanders, Ronald. *Shores of Refuge*. New York: Holt, 1988.

Shabtai, Teveth. *Ben-Gurion*. Boston: Houghton Mifflin, 1987.

Stone, I. F. *Underground to Palestine*. New York: Boni and Gaer, 1946.

Wasserstein, Bernard. *Britain and the Jews of Europe, 1939–1945*. Oxford: Oxford University Press, 1979.

Wechsberg, Joseph. *The Murderers among Us*. New York: McGraw-Hill, 1967.

White, Lyman Cromwell. *300,000 New Americans*. New York: Harper & Brothers, 1957.

Wischnitzer, Mark. *Visas to Freedom: The History of HIAS*. New York: World, 1956.

Wyman, Mark. *DP: Europe's Displaced Persons*. Philadelphia: Balch Institute Press, 1989.

Zweig, Ronald. *Britain and Palestine during the Second World War*. Woodbridge, Eng.: Royal Historical Society, 1986.

Reports and Pamphlets

Edelheit, Abraham J. and Hershel (eds.). *Bibliography on Holocaust Literature*. Boulder, Colo.: Westview Press, 1986.

———. *Bibliography on Holocaust Literature: Supplement*. Boulder, Colo.: Westview Press, 1990.

Sagi, Nana. "The Epic of Aliya Bet: Illegal Immigration to Palestine, 1945–1948." *Midstream*, Vol. XVII, No. 3 (March 1971).

Segev, Samuel. *Operation "Yakhin": The Secret Immigration of Moroccan Jews to Israel*. Tel Aviv: Israel Ministry of Defense, 1984.

Index

Index

Index

Index

Index

Index

Moravia, 151, 153

Morgenthau, Henry, Jr., 9, 11, 41–42, 46, 200

Morgenthau, Henry, Sr., 11

Morocco and Moroccan Jews, 59, 206, 208, 209–76, 309

Morse, Arthur D., *While Six Million Died*, 53, 54

Moscow, 140

Mossad, 5, 6, 16, 24–37, 43, 45–50, 61–70, 75–80, 83, 88–99, 103–4, 111, 113, 115, 118–21 and *n.*, 124–39, 146, 156, 201–2, 206–8, 210–14, 224–78, 281–307, 309, 310

Most Favored Nation (MFN) status, 278

Moyne, Lord Walter, 33

Náchod, 137–38, 150–68

Narkiss, Uzi, 241–42 and *n.*

Nasser, Gamal Abdel, 228, 234, 244, 281

National Association for the Advancement of Colored People, 73

National Liberation Front (FLN), 229–32

Nazi concentration camps, 8, 10, 12, 25, 32, 34–35, 52, 54, 69, 95, 96, 104–5, 116, 130, 136, 147, 150, 226

Nazi Party, 21, 28–35, 69, 144, 216, 239, 253, 309

Nebuchadnezzar, 215

Negev Desert, 192

Netherlands, 21, 39, 89, 164, 184

Neulander, Sylvia, 136

New York, 20, 21, 122, 205, 229, 299, 300, 305

New York *Herald Tribune*, 157

New York Times, The, 92

Nichols, Philip, 155

Nixon, Richard, 278, 279, 303

NKVD, 156

North Africa and North African Jews, 7, 8, 57, 59, 91, 187, 205–313; *see also* specific countries

Nosek, Václav, 141, 142, 156, 158, 195, 196

Novinsky, Stanley K., 112

Office of Strategic Services (OSS), 65

Operation Babylon, 206

Operation Documents, 119

Operation Ezra, 206

Operation Framework, 225–60, 281

Operation Magic Carpet, 208

Operation Moses, 297–98, 301

Operation Mural, 242–43

Operation Nehemiah, 206

Operation Solomon, 301–6, 312*n.*

Operation Yakhin, 249–52, 261–76

Operation Z, 149*n.*

Oran, 241

Organization for Rehabilitation and Training (ORT), 241

orphans, Jewish, 83–84, 108, 164–65

Ottoman Empire, 11

Oufkir, Mohammed, 266, 270, 273, 275

Oujda, 241

Pact of Omar, 215

Pakistan, 289

Palestine, partition of, 5, 175, 183–84, 189–93, 308

Palmach, 29, 37, 84–86, 121, 133

Palyam, 29, 121

Pan Crescent (ship), 185–88

Pan York (ship), 185–88

Paris, 18, 21–22, 25, 27, 60, 92, 97, 120, 178, 219, 230, 238, 241, 250, 251, 269

Pehle, John W., 42

Pelabon, André, 220

Perl, Willy Israel, 31*n.*

Perón, Juan, 232

Persian Gulf war, 287*n.*, 302, 311

Peru, 184

Pétain, Henri Philippe, 56, 59

Peter, Gábor, 199

Pilsen, 136

Piraeus, 83, 172

Pius XII, Pope, 51, 54, 164

Plasterek, Sigisbert, 222

pogroms, 127–30, 151, 152, 208, 225–26

Poland and Polish Jews, 12, 17, 28, 29, 44, 53, 54, 63, 80, 88–90, 106–8, 112, 118, 120, 124–30, 134–38, 148 and *n.*–69, 194–95

Port-de-Bouc, 174–75

Port Said, 245

Portugal, 22, 215

Prague, 62, 125, 130–35, 138, 140, 141 and *n.*–42 and *n.*, 144, 145, 154, 155, 161–64, 195–97, 201, 309–10

Qaddafi, Muammar al-, 283

Index

Index

Index

47–48, 54, 61
Warsaw, 17, 27, 62, 90, 120, 129, 165
Warsaw Ghetto, 23
Weiss, Shalom (Danny), 237
Weizmann, Chaim, 10, 191
Welles, Sumner, 10, 42
West Bank, 192
West Jerusalem, 192
White Paper (1939), 6, 8, 26, 31, 40 and
n.–41 and n., 43
Whittal, Arthur, 49, 50
Wilhelmina, Queen (of the
Netherlands), 164
Wingate, Orde, 18, 291
Wisliceny, Dieter von, 115
World Jewish Congress, 243–44
World War I, 9, 11, 13, 141, 143, 171
World War II, 8–69, 82, 103, 144–45, 216
Wroclaw, 150

Yale University, 20, 21
Yemen and Yemenite Jews, 205, 206,
208, 226, 280, 312
Yeshiva University, New York, 20
Yishuv, 23–25, 36–37
Yugoslavia and Yugoslavian Jews, 18,
29, 30–31, 36, 37, 63, 64, 67, 80, 88,
106, 173, 181, 184

Zagreb, 173
Zaire, 276
Zolli, Israel, 77
Zorin, Valerian, 155

Index